D1416955

Looking Back and Going Forward in IT

Looking Back and Going Forward in IT

Jean-Pierre Corniou

LCC SOUTH LIBRARY

First published in France in 2002 by Hermes Science/Lavoisier entitled "La société de la connaissance : nouvel enjeu pour les organisations"
First published in Great Britain and the United States in 2006 by ISTE Ltd
Translated by Tim Pike

Apart from any fair dealing for the purposes of research or private study, or criticism or review, as permitted under the Copyright, Designs and Patents Act 1988, this publication may only be reproduced, stored or transmitted, in any form or by any means, with the prior permission in writing of the publishers, or in the case of reprographic reproduction in accordance with the terms and licenses issued by the CLA. Enquiries concerning reproduction outside these terms should be sent to the publishers at the undermentioned address:

ISTE Ltd
6 Fitzroy Square
London W1T 5DX
UK

www.iste.co.uk

ISTE USA
4308 Patrice Road
Newport Beach, CA 92663
USA

T
58.5
.C684
2006

© LAVOISIER, 2002
© ISTE Ltd, 2006

The rights of Jean-Pierre Corniou to be identified as the authors of this work has been asserted by them in accordance with the Copyright, Designs and Patents Act 1988.

Library of Congress Cataloging-in-Publication Data

Corniou, Jean-Pierre.
  [Société de la connaissance. English]
  Looking back and going forward in IT / Jean-Pierre Corniou.-- 1st ed.
    p. cm.
  ISBN-13: 978-1-905209-58-3
  1. Information technology--History. 2. Management information systems. 3. Information technology--Social aspects. I. Title.
  T58.5.C684 2006
  004.09--dc22

                                                                    2006000869

British Library Cataloguing-in-Publication Data
A CIP record for this book is available from the British Library
ISBN 10: 1-905209-58-4
ISBN 13: 978-1-905209-58-3

Printed and bound in Great Britain by Antony Rowe Ltd, Chippenham, Wiltshire.

MAY 2 8 2007

Table of Contents

Foreword

Reality cannot be judged or properly appreciated if there are no bearings. One of the major strengths of this book is to put IT into perspective and trace its development through time.

Jean-Pierre Corniou's viewpoint gives rise to a first observation and a first surprise. Information Technology, which is said to be such a recent development, is in fact almost as old as the automobile. More than a hundred years of bustling history is hardly negligible! Many of us continue to blame system failures and computer bugs on youthful indiscretions. This could not be further from the truth.

IT is therefore more than a century old, and it has seeped into all the fields of activity on which each and every one of us has come to depend. And yet, for many company directors – myself included – it resembles a black box which has great difficulty in revealing its secrets.

This dependence can sometimes be difficult to bear because, unlike in other fields of activity, we do not have a set of intuitive parameters at our disposal that might enable us to appreciate the value and efficiency of the IT investments we make.

What we do know instinctively is that IT is a tool to aid productivity, and today, productivity levels – however little and however badly they are assessed – remain the primary justification for IT investment. Unfortunately, this productivity remains tied up to the image of factory automation or the mechanization of accounting operations, which have led to hours of work being cut down to mere seconds of processing. This simplistic vision does not suffice, because IT is also a tool which creates its own demand. Measurements of productivity are thus rendered difficult, if not to say impossible, most notably because of this continuous need, and because of the recurring dynamics between needs being created and satisfied. When a factory is automated, there is a "before" and an "after", and the two relatively stable states can be compared. With IT, there is no stable final state.

IT is thus an incredibly versatile object. Things have changed somewhat with the arrival of ERPs which are more systemic tools, but so far we have always built systems that are made-to-measure. This flexibility is further emphasized by the continuous creativity that is constantly pushing back the barriers of what is possible. The end-result is that IT always generates more hunger than it can satisfy. How then can actual, permanent productivity levels be measured?

The computerization of accounting systems is a fine example. Granted, processing has gained in speed, but that is not the most important point because, other than speed, we have come to expect details of cost prices, expenses, analyzes, etc. How can these be measured? Faced with this observation, it is best to acknowledge that quantitative measures are, in some cases, insufficient unless there is an absolute desire to create them artificially. Actually, the fact that it is so difficult to assess productivity has led us to manage IT from an expenditure point of view, by carrying out benchmark analyzes with other businesses and optimizing the use of the expenditure rather than its size.

These difficulties are also encountered in the technological choices we make. With a lack of distance and a lack of measurements, our IT choices are based on trust in the recommendations of our advisors. Perhaps other businesses have already used the product and can vouch for its effectiveness. Inevitably, there is a natural degree of uncertainty with this kind of procedure. However, this acceptable air of uncertainty is coupled with an unbearable element: agreements drawn up with the vendor through contracts which are far from perfect. From that point onwards, there is the distinct feeling that the vendor is taking you for a ride and that, at the same time, the client is acting in an irresponsible manner. If contracts have not been clearly formalized, the client can be tempted to review demands, and we are only too aware of the fact that reviewed demands bring about additional expenditure. In this area, we should be as thorough with IT as we are with the provision of other goods and services.

Choices and decisions: a manager's major responsibility. However, anyone who purchases a black box but lacks the necessary skills is bound to fail. This is applicable to the IT and automotive sectors alike. Today, 75% of a vehicle's cost price can be attributed to its bought-in components. If the manufacturer does not fully understand and master these various parts, efficient vehicles will not be produced. The same goes for IT. It is essential to master the architecture and the system and have a full understanding of the subject throughout time, which is not necessarily the same for every car manufacturer. The only rule is that, in a major corporation, production is a complex system, and if a number of elements can be bought in from outside, it will simultaneously be rendered simpler and more efficient.

Obviously, our understanding of IT has evolved, as has its organization within a corporate environment. At one time, it was thought that the computerization of a company defined a certain kind of internal organization, and that organization- and computerization-related tasks were naturally intertwined. Optimal IT system issues even became defined as optimal organizational issues. However, today, with the aid of the perspective proposed by Jean-Pierre Corniou, it is clear that all of this has no meaning.

In effect, the division between those who use IT and everyone else no longer exists. We all use one or more computers and thus all contribute to IT on a general level. The IT manager is therefore no longer in charge of a single sector, but is responsible for the technology which acts as the liaison between all company workers.

Jean-Pierre Corniou quite justifiably uses the image of IT bilingualism. It is a case of being competent in IT whilst simultaneously understanding and being familiar with the company's various business lines. A further difficulty is linked with the ambivalence towards the notion of in-house clients. The clients of CIOs are other company players, but these are not clients who are spending their own money. Within a company, the real money is that which comes in from outside clients. CIOs are unlike other suppliers because they also play an advisory role. Parallels can be drawn between the CIO-client relationship and that which exists between doctors and their patients: just because patients are prepared to pay their doctors a lot of money does not mean the latter can prescribe any old remedy! This leads to a relationship which is thus one of bilateral authority ... and this can indeed be rather complicated!

The idea of a new economy did not solve anything. I have always been annoyed by the opposition between the old and new economies. The lion's share of the mistakes made by non-IT experts – and sometimes by IT experts – could be traced back to their tendency to draw upward curves and build future scenarios without enough of a history behind them. This led to all the economic bubbles and disillusionment. With my experience gained as a company director, I am in a position to say that strategic thinking must be founded on long periods which provide more solid reference points, in order to assess the various possible scenarios. The erratic ups and downs of technological stocks in recent months have been a clear illustration of how short track records are judged. The growth rates experienced over an extremely short term had been excessively projected over too long a period. Failure was inevitable. However, there is another reason behind all this. The instigators of the so-called New Economy had forgotten the customers.

Let us take a look at what is happening in the automotive industry, and at Renault in particular. The e-vehicle on which we are currently working – featuring a mobile interface with the outside world and which is rich in information – is but in its early stages. The human/machine interface is the focal point of this e-vehicle, and the person on board is in most cases the driver, most of whose energy must be devoted to driving the car. Simple human/machine interfaces must therefore be designed, making use of the sole means available, namely speaking and hearing. Alas, we have a long way to go before achieving efficient voice control in a noisy environment. Furthermore, we do not yet have the slightest idea about what the true solvent market will represent – in other words, what the customer really needs. Whatever, in all cases, the product must be of genuine value if it is to attract solvent demand. Once again, this book clearly portrays the distinction between the dazzling rise of mobile phones, with a simple interface produced in response to a solvent need, and WAP systems, with their non-user-friendly interface and for which a solvent demand has yet to be identified.

We are aware of the fact that a company's efficiency rests on its ability to manage useful information. One of the issues in my eyes is the ability to provide access to data which has been sorted and prioritized. In this area, today's systems are a very long way from perfect. We have an unprecedented wealth of information at our fingertips but do not have the means of sorting it and providing it to the person who needs it at the time they need it. In this field, I have been struck by, for instance, the fact that the web has now become an accumulated mass of information that takes longer to read than traditional paper publications.

Therefore, Jean-Pierre Corniou's book is a fine starting point which can be read with interest and understood by all. However, what is most important is that it puts its subject matter in perspective. Different elements are put back into context allowing the surrounding scenery to emerge, and objectives and decisions to be redefined. This book does not provide answers to questions and does not say what should or should not be done. It is a reference book, and that is where its major strength and greatest usefulness lie.

Louis SCHWEITZER
Chairman and Chief Executive Officer, Renault

Introduction – All Set for an E-journey

As dawn broke over the 21st century, Information Technology officially celebrated its golden anniversary … it might be thought that the 50 year-mark would go hand-in-hand with the age of reason, but nothing could be further from the truth. In the extended family of innovation, IT is still the rebellious teenager: immature, incomplete and frustrating. Frequent counter-performances have left users irritated, while corporate board-members continue to be annoyed by the sheer unpredictability of results, despite the massive investments being made. So often in the world of IT, *arx tarpeia capitoli proxima*: high praise is swiftly followed by a sharp fall! The lack of foresight on the part of programmers led to record turnover being generated by the need to correct the Y2K bug and its actual or presumed effects. The overly-hyped stock market triumphs of the New Economy were followed by a nosedive which left investors in a state of shock; the very investors who had sought to plough their funds and put their unlimited trust in high-yield ventures which would seemingly be devoid of setbacks. Nevertheless, IT remains fallow ground for dreams of greater things, and is still behind many a success story. It continues to embody a new intellectual frontier, offering a world of ubiquity and unlimited exploits.

However, what do we mean by "Information Technology"? The term may suggest semantic singularity, when in fact IT now encompasses a wide and growing field of activities, competencies and products. The traditional "hardware" and "software" pigeon-holes – the former referring to physical equipment, the latter to programs – now fall short of accurately illustrating the types of product at stake. What really matters for today's end-users is the quality of service provided by the diverse objects on offer. As such, IT is constantly evolving, fading into the history of innovative technology only to re-emerge on a far more widespread basis, taking on new and hitherto unimaginable forms.

As the 21st century began, a new leaf was turned as the Y2K bug was laid to rest, and along with it one of the blemishes on the skin of IT's difficult early days. IT has entered a period of vast technical and social change, which is in line with the new perspectives faced by world economy. Indeed, two major shock-waves hit the world at the end of the 20th century: the fall of the Communist regime in 1989 and the bursting onto the scene of the web in 1993. Despite being the result of extremely different logical processes, the two were concomitant, and freed up convergent forces which, over a short period, have shaped a worldwide economic system in which rules seem to be laid down without any form of counterbalance. Economy, and now society as a whole, has come to be characterized by the free circulation of goods, individuals and ideas, instant and simultaneous access to unlimited information, and the bringing down of barriers between sectors, businesses and scientific disciplines. The movement, steeped in chaos and controversy, somewhere between Davos and Porto Alegre, appears to be irrepressible. But is it really? Is the model of this new economy – entirely focused as it is on short-term performance – the indisputable product of the third technological revolution?

For the world of IT, which had already undergone major transformations in the 1980s with the unharnessed development of micro-computing, the web has brought about a major upheaval, shaking in its wake players across the IT sector, whether manufacturers, software editors, service vendors and of course corporate IT departments. After the financial world had built them up with fever pitch enthusiasm, internet stocks were also the first to suffer a violent change of fortune. The IT world experiences the ups and downs of the business world with the accelerator full on. The IT world is a stage on which all the passion and drama of human activity is played out faster than elsewhere.

Ever since its earliest days, IT had been the affair of specialists who would sort problems out amongst themselves, using their own specific language. Nowadays, IT has made headway into ordinary, everyday life, the general public and mass-distribution media. Developments are dictated as much by mass-marketing policies as by technical evolution. All areas of the social and the corporate worlds now make use of IT tools. With the diversification of equipment, micro-computers have taken on multiple and hidden forms. Children and teenagers are no longer inhibited by the machines, which they make their own with unerring ease. Much like wireless telegraphy, cinematography and aircraft, which were fairground attractions before becoming mass phenomena, IT is now commonplace. However, the process is far from complete. There is still a mythical side to IT, which periodically continues to inspire when the boundaries are pushed further back.

The sole ambition of this book is to present the keys to understanding the technological world in which we live, and which has already deeply transformed our environment. Technological innovation, which shows no sign of letting up, will have an ever-stronger influence on our lives in the coming decades. History must help us to understand how and why we have reached this stage of development. Which opportunities have we drawn benefits from, and which have we wasted? Who and what economic forces can be found at the forefront of the movement? The advent of the information society is not the result of "generation spontaneity", but has been the fruit of many contributors over more than half a century. An historical approach – hitherto under-exploited in this field which tends to shelter behind a modern, instantaneous image – offers a new viewpoint. By tracking the paths of those who contributed to the design of modern IT, by going back over the dreams and analyzing the failures, an in-depth view of this complex sector will be forthcoming. By going back to the roots of IT, we can attempt to comprehend what lies ahead in the years to come, with a view to minimizing the risks and maximizing the potential of future progress.

This book is as much a result of my impassioned personal experience as of analysis in the cold light of day, and will not fail to take sides and make choices, however unfair or excessive they may at times appear to be. The aim is to find a way through the thick undergrowth and shed some light on the subject. Future progress can only be achieved if a clear vision is provided. Action is enabled by a jargon- and mystery-free understanding. Investigative efforts of the like are justified by the subject at hand. Excess and passion have surrounded the history of IT. Technical adventures often resemble fictional novels. IT entrepreneurs have always been ambitious individuals on a quest for glory and fortune. Market growth has offered them opportunities which have never existed in any other sector. No-one is indifferent to IT, which as a discipline is at the crossroads between science and technique, rationality and humanity, culture and business. Feared and ignored by previous generations, but entirely taken on board by today's children and teenagers who choose not to burden themselves with seeking a global vision, IT is now very much of our time: both the product and driving force of our era. In all fields, the 21st century will be marked by progress made in the deployment of information and knowledge processing techniques.

At what cost? In what conditions? With whom? Who will reap the benefits? Will IT cease to be studied and questioned? Or will transformations continue thus bringing about new concerns as well as new opportunities? We will attempt to understand yesterday's challenges to be able to picture those we will face tomorrow, by providing a lucid answer to the following question: *will IT die or be transfigured?*

Chapter 1

The First Information Revolution

1.1. Information: the catalyst for the development of the human community

To be able to comprehend the social and economic impact of a nascent industry destined to gradually turn the world upside down, it is essential to go back to the sources of the history of IT: beyond the simple yet fascinating story of inventors and the objects they invented. However, this does not imply doing the work of an historian, but simply involves putting the expansion of this technical universe into perspective. Particular political and social contexts – and major shifts in history such as World War II – have always precipitated innovative processes, invariably led by a handful of ambitious and creative individuals, seeking, whatever the price, to automate one of humankind's identity-forming activities: intellectual creation. Granted, what they created is essential. Without their efforts and their failures, we would not have the machines of today, which have become such a familiar part of our environment. Our attention will be focused on the uses that others then made of their discoveries. How did the use of calculating machines and intellectual production tools mould evolutions across society? A machine equates to nothing without the relevant education, training and work processes which render it operable. This socio-technical system will be considered, and, whenever necessary, ethical judgments as to the choices made will not be evaded.

Information is at the heart of all human and economic activity. It conditions all forms of exchange. From Sumer through Gutenberg, the cultivation of the rich layer of soil giving rise to the development of organizational progress and social construction has slowly resulted from the mastering of the signs and tools used to produce, disseminate and stock information. The milestones along the road are familiar to all: writing appeared around 3200 B.C., numbers and the first alphabet in Phoenicia (1100 B.C.), and then printing in 1450. Communication was made easier with each step forward. There was an upsurge in trade and commerce, as man learned to count and keep track of transactions. Knowledge continued to develop, as man began formalizing thoughts which had been enhanced by the ever-increasing number of viewpoints now available. There is a dialectic relationship between progress made in the field of material media and the ever-richer content being carried. The Phoenicians created their alphabet because trade could only be developed if faster information processing was available, hieroglyphs being deemed too slow and too little understood. Ease of distribution of the Bible multiplied with the invention of the printing press, far surpassing the low productivity of scriptoria in monasteries, and the development of literacy drove the diffusion of the very culture which would feed the Renaissance. If this determinism seems overly basic, it might nevertheless be acknowledged that innovation succeeds when it meets a real latent need, even if the latter has yet to be – or cannot be – expressed.

Let us travel through time to the second half of the 19th century. During this period, the tools destined to shape the tertiary world and those about to lay the foundations of the information society appeared simultaneously. The early ambition of the handful of men behind this movement was straightforward: to make the execution of basic functions learnt by children from the moment they attend school – writing, counting, sorting, classifying – faster, more reliable, and, if possible, automatic. The same process of innovation was then repeated for each product. Inventors would freely venture down every path opened up before them by the techniques and materials of their particular era, hand-crafting "their" machines, whether for calculating, typing or data processing, etc. With the aim of reproducing texts and figures, the rotary press was invented, as was … carbon paper! Inventors would then seek to industrialize their prototypes with the hope of striking gold. The necessary resources – funds and a pioneering spirit – were forthcoming, because the inventors in question were part of a young, up-and-coming nation that was eager to grow and craved discoveries: the United States of America. Indeed, even as early as 1890, this wave of research was being nurtured Stateside. The new machines were seized upon by establishments in such diverse sectors as banking, insurance, railways, trade and even the public authorities, leading to corporate activities being reviewed and new services being developed. It was not until the 1920s that such tools started to develop in Europe, as in the meantime clerks and managers alike had taken a great deal of convincing. The resistance of the middle ranks, as well as cultural misgivings, were already holding back the deployment of technology aimed at boosting performance and productivity.

The sources of the IT industry can thus be found at the end of the 19th century, at the time of the emergence, over a short period, of the first machines aimed at increasing the ability of individuals to conceive and diffuse thoughts.

1.2. Writing

Typewriters both spearheaded and symbolized the new office world. They made a major mark on the 20th century, shaping the social organization model and its hierarchical layers, archetypes and images. They also enabled the large-scale arrival of women in the workplace. More than a century down the line, our modern computers still incorporate the fundamental characteristic of typewriters: the keyboard, which conveys the bygone image of the typist, with the now pointlessly complex QWERTY or AZERTY arrangements of keys, which modern IT has yet to shake off.

One name is synonymous with typewriters: Remington. Its inventor, the Milwaukee publisher Christopher Sholes, was not the first to dream up a machine which would do away with the tedious manual chores associated with elaborating and reproducing documents, but he was the first to break the 25 words per minute barrier achieved by the best clerks. The chosen sequence of letters prevented the type-bars from getting stuck against each other in the machine, and writing became a swifter process. The next step was to find a manufacturer capable of overcoming the technical complexity of the machine within acceptable economic conditions, and after some unsuccessful attempts, light weapons manufacturer Philo Remington was responsible for putting the first thousand typewriters on the market in 1873. Sales were slow to pick up, and it took five years to shift the first batch of machines. In 1878, a second model was released which included a major innovation for its time, one we now take for granted: the possibility of shifting between upper-case and lower-case characters. By 1890, annual sales had hit the 20,000 mark, and a distribution and maintenance network taking in major cities was set up, as well as a beginners" and in-service training system, essential if the market penetration of Remingtons was to be ensured, given the fact that *bona fide* qualifications were needed in order to master the equipment. In 1900, the United States boasted 112,000 qualified typists, 76% of whom were female.

The fundamental activity of the office world is to produce documents. The essential complementary functions are the ability to classify, sort, retrieve and archive the said documents. While these secondary activities have never aroused as much passion as typewriters, many inventions have nevertheless greatly helped the rise of office work. In the early 1890s, the first vertical filing folders were introduced. However, with the escalating number of files, a means of rapidly identifying the desired documents became indispensable. Hence, the many inventions that emerged, including bank clerk James Rand's handy system of colored labels and strips. Spurred on by the fast-expanding economic climate, he soon set up his own company, Rand Ledger Co., which grew rapidly, becoming a multinational force in 1908. His son, James Rand Jr., invented a card-based information storage system, going under the name of Kardex. It was to be widely used for the best part of a century. Rand Kardex Co. went on to become the undisputed leader in document classification and archiving and – thanks to a daring mergers and acquisitions strategy – to master all office-work related techniques. Come 1925, Rand had 219 branches in the United States, and a further 115 offices overseas. After that fine start, the United States witnessed a whole host of considerable "information technology" developments in the 1890s, across a market which was hungry for innovations to feed its growth. American society was devoid of the inhibitions affecting European society around that time, and the US enthusiastically embraced the technical innovations which rapidly transformed the tertiary world.

1.3. Counting

The history of calculating machines stretches further back in time than that of the typewriter. It officially began with Blaise Pascal in 1642, even though, long before then, Leonardo da Vinci had outlined the basic principle, and in 1623 the German Wilhelm Schickard had built two prototypes. The "Arithmometer", the first mass-produced calculator – manufactured at a rate of one or two per month – appeared in France through the initiative of Thomas Colmar. The second generation of machines can be attributed to the Swede, Willgodt T. Odhner, who perfected a "pin-wheel" system. This particular innovation was later taken on by many other manufacturers. However, with the exception of sectors such as insurance, investing in calculating machines could not be justified, given that accountants were well-trained in the art of calculating by hand, without making mistakes and far more quickly than with a manually operated machine, tediously difficult to use. The market would only be convinced if data could be input quickly, and, above all, if the machine could provide written results.

Two men, Door E. Felt and William S. Burroughs, tackled these critical issues. The 1885 invention of the then 22-year-old Felt was a keyboard, which ensured that the dials of the Arithmometer or its rivals were no longer subjected to the hazardous handling of a stylus. A seasoned user could enter a 10-digit number in a single operation using the keyboard, made up of nine columns of eight figures. In 1887, Felt joined forces with a local Chicago-based manufacturer, leading to the founding of Felt & Tarrant Manufacturing Co., and the production of 1,000 "Comptometers" in 1900. This invention met with considerable success from 1915 onwards, and millions were manufactured by Felt & Tarrant, who also developed a youth training scheme aimed at increasing the market penetration of their product. The same machine underwent constant improvement, and continued to be manufactured until the end of the 1950s. F&T disappeared upon their 1961 merger with Victor Adding Machine Co., having failed to come to terms with the onslaught of computerization.

Around the same time, in 1886, the American Arithmometer Co. was founded, with a view to manufacturing and selling the first-ever calculating machine to feature a printing function, 28-year-old William Seward Burroughs" 1885 invention, the "Adder-lister". The company was re-named Burroughs Adding Machine Co. after the premature death of its founder in 1905, before becoming Burroughs Corporation in 1953 and going on to become a major name in the history of IT. By the end of the 19th century, Burroughs was shifting 8,000 units per year, thanks to an effective sales organization, and in the years leading up to World War I, production hit 13,000 per annum. By then, the various models on offer were being specifically designed for the sectors in which they were to be used. In 1906, the car manufacturer Ford produced a model which featured a rack large enough to carry an adding machine: the "Burroughs Special". By 1920, 800,000 Burroughs machines had been sold worldwide, and the one million mark was reached in 1926. These figures show the extent to which innovative products were already being met with growth rates that would send sales figures soaring. Burroughs also made headway abroad, and as early as 1925 were present in 60 countries, including Canada in 1917, Brazil, Argentina and Mexico in 1924, Belgium in 1925, followed by Germany in 1926. Burroughs extended operations by taking over a number of competitors and integrating their techniques. 1911 saw the introduction of the subtracting machine. The 1921 takeover of Moon-Hopkins brought about the launch of the first machine to combine an electric typewriter with a calculating machine, which could genuinely be deemed to be the ancestor of subsequent office calculators. Finally, a portable calculator, weighing less than 18 kilograms (40 pounds) was put on the market in 1925, and was an instant success.

In the US, Felt & Tarrant and Burroughs were joined in the race by dozens of other companies, entering this constantly developing market which was sustained at least as much by the sheer complexity of the fiscal system as by economic growth.

Date	Event
1898	Radio invented by Marconi.
1900	Paper clip patented.
1901	First transatlantic telegraphic radio transmission.
	First numerical keyboard for punching cards.
1902	Arthur Pitney receives a U.S. patent on the world's first postage meter approved for use by the U.S. Postal Service in 1920.
	First electric typewriter to be sold worldwide: the Blickensderfer Electric.
1903	Clipper Manufacturing Company, the first company to manufacture paper-fastening devices L. C. Smith and Brothers Typewriter Company formed (became Smith Corona Company in 1926
1904	Three-ring binder patented by Irving Piff Manufacturing Company.
1905	Star Furniture Company founded in Zeeland, Michigan (renamed Herman Miller in 1923).
1906	Stenotype machine invented by Ward Stone Ireland.
	The Haloid Company founded to manufacture and sell photographic paper (name changed to Xerox Corporation in 1961).
	Vacuum valve invented by De Forest.
1907	Telephotography inaugurated when Arthur Korn telegraphs a photograph from Munich to Berlin, Germany.
1908	Olivetti founded in Italy by Camillo Olivetti.
1909	Bakelite, the first totally synthetic plastic, patented.
1910	Lefax loose-leaf personal organizer invented by J. C. Parker.
1911	Computing Tabulating Record Co. founded (became International Business Machines – IBM – in 1924).
1912	Corona makes a portable manual typewriter.
1913	Edouard Belin invents the Belinograph, a portable facsimile machine capable of using ordinary telephone lines.
1915	First North American transcontinental telephone call between Thomas A. Watson in San Francisco and Alexander Graham Bell in New York City.
1947	Bardeen, Brattain and Shockley invent the transistor at Bell Laboratories.

Major milestones in the first information revolution[1]

---

[1] Sources: 'From Carbons to Computers', Smithsonian Institution: (http://educate.si.edu/scitech/carbons).

1.4. Sorting: Hollerith's tabulating machines

The first research aimed at developing machines to automate calculations was made in fields of activity that used specific calculation tables and formulae, such as shipping and sailing, astronomy and architecture. The tables they used were produced by networks of individuals and were not error-proof, despite systematic double-checking procedures. Indeed, it might be noted that the word "computer" originally referred to the person whose specialty it was to compute! It was not until the 1960s that the term took on its current meaning. It was one of the major projects of the early 19th century which showed up the need for means of calculating, namely Napoleon's decision to overhaul the land registration system in France. He called on a gentleman by the name of Gaspard de Prony to handle the assignment, which involved converting the measurements made under the monarchy into decimal units. To achieve this, de Prony set up what amounted to a veritable calculation factory, based on the sharing of the tasks at hand. British mathematician Charles Babbage found the experience particularly appealing, and it inspired him to conceive the "Difference Engine", aimed at reducing the inaccuracy of mathematical tables and enabling them to be printed directly. Unfortunately, the machine designed by this whimsical authoritarian was somewhat in advance of what 1820s technology would permit. Babbage was not destined to achieve his goals, and succeeded only in squandering a considerable amount of money … although in 1991 engineers from the British Museum did manage to build a machine based on one of his plans. Another Englishman, George Boole, a contemporary of Babbage who once crossed paths with him in 1861, was to play a major role in the history of IT. Boole's "The Mathematical Analysis of Logic" formed the theoretical basis of binary language. The quest for techniques enabling tools and automatons to be programmed can be traced back to Antiquity and the camshafts used in hydraulic organs by engineers in Alexandria. Later, the technique was perfected in automatons designed for the purposes of entertainment, and, later still, French silk-weaver Joseph-Marie Jacquard used punched cards to control the warp and weft threads on a silk loom.

The first large-scale use of mechanical tools to process data occurred in the United States during the 1890 census. Demographic growth in the US had taken off to such a degree that a census could not be carried out using manual means of calculation. Between 1840 and 1860, the population had risen from 17.1 million to 31.4 million. The mechanical punch-card machine which enabled the census forms to be processed was the invention of one Herman Hollerith, an engineer born to a couple of German immigrants in 1860, and who had been heavily influenced by Jacquard's system. In August 1890, after a mere six weeks, the Census Bureau proudly announced that the American population totaled 62,622,250. This feat was the source of much pride for the young American nation, now ranked the world's leading state. However, the invention of the punch card and its large-scale use to draw up concrete results, rather than simply to assess laboratory experiments, paved the way to today's modern automatic data-processing tools. In terms of productivity and measurable gain, the Census Bureau saved $5m by making use of the Hollerith Machine. The world of banking, insurance and industry then took up Hollerith's offer to utilize his machines, which would otherwise have remained unused until the next census.

Not only did Americans take to the tools which made everyday, repetitive chores easier, but they also unearthed a whole new breed of company workers who would mark the corporate world in years to come: "systematizers", whose mission it was to restructure office tasks, following the example of the work carried out by Frederick Taylor in the industrial world. Systematizers introduced typewriters, calculators and filing systems, thus increasing levels of productivity in banks, insurance companies and corporate head offices. They were the forerunners of today's organizers and consultants.

1.5. Europe lagging behind ...

In Europe, the sheer weight of cultural habits and social groups, together with slow-moving state administrations, meant that office techniques failed to evolve at the same pace as in the US. However, American companies were rapidly setting up subsidiaries in Europe, and left little or no room for European innovators. Hollerith's company, Tabulating Machine Co. (TMC) expanded throughout the continent. The British Tabulating Machine Co. was founded in the UK in 1907. The German branch, Deutsche Hollerith Maschinen Gesselletstaft (Dehomag), followed in 1910, and citing national integration was controversially involved in the Nazi regime[2]. On 15th July 1914, TMC created "International Time Recording", its French subsidiary. Prior to that, 1913 had seen the arrival on European soil of Powers, TMC's major competitor. It was in Germany that the typewriter really began to develop, with the 1904 launch of AEG's legendary Mignon typewriter. The work carried out by the Italian Camillo Olivetti also deserves recognition. His M1 machine was put on the market in 1911, and was an innovative step forward both in terms of its design and the mass-production processes used in its manufacture. The M40, launched in 1930, was a direct result of Olivetti's concern for technical perfection, and already traced the shape of modern machines. Swedish calculator manufacturer Facit should also be saluted. Founded in 1918, the company went on to dominate the market until the end of the 1950s.

World War I left Europe listless, while the US basked in triumph. The war gave opportunity for women to obtain work in factories and offices, but the Taylorization of the tertiary world limited them to menial duties. "We will recruit female operators

---

[2] Edwin Black, *IBM and the Holocaust*, Time Warner Paperbacks, 2001.

aged between 15 and 20, and basic primary-level education will suffice. They will be drafted in from outside the company. Existing staff, however, will be employed either for codification or graphical purposes, in other words before and after but never during machine operations."[3] The quaint stereotypical image of the cultured, piano-playing lady was long-gone! The office world was split down the middle between everyday members of the typing pool, whose mission it was to increase the rate at which documents were produced without trying to understand what it was they were writing, and shorthand typists, the *élite* secretaries. The office world thus left a durable mark on the perceived image of the roles of workers, and contributed substantially to stifling the potential transformations brought about by technical innovation.

While the mechanization of office tasks struggled to progress in Europe, the thinking that surrounded the organization of tertiary work met with relative success, albeit limited to some circles. In France, Henri Fayol began reflecting upon methods for corporate management, and declared before an audience of fellow company directors that "we must strive to discover the laws that will make the organization and workings of management machines as flawless as possible". Fayol, an experimentation and measurement enthusiast who was intent on pinpointing the rules for command and organizational principles in companies, published "General and Industrial Management" in 1916, and three years later founded the *Centre d'Études Administratives* (Center for Management Studies), which remained operational until 1925. This center was entirely given over to experimental research into corporate organization, and ensured that Fayol's thinking exerted its influence over the up-and-coming generation of 1920s company directors.

By the end of World War I, the various players had taken up their positions, and the balance of power was not to shift throughout the 1920s: the United States dominating the field of data-processing, gaining a foothold all over the world, and holding a position of leadership that nobody could contest.

---

[3] *Revue du Bureau*, No. 294, dated August 1935.

Chapter 2

From Electromechanics to Electronics

2.1. The NCR crucible

The IT world was soon being shaped by innovative management methods in areas such as marketing, sales, user training and funding. Success in the sector depended not only on the attractiveness of data-processing tools and the increased productivity it was claimed they brought, but above all on the constant and extraordinarily creative marketing which has always gone hand-in-hand with IT. The occasional genius has shown the way down this particular avenue by defining models which have only been subject to minor subsequent adjustments. In the history of IT, the position held by NCR can be attributed not only to the company's technical exploits, but also to the implementation of a brilliant sales system, which came to be regarded as a marvel by the industry. And the filiation between NCR and IBM comes down to one man. Thomas J. Watson took the NCR model and methodically refined it for IBM, thus ensuring the commercial and financial supremacy of "Big Blue" for a number of decades.

The NCR story began towards the end of the 1880s, when the National Cash Register took on board the idea of one James Ritty, a gifted restaurant owner who lacked the means to develop his invention. The first man to understand what was at stake on the market was coal merchant John H. Patterson. This 40-year-old entrepreneur enthusiastically dived headlong into the nascent cash register market, taking a dual gamble on ever-evolving innovative technology and an effective sales organization. Patterson's personality made him the undisputed pioneer of the managerial methods of modern IT. He launched the large scale development of sales force motivation techniques which still constitute the major strength of companies in the information processing sector. Patterson was also the first to draw up individual sales quotas, and would elevate his best salesmen to the ranks of his "Hundred Point Club". He would bring his sales agents together once a year for lively gatherings at the Head Office in Dayton, Ohio. He also set up the first sales training school in 1894, drew up sector-based marketing documents adapted to each form of trade, inspired his teams with passionate motivational talks, and coined the term "prospective customer". In 1888, he created an "inventions department" which over the next 40 years would become a benchmark example for research and development laboratories across the industry. The Patterson school of thought had a tremendous influence on the elaboration of American management culture between 1910 and the 1930s. It has been estimated that during that period, one in every six American directors had passed through NCR. Among those determined salesmen, one exceptional young man, a former piano dealer from rural Pennsylvania, quickly climbed through the ranks. He was spotted by the boss himself in 1903. Thomas J. Watson was then aged 29. In 1908, Watson was appointed Chief Sales Executive at NCR, and came up with the NCR slogan: "THINK". In 1911, his faultless ascension was complete, the 37-year-old becoming Managing Director of NCR.

John Patterson not only invented modern sales techniques, but he also developed a social management policy which was innovative for its time, with staff canteens, medical rooms, vacation trips, activities for children and an employees" country club. In 1893, he built the first modern factory designed to let in ample fresh air and daylight. Paternalism and indoctrination were never far behind. Slogans were ubiquitous in factories and in the "house organ" known as The Factory News. The cloak of modernism hid a brutal policy towards competitors, Patterson urging his sales executives to "kill" them. At times, these forceful methods approached the boundaries of legality. In 1912, the federal government met NCR head on, charging Patterson, Watson and other company officers with anti-trust and restraint of trade violations. In 1913, they were found guilty and received a one-year prison sentence and a $5,000 fine. However, Patterson and his teams were bailed out by an act of God. Their actions were exemplary when Dayton was hit by a tornado and floods in March 1913, as they provided massive relief support for the inhabitants of the city. They thus gained the sympathy of the general public and a pardon from the government. And then Patterson, no doubt irritated by this double victory, decided to fire Watson! Watson found himself jobless, but soon became President of CTR (the Computing-Tabulating-Recording Co.), the company which had acquired rights to the Hollerith Machine. Despite this split – which was a milestone in the history of IT – NCR continued to thrive: 25,000 units sold and 2,500 employees in 1900, rising to 100,000 units sold and 5,000 staff in 1910. By the time of Patterson's death in 1922, NCR had manufactured 2 million machines!

2.2. A company named CTR

The Census Bureau contract had enabled Hollerith to enjoy a comfortable lifestyle until 1893, but between censuses, he had to find other ways of generating income through the commercial use of his machines. With this purpose in mind, in 1896, he founded the Tabulating Machine Company (TMC), and contracts with railway companies soon followed. However, the 1900 census once again engaged all his energy and resources, until the definitive end of the agreement in 1905. From this point, he had little choice but to devote himself to the commercial development of his business, by working on a whole range of machines including punch-card perforators, sorting machines and tabulators for operations.

Although success was forthcoming, the industry only touched a few hundred customers such as insurance companies, electricity firms and department stores. The ageing and ailing Hollerith accepted the friendly takeover bid made by venture capitalist Charles Flint, who masterminded the merger between TMC and two other companies: the Computing Scale Company, which made scales, and the International Time Recording Company, which specialized in control dials and clocks. Hollerith left the scene $1.2m better off. Flint appointed Thomas J. Watson Chief Executive Officer, and then President in 1914. Watson had no intention of letting CTR stagnate. His utmost desire was to become extremely rich, and to have his way he went on to exploit Hollerith's patents on a worldwide scale. Having signed a work contract with a moderate basic wage but a 5% cut of profits, Watson's wealth depended on the growth of the company.

At CTR, he immediately implemented the methods which had borne fruit at NCR, with sales quotas, new sales territories and spectacular launch campaigns for new and innovative products … without forgetting the pompous sloganeering and the constant pressure exerted on staff to create a clan-like culture. In 1924, CTR made way for International Business Machines, and Watson proudly declared "Everywhere there will be IBM machines in use. The sun never sets on IBM". At this stage, the IBM system was nothing other than a faithful reproduction of the lessons learned at NCR. However, it worked wonders: a three-fold increase in turnover over a five-year period and the in-house corporate culture turned upside-down. What is more, the annuity model invented by IBM ensured constantly renewable income. Rather than sell machines, IBM leased them to customers, and the sale of punch-cards generated substantial profits. By 1930, IBM was selling 3 billion punch-cards per annum, making up between 30 and 40% of the company's profit.

IT was not yet on the agenda. Electromechanics were in control of what was a prosperous and lucrative market. Orders for punch-card accounting machines came from all major US companies, and a confident Watson maintained factory activity throughout the Great Depression, even if this meant stocks building up. In 1927,

Watson's sole real competitor, Remington Rand, took over Powers, the firm which had won the profitable national census contracts in Hollerith's wake. Competition between the two rivals was ferocious. In 1928, IBM introduced 80-column cards, to replace the then standard 45-column cards. Remington counter-attacked two years later by releasing 90-column cards. Each step forward brought improved performance, but increasingly blurred standards. The battle was fought all over the world, the planet having become the theater of operations for the two US companies. IBM edged into the lead by launching the 400 series, which continued to be produced well into the 1960s. This time, IBM was penetrating the bulk volume market, with more than 1,500 Model 405s being produced per year. The Model 405, with its 55,000 parts and 100 kilometers of electric cable, took the punch-card machine to its pinnacle.

IBM went on to dominate the market thanks to their reliable machines, high-quality maintenance schemes and an extraordinarily dynamic sales force. In 1935, IBM boasted an 85% market share! Thomas J. Watson was also astute in his handling of relations with political powers. President Roosevelt addressed many a letter full of admiration to his friend Watson, and IBM still exhibit the missives at their Armonk headquarters. IBM became supplier to the federal government, and in 1936 the latter purchased much of IBM's stock – 415 machines – in order to draw up employment statistics for the working population who would contribute to applying the 1935 Social Security Act. This was but the first of many major contracts for the federal government, who, as part of the New Deal, had implemented numerous projects across the state and private sectors that necessitated statistical processing. By the eve of World War II, Watson had met his objectives: IBM's sales figures had doubled between 1936 and 1940, rising from $26m to $46m, while the work-force was now 12,000-strong. IBM was yet to become the giant which we know so well, but already the firm far outclassed other companies in the same sector.

War was to be the springboard which would bring the industry into the IT era.

2.3. IT: a product of World War II

Throughout World War II, the considerable efforts made to exploit advances in science as a weapon destined to gain total supremacy over the enemy far surpassed those made during all other conflicts. The Manhattan Project, aimed at building an atomic weapon, and developments in radar technology were the best-known of the Allies" programs. The military context enabled IT research to progress, with a view to catering for the calculation-related needs of the major projects. However, 1940s IT was nothing more than a laboratory matter confined to the world of calculations, and far-removed from notions of civil usage. Priorities lay elsewhere, as was the case at the time of the US census. It can be noted that choices made by public authorities played an essential part in the development of the data-processing industry, both in the US and in Europe.

A dozen machines which could loosely be termed computers were built during World War II, mainly to decipher secret codes or to make calculations relating to ballistics. All the major US corporations of the era set up such projects: Remington Rand, NCR and IBM, but also RCA and AT&T. In Europe, Louis Couffignal can be regarded as one of the first between-the-war scientists to work on a "universal machine" which would incorporate mechanical configurations able to perform sequences of calculations. He introduced the idea of using the binary system to carry out such operations. A prototype binary calculator was even produced, and in early 1939, its potential for ballistic calculations attracted interest from the army. The German Konrad Zuse conceived the prototype of the Z1, a programmable machine, and was met with indifference. British researchers, under the leadership of Alan Turing, specialized in encryption and cryptography tools, which resulted in the 1943 Colossus project, during which the codes of the German army were deciphered. However, these efforts could not stay afloat while Europe was at war, and only picked up again when peace was restored.

Meanwhile, the United States benefited from their situation and resources, and the Harvard Mark I, built by IBM for the University of Harvard between 1937 and 1943, became the symbol of the progress made by researchers. Thomas Watson's interest in research was nothing new. In 1929, he had donated a large amount of laboratory equipment to the University of Columbia, and had supported the work being done by Howard Hathaway Aiken, a Harvard researcher who had been inspired by the Babbage machine to build an automatic programmable calculator. Aiken gained the financial and technical backing of IBM, and in 1941, his program was included in IBM's military development scheme. The first tests of the machine took place in January 1943. The slow and noisy contraption was also enormous: 15 meters across. Its active service in the US Navy began in May 1944, and it was used to calculate tables. One hundred years on, the classical architecture of Babbage's remarkable vision had been retained and everyone was impressed by this marvel of technology ... which carried out a mere 200 operations per minute

Other than the emblematic success of Mark I, it was at the Office of Scientific Research and Development (OSRD) – responsible for co-ordinating US science projects at the time of the war – that researchers began mapping out the concept of the modern computer. A committee made up of 12 scientists, the National Defense Research Committee (NDRC), handled the central co-ordination and validation of the myriad local projects that were at the root of the intense research being made, enabling resources to be merged, ideas to be shared and, consequently, research to gain pace.

The names of those involved in that particular revolution never went down in history alongside those of their illustrious predecessors. The Moore School of Electrical Engineering at the University of Pennsylvania was at the heart of developments. Prior to war breaking out, its duty had been to train scientists considered essential for the development of military operations and to make calculations for the Ballistics Research Laboratory (BRL). Researchers were faced with having to go through the slow process of making the calculations needed to draw up ballistic tables, and lacked the kind of equipment that would have speeded up the tedious task. This led to the heated exchange of ideas between researchers, mathematicians and physicians, and the inception of a project for an electronic calculator. In their ranks, the visionary John Mauchly and the 24-year-old engineer John Eckert worked on the development of a method for tracking moving targets by radar, and considered using vacuum valves to process the necessary data. In April 1943, the project was met with a favorable response from the BRL, through the impetus given by the mathematician Lieutenant Herman Goldstine, and a development contract was signed to build a machine: the ENIAC (Electronic Numerical Integrator And Computer). The complex project – 18,000 valves were needed – was launched in the fall of 1943. There was then a chance encounter between the project team and the Hungarian mathematician John von Neumann, who was working on the Manhattan Project and seeking powerful means of making calculations. Showing great enthusiasm for the ENIAC project, Von Neumann immediately began work on eradicating its weaknesses, most notably the inability to easily re-program the machine, given the machine's internally-stored fixed program. The basic idea was to store program data and instructions in a single manner. Von Neumann designed the architecture of the new machine, the EDVAC (Electronic Discrete Variable Automatic Computer). While work continued on building the ENIAC, he identified five basic functions which continue to define the very backbone of computer architecture: the central control unit, the arithmetical calculation unit, memory, and input and output systems. The team also chose to use binary rather than decimal numbers. On 30th June 1945, von Neumann published "A First Draft of a Report on the EDVAC", which is without doubt the birth certificate of IT.

On 6th August 1945, Hiroshima was bombed, while the ENIAC would only be completed a few weeks later, in November of that same year.

2.4. IT: a complex, precious and expensive commodity

When the ENIAC was unveiled with great pomp on 16th February 1946, the Mark I, a thousand times slower than the new arrival, became history. Enthusiastic press coverage even coined the term "electronic brain". The whole world was fascinated by the invention, which appealed to scientists, researchers and industrialists alike, and left the general public speechless.

With war over, business picked up again. And yet, with the exception of Great Britain – where the world's first commercial computer, the Ferranti Mark I was produced in 1951 as a result of work done at Manchester University – no country had the means to launch into the commercial development of IT. Europe, which had nurtured the likes of Boole, Babbage, Turing and, of course, von Neumann, was unable to pull together and develop a strong IT industry, unlike other sectors such as aeronautics and aerospace, which have capitalized on the boost given by pan-European creation. Therefore, once again, the US market – with the backing of US state authorities – enabled the large-scale development of IT.

Thomas Watson has been quoted as saying that he estimated the worldwide market for computers as being limited to a dozen, and that the market was thus too limited to be of any interest to IBM. Nevertheless, IBM did not make the mistake of turning their back on the nascent market for long, and after a few years of observation, entered the race alongside the other office equipment manufacturers Remington Rand, Burroughs and NCR. These companies were up against the major players in the electronics sector, firms such as RCA, General Electric and Honeywell, who viewed the computer as a natural extension of their own activities.

They were soon joined by experts in innovation such as Eckert and Mauchly, who founded the Electronic Control Co. in 1946, and Engineering Research Associates (ERA), one of whose founders went on to start up the Control Data Corporation.

2.4.1. The UNIVAC venture

Eckert and Mauchly were the first to enter the market in the spring of 1946. Negotiations had led to an agreement with the Census Bureau (yet again! …) and the payment of $300,000 for a machine before it had even been built. At their Philadelphia laboratory, the scene was set for everything to be started from scratch. If they were to build a machine for industrial rather than experimental use, they would have to get around every technical and material obstacle in their path. They experienced the typical torments of technological start-ups: having to root around for funding while keeping clients waiting. They were faced with immense hardship, but were rewarded with new orders, and major investment in their new company, Eckert-Mauchly Computer Corporation (EMCC), was forthcoming. Unfortunately, their generous benefactor died in a plane crash, and once again they were threatened with bankruptcy, throwing them into the arms of the highest bidder, namely Remington Rand who thus gained control of EMCC. Work on building the

UNIVAC (the UNIVersal Automatic Computer) could therefore proceed in a healthier climate, and on 30th March 1951, the first machine was finally operational, having successfully passed a series of tests. It was delivered to the Census Bureau, the government also receiving the next two machines to be manufactured. The UNIVAC made history when it was used live on CBS to produce the first estimated results of the 1952 Presidential election, which saw Eisenhower's landslide victory over Stevenson.

2.4.2. The IBM riposte

IBM could not accept the fact that a competitor was making headway in such spectacular fashion. Spurred on by the energetic leadership of Watson Junior, IBM began work on three different computers, the Defense Calculator, the Tape Processing Machine and the Magnetic Drum Calculator, which gave rise to the birth of Models 701, 702 and 650 in December 1952 and 1953, although actual delivery only followed from 1955 onwards. With a canny sales policy and an ability to produce modular machines which were not only easy to transport and install, but also more reliable, IBM quickly gained the upper hand over UNIVAC. In 1956, Thomas J. Watson passed away aged 82. At that time, there were at most 2,000 computers around the world, with an average processing speed capacity of 10,000 instructions per second, and thus a total combined processing speed of 20 million instructions per second (mips). The embedded system of a modern Rafale fighter jet has a processing speed of 300 mips!

Even with their founder now gone, IBM's growth-rate remained remarkably high, and spectacular success ensued. Major achievements included the 1958 release of the first major real-time operating system, SAGE (Semi-Automatic Ground Environment), built for the North American Air Defense System by the Massachusetts Institute of Technology. The foundations of this system were laid as early as 1949, and the $8bn project went on to use the services of 700 of the 1,200 programmers trained in the US, in turn ensuring the total supremacy of the US hardware and software industries. 1962 saw the launch of SABRE, the first airline booking system, produced for American Airlines. SABRE was implemented across 50 cities and operated using two centralized 7090 computers.

Success was fuelled by an audacious innovations policy. In October 1959, IBM launched the 1401 computer, which was much more than a straightforward machine. It was, in fact, a very complete, high-performance system in which valves had made way for transistors and which incorporated a high-speed printer that ran at 600 lines per minute. It also introduced RPG (Report Program Generator), a completely new programming system, which went on to achieve lasting success. The system was astoundingly well-received. 12,000 1401 systems were distributed. In 1964, IBM launched the SYSTEM/360 range, which was the first to feature integrated software and hardware. It was the first such third generation machine to use integrated circuits. The full range of goods on offer was made up of six different central units, 44 types of peripherals and software tools, the OS/360 operating system and the PL/1 programming language. Launched in a blaze of publicity, it rendered all other computers virtually obsolete overnight. Orders came flooding in and delivery periods reached several years, while the 250,000-strong IBM's turnover hit $5bn. IBM's supremacy was complete with the release of the 360, which, despite its ambitious software and inability to cater for then in-vogue time-sharing demands, was the first modern computer. At the end of the 1960s, IBM laid claim to 75% of the mainframe market.

2.4.3. *The BUNCH*

IBM's opponents consisted of a group of firms which came to be referred to as the "BUNCH": Burroughs, Univac, NCR, Control Data and Honeywell. The opposition also included the US market-focused General Electric and RCA. The seven manufacturers picked up the little that was left of the mainframe sector, each having a market-share ranging from 2 to 5%, and unable to reap the enormous profits made by IBM, estimated at 25% of overall turnover. This peculiar situation led to players on the mainframe market being nicknamed "IBM and the seven dwarfs"! The fate of IBM's various rivals has been far less enviable than that of Big Blue, but they all left their mark on the history of North American IT in their own way, without having been able to draw benefit from the ever-expanding and increasingly democratic markets. European companies have had an even rougher and stormier ride.

And yet, the contest was far from being a walkover: IBM had to face up to many an onslaught from competitors. IBM products were not perfect, particularly as far as software was concerned, which left space for competitors to come up with both better and cheaper products, or to discover their own sales niche.

The release of Honeywell's IBM-compliant Model 200 in 1963, available in a number of different versions and capable of considerably higher performance levels with the IBM 1401, was in line with Honeywell's new policy as regards compatibility. RCA's response to System/360 came in 1964 with the Spectra 70 series. As for Burroughs and NCR, the former released the non-IBM-compliant 500 series in 1966, and the latter the Century Series in 1968. UNIVAC specialized in the airline bookings market. Control Data aimed for the major applications market, particularly in the military defense field, and produced high capacity machines. Finally, Burroughs remained centered on the banking sector.

Ultimately, the playing field was far from level, the "dwarfs" were losing more and more money, and the 1970-71 recession led to RCA and General Electric dropping out of the race. The BUNCH survived into the 1970s, but subsequently ran aground as they sought to safeguard their ecological niche.

Rank	Company	Output	Market Share
1	IBM	4,806	65.8
2	Rand	635	8.7
3	Burroughs	161	2.2
4	Control Data	147	2.0
5	NCR	126	1.7
6	RCA	120	1.6
7	General Electric	83	1.1
8	Honeywell	41	0.6
	Others	1,186	16.2
		7,305	

Computer manufacturer statistics, 1962

Rank	Company	Output	Market Share
1	IBM	19,773	49.6
2	Rand	4,778	12.0
3	NCR	4,625	11.6
4	Control Data	1,868	4.7
5	Honeywell	1,800	4.5
6	Burroughs	1,675	4.2
7	RCA	977	2.5
8	General Electric	960	2.4
	Others	3,420	8.6
		39,876	

Computer manufacturer statistics, 1967

2.5. The trials and tribulations of IT in Europe

Coming out of World War II, Europe realized how powerless she was at conducting formative economic policies to face up to the rise of the US, and in the quest for convergence, cutting-edge technology was certainly not going to be a priority, with more emphasis being put on the core industries essential to rebuilding the general infrastructure, as specified in the 1948 European Coal and Steel Community Treaty. Information and communications techniques were within the competence of each individual state, and whilst pre-war efforts had not resulted in a solid industry, the outcome of post-war ambitions proved hardly more convincing. The Gaullist vision of national independence, with the ups and downs of state intervention in the IT sector, gave rise to much criticism and irony. However, it must be recognized that the IT policies of the various European countries, which had veered off in different directions, scarcely shone. The failure of IT to take off in Europe could be attributed as much to the lead held by the US at the end of the war as to the strong presence, in Europe, of US companies, who had followed in the wake of the IBM flagship. Factors of the like were at least as decisive as the ignorance of political leaders and the lack of interest demonstrated by company directors. Remember that in the 1950s, the various US defense and military departments ploughed $400m into research and development at IBM alone, accounting for 60% of the firm's research budget. At that time, efforts made by European governments were derisory. Over the same period in the UK, the National Research Development Corporation had invested the equivalent of $15m across the whole of the nation's industry!

And yet the situation merited a vigorous turnaround. As of 1st January 1959, there were 2,000 calculators in the US, 110 in the UK, 98 in Germany and just 20 in France[4].

Country	1959	1967
Germany	94	2,963
UK	110	2,252
Italy	16	1,360
France	20	2,008
Total Europe	265	9,543
USA	2,034	39,516

Numbers of systems installed (regardless of size)

2.5.1. *France: caught between state intervention and US domination*

The figurehead of the movement in France was the Egli Bull Corporation, founded in 1931 and whose mechanographic machines were widely used by railway and insurance companies. Those very clients, aware that Egli Bull had hit hard times, acquired a 50% stake in the company's capital in 1933. Bull thus became "*Compagnie des Machines Bull*", and struggled until the war. However, in the post-war period, the company grew steadily, the workforce rising from 200 in 1935 to the 15,000 staff in 1964 engaged in producing a whole range of electronic calculators. However, hit by further financial shortcomings in 1960, Bull turned to General Electric, who gained 51% of capital in 1963, and later 66%. Bull became Bull General Electric, and then Honeywell Bull in 1970, when General Electric withdrew from the IT market.

---

[4] Figures quoted by Pierre Lhermitte in "*Le Pari informatique*" ("The IT Gamble").

In 1966, IBM's share of the French calculator market stood at 60%, followed by Bull GE (20%), Control Data (5%) and UNIVAC (2.8%). With 3.1% and 1.1% respectively, the two entirely French manufacturers SEA (*Société d'Electronique et d'Automatisme*) and CAE (*Compagnie Européenne d'Automatisme Electronique*) claimed less than 5% of the market. SEA played a singular part in the development of IT in France. The company was founded in 1948 by a group of engineers spurred on by one François-Henri Raymond, a visionary who, in 1947, had followed the example of others by making an initiatory voyage to the United States. SEA was a research unit – a veritable consultancy firm before the term had been coined – as well as a manufacturer of technical and scientific goods, and later of office computers with the CAB 500. Another peculiar case was that of IBM, who had a major foothold in France with 12,000 staff divided between plants in Montpellier and Corbeil-Essonne and in their research and development center in La Gaude. They intelligently opted for a more national approach – a firm rein being kept on American aspects of the corporation – and yet still failed to break into the public sector.

In the light of the US refusal to authorize the export of Control Data computers needed for calculations – most notably in the military and energy sectors – France's political desire was to be endowed with an IT industry which might be able to uphold the need for national independence and strengthen the resistance against American domination, hence the launch of *Plan Calcul* in 1966. In September of that year, an IT Commission was set up. Accountable to the Elysée Palace and under the leadership of Robert Galley, its mission was to federate the electronics industry and to promote the use of IT within state institutions. The scheme obliged the French companies in the sector – namely the Schneider subsidiary SEA, and CAE, the joint subsidiary of CGE and Thomson CSF – to come together as CII (*Compagnie Internationale pour l'Informatique*). CII was placed under the responsibility of a pool of private corporations (CSF, Thomson, CGE and Schneider). SPERAC was also set up to deal with the development of calculator-related systems and peripherals, and was a joint subsidiary of *Compagnie des Compteurs* and the French company Thomson-Houston. 1968 saw the delivery of CII's first calculator, the Iris 50, followed by the Iris 80. Then the French government urged CII to draw up alliances with European partners, to gain the international dimension which had hitherto been distinctly lacking. An agreement was signed on 4th July 1973 with Siemens and Philips, but the Unidata consortium, as it was known, was never to be. The next idea was for CII to merge with US firm Honeywell Bull in 1974, resulting in CII Honeywell Bull, thus shattering the dream of independent European IT. Sems, the subsidiary of Thomson, and *Télémécanique Electronique* also joined CII-HB. Within the framework of a risky and short-lived diversification policy, Saint Gobain became a stake-holder alongside Honeywell (1980) as part of a complex arrangement with Olivetti.

In 1982, Bull was nationalized by the Socialist government of the time. The state acquired 65% of company capital, and later 75.8% to which was added France Telecom's 17% stake. The tacit objective was as much one of saving jobs through palliative measures as of developing a genuine industrial tool, however outmoded it might have become in the worldwide climate of the day. Because of a lack of managerial leadership, development teams took a long time to merge, corporate culture remained heterogeneous through the overbearing influence of the state, and Bull never gained a long-term strategic vision or steady, committed shareholders. Had the state, by means of the *Commission Centrale des Marchés Informatiques* (Central Commission for IT Markets), not encouraged civil service departments and public sector companies to systematically purchase Bull goods, the ill-assorted and incomplete range of equipment on offer would not have survived as long as it did, regardless of the (genuine) quality of some isolated products, such as the Mini 6. In 1979, Bull was a pioneer in the development of the CP8 chip card. Many of the company's initiatives met with unfortunate consequences. These included the forced takeover of the IT operations of Honeywell, who supplied the GCOS mainframe operating system, and in 1989, the €600m (equivalent) takeover of US micro-computer manufacturer Zenith Data Systems, who until then had had a strong foothold in the US public service sector but immediately lost that lucrative market.

IT history in France has also been marked by successive attempts to develop the subject in schools. As early as 1970, the *Mission à l'Informatique* and the National Education Ministry launched a secondary school operation aimed at pupils" IT awareness. 500 teachers were put on a one-year training course, and 58 high schools were equipped with CII Mitra 15s and Télémécanique T1600s. A specific language was even developed for the scheme. Indeed, L.S.E. (*Langage Symbolique pour l'Enseignement*) isolated the teaching community from the outside world. In 1971, the *Institut National de Recherche Pédagogique* (National Institute for Pedagogical Research) founded an "IT and Teaching" department, to develop an experimental approach to the introduction of IT into teaching, but the *Center National de Documentation Pédagogique* (National Center for Pedagogical Documentation) only set up a software unit in 1982. Budgetary cuts in 1976 meant the first program was heavily compromised. However, the government renewed the scheme in 1978, and it became known as the "10,000 Computers in High Schools" operation. The "IT for Everyone" program launched by Laurent Fabius in 1985 was constructed around specific material solutions: Thomson's MO5 and TO7 micro-computers. However, the equipment did not have the necessary support at its disposal, nor did it have a satisfactory range of software, given the proprietary nature of its operating system. The ambitious project involved purchasing 120,000 machines and training 110,000 teachers. The plan soon proved to be a failure, both in terms of its pedagogical content and its industrial aspects, as Thomson ceased producing micro-computers in 1989 after the aborted attempt to merge with Olivetti. In 1988, the French Education Board purchased a further batch of machines – which this time met the common

13000 standard – for secondary schools and technical colleges. However, all these costly and spectacular operations were also short-lived, due to the lack of genuine pedagogical integration of the IT tools within learning processes.

The stormy and as yet unfinished history of the national figurehead, which has allegedly cost the country €7.5bn, has shown the French state's inability to conduct an IT policy, content for a long time as it was with playing industrial Meccano with the clumsy initiatives of ministers and their advisors, far-removed from the logic and the technological realities of the market. IT use and training, the last resorts of competitiveness, were neglected in favor of focusing on industrial factors. Other sides of the French IT policy, such as the major levels of public research around IRIA, which later became INRIA, the *Institut National de Recherche en Informatique et en Automatique* (National Institute for Research into IT and Automatics), and the experiments in implementing IT training at school with the "IT for Everyone" scheme, have also illustrated the gap between awareness of IT stakes and the concrete ability to support durable operations out in the field.

2.5.2. *Great Britain's vanishing greatness*

Despite a previously promising track record, Great Britain fared no better in preserving a strong identity in the IT field. Indeed, during the pre- and post-war periods, the British had developed remarkable IT skills in the domains of industry and academia, particularly at the Universities of Manchester and Cambridge. The EDSAC (Electronic Delay Storage Automatic Calculator), a digital and electronic machine with a stored program and which became operational on 6th May 1949, had been conceived in laboratories at Cambridge University, opened in 1936. Manchester University designed and produced the Small-Scale Experimental Machine (SSEM) – also known as "Baby" – which operated for the first time on 21st June 1948. Baby was the first machine to be built around a complete architecture and the first case of a machine being able to store both data and a program in its electronic memory. The following year, it served as the basis for a more powerful machine, the Manchester Mark 1, with an integrated high speed magnetic drum. This was put into service at the University for various scientific calculations. The Mark 1 provided the foundations for the industrial development of the Ferranti Mark 1, launched in February 1951 and widely regarded as the world's first-ever commercially available computer. In 1959, the Atlas I computer, designed by Manchester University and Ferranti Ltd., introduced two new types of technology which have become a fundamental element of modern computers: virtual memory and multi-programming. A pipeline system was implemented for running instructions, the machine incorporating a calculation unit for whole numbers and another unit for movable decimal points. Its processing power was of 200 kFLOPS (floating operations per second).

One unique and edifying event in the history of IT deserves particular recognition: the story of J. Lyons & Co, who made tea and cakes and ran tea-rooms. Wanting to develop the idea of scientific management systems, and given the lack of suitable offers on the market, the company directors began work on the realization of an integrated IT-supported information system. Again, this was sparked off by a far-reaching fact-finding trip to the US, during which the two directors had seen the ENIAC and met Eckert, Aiken and IBM. They immediately became aware of the very real potential that such "electronic brains" – then, being used to make calculations for scientific and military purposes – might have if applied to the management of companies. They enthusiastically reported back to the board, and, in May 1949, the decision was made to design and build their own system, on the basis of the work done in Cambridge on the EDSAC. So, the Lyons Systems Research Office was set up, and headed by David Caminer. It brought together a 20-strong team of youthful talents whose achievements in this unique experience, in which everything had to be started from scratch, served as launch-pads for their respective careers. On 17th November 1951, the system functioned for the first time using genuine production, manufacturing and stock data. In February 1954, LEO (Lyons Electronic Office) produced its first payslips. The system could be regarded as the first-ever computer-stored corporate application. The sole objective of the Lyons teams was to improve efficiency within the company. Their goal was certainly not to enter the world of IT. Nevertheless, the venture met with such success that, after LEO I, the Lyons board chose to pursue operations and started up a dedicated subsidiary, LEO Computers Ltd., who went on to produce LEO II in 1957. The system was a *bona fide* success across the country, in industry, retail and public services, most notably because of its wages application. In 1961, LEO III was released, and was the first machine to feature transistors, multi-programming and high-level language, all of three years before … IBM. In 1962 and 1963, 10 orders were registered for the LEO III, despite the competition from IBM. In February 1963, Lyons shareholders decided to merge LEO Computers Ltd. and English Electric. LEO's biggest coup then came with the General Post Office's purchase of the most powerful computer in the range, the LEO 326, which remained operational until 1981. A total of 73 machines were produced between 1954 and 1963.

The merger was but the prelude to a long movement of concentration within the British IT industry. The Labour government formed after Harold Wilson's 1964 general election victory was particularly concerned about the country's brain drain, as brilliant scientists crossed the Atlantic in droves. It was decided that the commercial spin-offs of new technology should be developed in order to revitalize the British economy. The government set up the Ministry of Technology, which was handed to Frank Cousins, and which brought together several state departments, agencies and laboratories, with the prime mission of saving the British IT industry, hence, the creation of the National Research Development Corporation, to finance the commercial applications of research, and particularly the introduction of new computers. Among the most influential researchers was one Donald Davies, who in 1966 began a longstanding fight to equip the UK with a business-oriented packet data transmission network. Starting out with Plessey calculators for the communication nodes, he launched Mark I, an experimental network within the National Physical Laboratory. The network was soon to be followed by Mark II, and enabled NPL researchers to work in an operational network environment until 1986. However, Davies failed to persuade the General Post Office to set up a packet switch network, which they only eventually implemented on an experimental basis in 1977.

In 1964, English Electric and Marconi merged to form English Electric Leo Marconi Computers. By selling off LEO-related assets, Lyons were able to cover the costs incurred throughout their IT venture. In March 1967, Elliott Automation joined the group, and in July 1968, the new entity, English Electric Computers Ltd., merged with International Computers and Tabulators (ICT) – whose 1900 series had had some commercial success – to form International Computers Limited (ICL). ICL began producing computers which were not compatible with the IBM 360, unlike English Electric's System 4. ICL struggled in the 1980s, and were taken over by the Japanese group Fujitsu in 1990. In 1996, ICL ceased all manufacturing activities and focused on services, with a 20,000-strong workforce.

LEO's exploits brought the limited nature of the enterprise to the surface. In the complex world of IT, an industrial gamble will never be successful unless it goes hand-in-hand with the staunch desires of the management team, stability as regards shareholders, not to mention international footholds. Although, historically speaking, British IT had little in common with the situation in France, both ended up in a similar national *cul-de-sac*.

It might be remembered that Britain played a pioneering role in the development of micro-computing, with the Sinclair Z-80. Even the BBC got in on the act, with an educational micro-computing project in the 1980s, the commercialization of several models of BBC micro-computers and, above all, a high number of software programs. Psion, who pioneered and then played a leading part in the development of personal digital assistants, surrendered much of the market to Palm, and have since, as part of the Symbian Consortium, focused on their operating system, as well as on professional and portable data capturing tools.

2.6. Centralization of IT power and work organization

Major IT systems really came into their own with the growth of tertiary occupations within public and private organizations. The Taylorization of tertiary work was further emphasized by the implementation of rigid IT systems which froze organizations, not by choice but because of their inability to escape associated technical constraints. The complexity and cost of implementing home-made IT systems rendered the rapid evolution of structures and policies impossible. "The implementation of a corporate IT system should lead to the elaboration of long-term methods and the construction of consistent reasoning that is sufficiently shielded from accidental disturbance (...) This basic schema is to cater for fluctuating situations and must not be subject to any individual decision that might call the laboriously engineered program and adjustments into question" wrote CIGREF[5] founding President Pierre Lhermitte, thus putting into words the concerns of contemporary computer engineers that their complex and fragile edifices – which had been so painful to deliver – should not be altered.

The material installation of the first central computers meant considerable financial investment for the few major companies capable of withstanding such an outlay. Indeed, computer rooms needed to be fitted with suspended ceilings and raised floors to house electric cables, inter-unit wiring and the air conditioning systems essential for cooling the enormous valve machines. The rental costs for early equipment, such as the IBM 704 or 705, came to $40,000 per month around the end of the 1950s.

Other than the technical complexity involved in installing and fine-tuning the equipment, its introduction brought about a sea change in organization and practices. This complexity left a longstanding mark on the IT world and its ambiguous relationship with both managers and staff. Technical adjustments would stretch out over several years, costs would be unpredictable, and the frequent errors gave rise to the simplistic but common tendency to blame the computer for everything. Even today, at a time when the democratization of IT has led to the belief that everything has become simple and reliable overnight, the image of IT continues to suffer from the painful early adjustments that had to be made.

Centralized IT was organized around a single computer linked to non-intelligent terminals by a proprietary network. By necessity, the whole system would be governed from the center. Such systems did not gain immense popularity as they solely catered for the kind of numbered data handled by administrative departments, considered to be a costly but inevitable facet of corporate life. That is why the first major IT systems were confined to applications for accounting purposes and aimed at "administrative automation". And still today, as a result of these links, the IT department – whose missions now encompass all fields of corporate operations – are often linked to the financial branch of the enterprise. Until the 1980s, most of the major systems that were introduced did not bring about changes that affected work

---

5 CIGREF, currently presided by the author, is the *Club Informatique des Grandes Entreprises Françaises*, the French corporate IT users association.

processes and methods. In fact, they functioned using deferred batch systems that processed and restored the basic data passively fed into machines by users. Real-time operations alone opened up new areas for improved performance, by introducing direct dialogue between users and their machines, and by enabling the penetration of IT on the market at large for industrial applications.

Major 1970s information systems, many of which are still in use in legacy corporations, have taken on board the various strata of successive organizational practices within their companies. They bear the scars of their manual beginnings and of the paper-based monitoring and publishing methods that corporations still consider essential, encouraged as they are to pursue such archaic practices by the sheer weight of administrative controls and laws.

Just as it took 30 years for the electric engine to be decentralized in workshops and provide a definitive substitute for belt-based central engine energy distribution systems, 30 years had passed before informational energy was produced by local networked workstations.

The 1960s were overshadowed by the centralized IT model as personified by IBM. Still the decade saw the development of a number of alternatives which paved the way for the eventual advent of the digital age. With the arrival of integrated circuits, new players were able to make headway on the market segments which had been abandoned by IBM. Digital Equipment Corporation (DEC), and other minicomputer manufacturers such as Prime Computer, Data General and Scientific Data Systems, aimed at the market for industrial and scientific applications, and the small and medium-sized enterprise sector. However, the worlds of academia and research, both in Europe and the US, were also behind advances in new hardware and software solutions that were newer and cheaper than central systems, and opened more doors towards whole new IT and corporate cultures. Over a 15-year period, this was the breeding ground for the competencies and practices that would lead to the digital revolution.

One of the main vectors for the emergence of new markets was not a machine but an operating system. In 1965, Bell Labs, in collaboration with MIT and General Electric, were working on an ambitious program for the development of a new mainframe operating system which would support time-sharing. The system in question was MULTICS (MULTiplexed Information and Computing Service), which Bell relinquished in 1969. It was then commercialized by Honeywell, and heavily influenced the GCOS 6 series of systems, used by CII HB for the Mini 6 and then on the Bull DPS-6 until 1982. This scenario is indicative of the complex relationships between players in the closed world of IT. After pulling out of the MULTICS project, Bell Labs authorized two of their talented programmers, Ken Thompson and Dennis M. Ritchie, to look into the development of a new, compact and elegant operating system which they called UNIX. Using a tiny DEC PDP-7 for their tinkering, within months they had designed a system that was re-written in the programming language C. This language, which was itself a major innovation at the time, had also been conceived by Ritchie so that his system could be carried by several IT platforms. Bell Labs were wise enough to offer the system to universities and research laboratories at a very low price, leading to the overnight popularity of UNIX in the academic world where young engineers were busy learning their trade. Over a few short years, a whole budding UNIX culture took shape, which would lead to even more powerful versions of the tool. By the end of the 1970s, UNIX was well-established as the sole credible major platform-compliant alternative to the IBM world.

The arrival on the scene of minicomputers is also a direct consequence of the development of integrated circuits, and later of micro-processors. By providing the same power for a tenth of the cost of an equivalent mainframe system, minicomputers were a straightforward response to the decentralization of organizations by taking the processing power closer to users. Prior to the micro-processing revolution, Ken Olsen, an MIT engineer, took it upon himself to develop an IT approach that would rival that of IBM. He gained the support of the first modern-style venture capitalist, the French General George Doriot, who taught at Harvard and had founded American Research and Development (ARD). Olsen began by producing electronic circuits, before announcing in 1960 the launch of the PDP-1, the first cheap, no-frills calculator designed for the scientific market and priced $125,000, around a tenth of the usual price. However, this economic breakthrough failed to produce a stampede of potential clients, and it was not until 1965 and the PDP-8 that success was finally forthcoming. The PDP-8 marked the history of IT, and was sold in its thousands, particularly to universities and industry, who turned to the machine for the purposes of process automation. It also marked the true beginnings of DEC and the minicomputer concept. DEC continued to play a major part in the history of IT, thanks to the performances of the PDP and later the VAX series, the quality of their VMS operating system, and their understanding of the stakes associated with relational databases. Come 1989, the Massachusetts-based engineering firm employed 125,000 staff, before a period of decline in the 1990s led to the humiliating acceptance of Compaq's 1999 takeover bid. In the present market, turned upside down by the rise of Intel micro-processor-based solutions, the same fate has overtaken most of the other minicomputer era manufacturers, before they ever achieved the levels of success and glory experienced by DEC.

Chapter 3

The Dawn of the Digital Era

3.1. The quest for new freedom

The "digital era" began at the beginning of the 1970s at the time when, focusing on micro-processors, innovators freely began to dream up all the new ways of using IT which were both cheap and easy to implement. They were guided by their strong technical desire to split from weighty centralized IT processing by exploring new, reliable and approachable means of sharing information. They also wanted to picture new practices which would break free from the domineering "grey-suit" model of the East Coast. The digital world was the fruit of the work and dreams of a generation of scientists who built, piece by piece, the tools which we now know so well. A great deal of dogma and inertia had to be eliminated if a world of lateral innovation was to be conceived, in which all kinds of information, images, voice and general data might be digitally generated, broadcast, mixed, stored and re-used *ad infinitum*. Beyond the technical challenge at stake lay commendable societal ambitions. By enabling complete interoperability between different contents[6], regardless of their forms, digitalization has indeed removed the burden of constraints brought about by multiple entries and physical storage, by opening the gateway towards the genuinely unlimited distribution of information, and, as a consequence, the overall growth of knowledge potential. It is far more than just another stage in the progress of calculation power. Digitalization represents a break with the past that opens up whole new perspectives in all fields of human activity.

---

[6] With the single but notable exception of compatibility between formats and ... electrical plugs!

The construction of the digital economy progressed by gaining from – and simultaneously breaking away from – the experience gained by the IT industry in the 1960s. The transformation process affecting the worldwide economy has been powered by the initial speed, methods, tools and laboratories of the IT industry, thus leading to faster-evolving IT and widespread distribution of technology in all other industries. IT is now present in all sectors of activity, both through the design and manufacturing stages, and within the products themselves. Given the fact that its diffusion is not linear, the slow process is still in its early days, even though it has been under way for more than 30 years. As in all major shifts of this kind, multiple factors have made up the conditions which have brought about these changes. Some believed the concomitance of the 1974 oil crisis and the US deployment of the embryonic digital economy triggered a major shift in long-term development phases from which the US would benefit. The European world of the first and second industrial revolutions, first steam then electricity, was forced to retreat before the onslaught of the third technical revolution, definitively destined to consolidate the foundations of America's dominant technological supremacy. It is important to remember the context at the time. The Cold War was still in progress. The arms and space races – which were such prominent elements of the competition between the Eastern and Western blocs throughout the 1960s – led to public research programs needing the very basic technologies that the information society at large would also require. In 1962, all the integrated circuits produced in the US were used in military and space. In 1964, the Minuteman II launch control facility was the first military program to feature a calculator which made use of integrated circuits, and the guidance system used by Apollo in 1965 followed suit. The US Federal Government played a considerable role in the rise of a whole generation of scientists and researchers who went on to spread their wings and start up their own companies. ARPA (Advanced Research Projects Agency), founded in 1958, was part of the US Department of Defense. Towards the end of the 1960s, through the channel of IPTO (Information Processing Techniques Office) which had been launched in 1962, ARPA funded the development of computer science educational programs across four universities which subsequently went on to play a major part in the history of IT in the US[7]. However, we should take care not to over-simplify the demonstration, for when clarifying things after the event, determinism is an easier option than the rigorous search for causalities. Breaks with the past can never be that decisive, and the digital world, leaning heavily on previous revolutions, combined the effects of both major shifts and continuity. It sought, indeed, to bring complementary factors on board rather than to exclude – rather AND than OR!

The development of the digital economy rested on two complementary but dissymmetrical forces. Supplier-side, technical innovation meant that more powerful

---

[7] University of California at Berkeley, Stanford University, Carnegie-Mellon Institute, University of Utah.

machines could be put on the market at lower prices, and improved performance led to the promise of new services through the software on offer. User-side awareness of what the tools could do aroused the desire to put them to good use, either to improve what they were already doing, or to bring new ideas for products, services or organizations to fruition. The movement has remained uneven most of the time, because the well-organized forces of innovation, endowed with powerful and accomplished marketing programs, have a natural tendency to commercialize the high-return solutions that they want to see on the market, while users, in their undefined world of contradictory interests, have very few means at their disposal to be able to lead providers in the direction that might be the most useful for them. What is more, different cycles are at play. The rate at which new products – not to be confused with technological innovations – are put on the market is faster than it is possible for new practices to be invented and diffused.

Even with its excesses, this dialectical movement has, over the past 30 years, produced a powerful industry and arguably more transformations than during any other era. However, despite the visibility of its performances, the process for introducing and metabolizing change has not always been considered to be mastered or to have satisfied users. IT is still regarded as a complex and even hostile universe, which destabilizes organizations in an unpredictable manner without respecting its prior commitments. The distortion between the promises made and the quality of eventual realizations is very much the result of the IT industry business model, and the sector's modes of construction and destruction. The 30 year boom in the IT industry, which stretched from 1971 to 2000, provides a wealth of lessons to be learnt through the analysis of successful transformations and missed opportunities alike, and sheds some light on the future.

3.2. The colorful saga of major firsts

A new leaf was turned in United States post-Vietnam ... the scene was set for a storybook tale featuring the Volkswagen vans of former hippies, garages, forgotten inventors and brilliant young people with sound business knowledge and solid PR acumen. The adventure is worthy of a Hollywood movie, and will undoubtedly inspire scriptwriters to piece together a revised version of *The Right Stuff* with a whole host of colorful characters, a lot of money, a good sprinkling of power struggles, and a fair share of paranoia and schizophrenia. A number of locations have taken on mythical status during the saga: Silicon Valley in California, Route 128 in Boston, and the suburbs of Seattle. A number of splintered families have to share space in the hall of fame of modern IT: institutional players, founding fathers, clumsy innovators, skilful copycats, martyred entrepreneurs, etc. Although the families have been torn, they often enthusiastically come together to wallow in the self-congratulatory praise of their values, and are uniform in their ability to hate each other one day and co-operate the next, so giving rise to the charming neologism "co-opetition".

But let us go back to the "new" roots …

Just as those generations of young people were keen to rid themselves of the old world, they also tackled central computers which they deemed to be patronizing machines served by zealous high priests. The old East Coast firms, characterized by IBM and ATT's grey-suited executives[8], were conformist and symbolized the White Anglo-Saxon Protestant work ethic. They personified a rigid vision of technology in a stable world. And yet the idea that computers might be able to lay down the law had become unbearable for many. It is no longer possible to conceive the extent to which it was difficult to access the invaluable, priceless and complex resources of a central computer, when the need for information was constantly growing. Users were intensely frustrated, as were the IT engineers whose creativity was being stifled. To gain freedom from the guardianship of central computers and associated structures, the "liberators" cleared a number of different ways during the 1970s. They themselves are now in the process of being ousted by the web generation. History – progress? – marches on …

3.2.1. *The first micro-computers*

With the invention of the micro-processor in 1971[9] came a revolution within the revolution. By enabling all the functions of a full computer to be featured in a single component, the micro-processor paved the way towards major changes which would have an ever-growing effect. Increased miniaturization and a decrease in electricity consumption led to a multiplication in the number of possible uses of IT, by integrating micro-processors in a large number of tools. With lower costs, the thresholds for entry into the world of digitalization were also lowered, allowing schools, SMEs and private households to gain access to equipment which had previously been limited to large businesses. The democratization of IT widened the existing base and enabled software editors to secure returns on their products and invest more heavily in research and development. The virtuous spiral has now been spinning constantly for 30 years, although the micro-computing market is currently faced with problems because viable projects have reached saturation level, and imagination has come to a halt.

---

[8] IBM's head office is in Armonk, in the state of New York, AT&T's head office is in New York and central activities in New Jersey, while Digital had its headquarters in Maynard, in the suburbs of Boston (Massachusetts).
[9] Intel 4004.

As early as 1972, prototypes of micro-computers, with little or no commercial future, were being developed by Xerox, Digital and the French company R2E. R2E had been founded by André Truong Trong Thi, who could legitimately claim to be one of the fathers of micro-computing with the Micral, based around an Intel 8008 processor. The market was flooded with individual calculators. Costing $400 in 1970, by 1976 the price tag read $50. The fact that they could be programmed made them *bona fide* "personal computers", as Hewlett-Packard proudly proclaimed when launching the $765 HP-65 in 1974. While the IT giants remained generally indifferent, the micro-computer market developed thanks to amateur radio, electronics and IT enthusiasts, who looked to specialist shops and magazines, particularly *Popular Electronics*, for the necessary plans and components. The micro-computing venture really came into being with the 1975 launch of the first micro-computer, the Altaïr 8800, which took its name from the TV series Star Trek. Its inventor, Ed Roberts, had started a small company – MITS (Micro Instrumentation Telemetry Systems) – in Albuquerque, New Mexico. The primitive machine had a 256-byte memory, was built around an Intel 8080, and put on the market in kit form for $367. Working from their Menlo Park garage in what has since become Silicon Valley, Steve Wozniak and Steve Jobs were inspired by the small size of the Altaïr to produce the first Apple I and later the legendary Apple II.

The market took off, dozens of companies launched micro-computers for the hobbyist market and the distribution of machines and peripherals came together with the arrival of the ComputerLand chain of shops, and, in the press, with the magazines *Byte and Popular Computing*. Commodore and Tandy entered the market with powerful promotion and distribution resources. The market soared, and the often ephemeral market players mushroomed. According to figures published by French magazine *L"Ordinateur Individuel* in their 1982-1983 guide book, there were no less than 124 different models of desktop machines, 21 types of pocket computers and 1,000 miscellaneous suppliers … on the French market alone! Prices started at the equivalent of €102 for a Sinclair ZX81, which was purchased by thousands of satisfied customers. Computers designed for the corporate world were far more expensive, costing the equivalent in today's prices of between €13,000 and €18,000. The equivalent of €14,500 would buy an HP-87XM, with 128 kilobytes of RAM (random access memory), 48 kilobytes of ROM (read-only memory), a QWERTY keyboard, a 9-inch screen, two floppy drives, run with BASIC programming language and an HP processor. Reference to the subsequent democratization of IT is therefore not in vain, certainly as far as the price/performance ratio of personal computers is concerned!

High school friends Steve Jobs and Steve Wozniak worked for Atari and Hewlett Packard respectively. Together they created, in 1976, the Apple I, of which they sold 200 models. With start-up capital of $91,000, Apple Computer was created in 1976, and achieved rapid success with the April 1977 launch of the Apple II, a fine springboard for the company which, by 1982, had registered a turnover of $583m! However, at the end of the 1970s, serious IT professionals, even in the US, still regarded the micro-computer as nothing more than a toy for amateur enthusiasts. IBM counter-attacked in 1981 with the IBM 5150 PC[10], a lackluster machine which, at least, managed to make micro-computing respectable in the eyes of the traditional IT milieu. Nevertheless, Apple can be credited with having fathered the first real personal computer to go down in history, the Macintosh. The compact, user-friendly Macintosh was launched in a blaze of publicity on Super Bowl Sunday in 1984. Learning from the frustratingly incomplete experience they had gained from LISA, an innovative but overly expensive machine which had been released in 1982, this time, Apple had put into practice a number of concepts developed by Xerox at PARC, the Palo Alto Research Center, with levels of consistency and ease of use made possible by the Mac's compact and (almost) portable material architecture. It should also be emphasized that all this was available at a highly competitive price. The Macintosh, with its 128 kilobytes of memory, a Motorola 68000 processor running at 8MHz, and a 9-inch integral screen, was put on the market for $2,495, compared with $9,995 for LISA. In September 1985, Steve Jobs was forced out of Apple with a $150m golden handshake from John Sculley, a regular shareholder who had arrived from PepsiCo. Jobs moved on to a new venture: NeXT Software. The NeXT Computer System was a potent, user-friendly machine, with exceptional image- and sound-processing ability, powerful software (for word-processing, messaging, databases and calculations) and a rewritable optical drive with 1 gigabyte of storage space. The NeXT took the same path as the Xerox Star did in its time, and although it remains a splendid machine that broke the mould, it was not adapted to the market and was destined to have but limited success, academics being alone in footing the $6,500 bill for the cube-shaped computers. NeXT ceased hardware production activities in 1993, having shipped 50,000 units, and concentrated on software developments until, in 1996, they were taken over by … Apple. NeXT served as software backbone for the superb MacOS X operating system, the only accomplished alternative to the Wintel world!

The market for workstations built for computer-aided design purposes developed in the early 1990s. Their architecture and graphic interface were identical to those on micro-computers, they used the same processors (Motorola 68000), and ran under UNIX. They were costly, top-of-the-range machines, and were associated with advanced peripherals such as plotters. The first major player on this nascent but rapidly flourishing market was the Massachusetts-based Apollo, started up by one Bill Poduska, who had also founded Prime Computer. Workstations priced at $40,000 were successfully shifted before the company was acquired by Hewlett-Packard in 1989. Another key mover, and one which has survived the upheavals in

---

[10] Standing of course for "Personal Computer", which became synonymous with IBM-compliant PCs, in other words, those using Microsoft operating systems.

the IT world, is Sun Microsystems. One of Silicon Valley's veritable child prodigies, Sun Microsystems started out in Mountain View with a team of four Stanford-educated employees, running the Berkeley UNIX operating system. In 1982, the $20,000 SUN-2 workstation was put on the market. Success soon followed, and turnover achieved by the dynamic company hit $1bn in 1988. In 1990, Sun introduced the SPARCStation 1, the first workstation to be sold for less than $5,000. Sun went on to introduce Java technology, the historic universal software platform.

In the 1990s, the market settled into a three-tiered pyramid of solutions for separate application fields. The top layer was made up of professional management mainframe systems (IBM, BUNCH or similar). Then came specialized machines (DEC, Tandem, and Silicon Graphics, Apollo or Sun workstations). At the bottom of the pile was the PC, serving a blurred and unstable sector in which it took a decade before consistent main lines based around lasting standards emerged.

3.2.2. Sources of inspiration

Information Technology has always known how to put the major companies responsible for its birth and development in the spotlight, and praise the brands which have personified the boom in the industry. However, in fact, IT owes much more to researchers in the academic world, who have taken technology onward and upward, than to the businessmen who have transformed ideas of the like into commercial successes. Without fundamental and assiduous research, which as we have seen was largely funded by state authorities, and without the creative imagination of communities of researchers, IT would never have been able to generate such achievements. The world of computer science has been largely outshone by the triumphs of IT firms. Let us think back to the sources of inspiration whose work brought about the development of the products of the industry we now use.

3.2.2.1. PARC

Palo Alto, in the heart of what was to become Silicon Valley, was the setting for what can be regarded as a major source of inspiration for modern IT. At the end of the 1960s, the Xerox Corporation were concerned by the threat of the "paper-free office" on their core reprography activities: hence their decision to constitute an exceptional team of researchers whose mission it was to create the "information architecture" with no targets in terms of deliverables or immediate profits. At that time, the 1970 Mansfield Amendment had stopped the flow of military defense funds to civil research programs, and Xerox, who had achieved great success with the 914 photocopier, invested heavily in the research project. Researchers were attracted with the greatest of ease and flocked to California. They came from MIT, from the corporate world, and from the four ARPA-supported universities, including Robert Metcalfe, who would go on to invent Ethernet. Led by George Pake, the researchers tackled the vast assignment at hand and in the process laid the foundations of contemporary micro-computing. The slogan of PARC researchers was "The best way to predict the future is to invent it". As early as 1973, they were developing a micro-computer, the Alto, of which a thousand or so models, costing all of $18,000 each, were produced for Xerox's in-house needs. The Alto introduced the first bit-mapped screen (72 pixels per inch), vertical full-page display, graphic user interface (GUI), the mouse, multiple windows, and the first WYSIWYG[11] word processor. A second model, designed for the professional market, was produced in 1981: the 8010 Star Information System. However, it was a commercial failure, due to the fact that it was ahead of its time in terms of its sophistication and its sheer strangeness in a market which was dominated by cheap hobbyist PCs. However, the objective was far more ambitious. The goal was not to deliver an isolated machine for personal use, like IBM's PC, but to provide a complete networked system which would be able to exchange mail and produce, classify, and print varied documents. Tools as a whole had to be easy to use, and the computer itself was to be virtually invisible ... the objectives were met on that score, although it was the Macintosh which rendered the concepts accessible for the general public. PARC's most notable contributions include XNS protocol network architecture, Ethernet, laser printing, page description languages, perfected lasers and object-oriented language (Smalltalk), which was developed by Alan Kay who went on to join Atari and then Apple. Smalltalk made the Macintosh interface possible.

PARC is still an active fundamental research center and is now focused around three areas: smart matter (based on MEMS[12], techniques for the extreme miniaturization of components and equipment), major networks and documents, and knowledge ecologies (management of interaction between man and document, evolving interfaces, natural language, etc.).

3.2.2.2. MIT

The other hotbed of computer science was, and still is, situated on the East Coast, in Cambridge, near Boston, at the heart of one of the most exciting and powerful campuses in the United States, which is home not only to MIT, the Massachusetts Institute of Technology, but also to Harvard. When Project MAC (for Multiple Access Computer and Machine-Aided Cognition) was launched in 1963, under the leadership of Fernando Corbato and Bob Fano and with the aid of a $2m grant from the inevitable ARPA, no-one imagined that one day computers would be

---

[11] What You See Is What You Get.

[12] Micro-Electro-Mechanical Systems: these are complete silicon-supported micro-systems, which capture and process data, and influence their environment.

used to develop inter-personal relations, to access shared databases for educational purposes, and even, perish the thought, to have fun! The project subsequently progressed, drawing in researchers who then branched out in numerous directions, before becoming a single research institute: The MIT Laboratory for Computer Science. In the 1960s, computer scientists aimed to find ways to share the power of a central computer, whose use had become both costly and severely limited by batch-related constraints. The first generations of programmers were subjected to tedious rituals: they would first write the instructions of the program on paper, then punch the data onto perforated cards (without making any errors …), before transporting the series of perforated cards to the calculation center (without dropping them!), where an operator would enter the data onto magnetic tape with the use of a punch card machine. And finally, if and when the computer was available, the program would run, so that the author could retrieve the program on paper … complete with program-generated errors! The cycle would then be repeated until the programmer was satisfied … The system was slow, ineffective, and was the ultimate nightmare of programmers who had but one dream: to be able to split the time machines spent calculating – which amounts to a minute proportion of overall cycles – in order to speed up the processing sequence of the program, hence the notion of "timesharing". The ambition of teams at MIT and elsewhere was to build a robust, open, easily-accessible, shared system. They believed that the interest of such a system would be to enable a team working on a single subject to share knowledge and skills, 24 hours a day, seven days a week. To deal with interruptions brought about by maintenance, the system had to be built with incorporated extraneous sub-sets. These concepts, detailed in a forward-looking article by Fano and Corbato in the September 1966 issue of *Scientific American*, formed the very basis of the research being carried out by MIT in partnership with Bell Labs and General Electric, which in 1968 gave rise to the Multics mainframe timesharing operating system project (Multiplexed Information and Computing Service). Multics was put into service at MIT in 1971, despite the two partners dropping out of the project, and the appearance of UNIX. It met the initial demands for a system that would be totally available to a community made up of 500 users. However, with the success of Digital and the introduction of micro-processors, researchers began to have doubts about the future of major IT systems.

In 1970, the laboratory split into two, giving birth to another branch, the MIT Artificial Intelligence Laboratory, and in 1975 Project MAC thus became the MIT Laboratory for Computer Science, focusing on micro-processors under the leadership of one Michael Dertouzos. This research resulted in the principles behind an extremely simple expansion bus, the NuBus, which was, then, used by Apple for the Macintosh II, and the delivery of UNIX on key micro-processors of the era, the Intel 8086, Motorola 68000 and Zilog Z8000. Their next main mission was to contribute to laying the foundations of the web.

3.2.3. *The first groundbreaking software*

In the 1960s, computers were programmed using low-level proprietary language which was close to machine language. With the appearance of machine-independent programming languages such as FORTRAN (1956) and COBOL (1957), which were then compiled or translated into machine language, the computer program development industry came into being. It was not until 1969 that IBM decided to sell machines and software separately. However, the growth of the autonomous software industry came about at the end of the 1970s with the development of major operating systems other than OS/360, in other words, UNIX, DOS, Windows and Macintosh OS. The first moves towards bringing "users" into the secret and closed world of IT were the introduction of straightforward programming for enthusiasts, swiftly followed by office tools. Micro-computers provided both the means and a symbol as users freed themselves from the authority of centralized IT. In 1982, a special issue of the French publication *L'Ordinateur Individuel* stated: "Just a few years ago, the association of computers and companies could only be conceived as part of an IT world under the control of white-coated technicians. Times have changed, and while powerful machines still have an important part to play, the major asset of computers that are now appearing in offices is that they are indeed *personal* computers". The use of easily operated software – word processing and spreadsheet programs, database management systems – and controllable printing functions meant that the bell tolled for dedicated word processors and, once the charm of the solitary personal computer began to wear off, their use as units within networks became essential.

3.2.3.1. *The spreadsheet revolution*

In 1978, a Harvard MBA student was tired of calculating the financial data of his case studies on paper. Dan Bricklin, for it was he, attempted to use a DEC computer to simplify the task. He quickly realized that it would be just as tedious to have to rewrite the program of instructions for each calculation. Along with Bob Frankston, a friend from MIT, he spent months seeking a more efficient solution which would make it possible to construct tables made up of rows and columns of numbers, in which calculations would be carried out automatically whenever data was edited. Their invention was given the name VisiCalc, for VISIble CALCulator, and it was put on the market in combination with the Apple II in 1979. From its humble beginnings, VisiCalc rapidly achieved commercial success, and in its wake brought success to the machine without which it could not work, and which, at the time, cost 20 times more. Once again, innovators – working without preconceived constraints on a quest for an effective and elegant solution to a practical problem – enabled progress to be made. However commonplace it may now seem, this product is probably responsible for the greatest advances in data processing, thanks to its simplicity and its efficiency, as proved by the millions of users every day worldwide. VisiCalc took off quickly, but the competition soon became stiff, its founders quarreled, and the company fell by the wayside in 1985.

Constant improvements were made on electronic spreadsheets from 1978 onwards by Lotus and their 1-2-3 spreadsheet program, and by Microsoft with Excel and Multiplan. Spreadsheet programs are now regarded as flagship software and have become an essential tool for most business analysts, who have far more costly software packages at their fingertips and yet still resort to the straightforward calculation functions and no-frills graphics of such a simple, widely available system. Spreadsheet programs have also been a major vector of the professional deployment of micro-computing, as they have led to substantial cuts in the costs generated by processing accounts, and have done so by rendering operations accessible without the need for expensive infrastructures or training programs.

Finally, VisiCalc was the first low-cost software program to sell in high numbers (700,000 copies sold over a 6-year period), and it shaped the mass-distribution software market. On the French market in 1982, Visicalc cost the equivalent of €340.

3.2.3.2. *An e-mail odyssey*

Electronic mail officially came into being with the first message sent by Ray Tomlinson (to himself) between two remote computers, the two being connected to ARPANET. Tomlinson, an engineer working for one of ARPA's main sub-contractors, was the first to use the "@" sign to designate an electronic address situated beyond the local network ... and success came instantly. Within two years, electronic mail accounted for 75% of the activity on ARPANET. This "invention" paved the way for one of the most significant IT developments of the information society. E-mail is now the means by which users have discovered IT in all its glory, and they have made the tool the most natural way of tapping into the full potential of networks. Products which have marked the development of e-mail include IBM's Profs, Microsoft Mail in 1987 and Lotus Notes, launched by Lotus in 1989 before being acquired by IBM in 1995. The advantages of e-mail are the reasons behind its success: the tool is straightforward, economical, meets the needs for asynchronous communication, lacks formality and, what is more, leaves a written copy. In the space of 30 years, e-mail has revolutionized the business world, enabling remote users to exchange complete documents within seconds, which no other form of communication would allow. Granted, e-mail has not completely eliminated the use of paper in offices, but it has directly contributed to a radical drop in the quantity of standard mail being sent, while its asynchronous virtues have led to a decrease in telephone usage ... and less disturbance of contacts by untimely phone calls! However, as with all innovations, e-mail has been the victim of a number of excesses which have tarnished its reputation, such as "spam" mail, bulky attachments and overabundant mailing lists. Filtering tools can be used to thwart excesses of the like, as can increased user awareness and careful thought as to how best to use this sometimes overly simple system, which may otherwise be devalued by over-use.

3.2.3.3. *The birth of Bill Gates and Microsoft*

As success stories go, the all-comers" award has to go to a young entrepreneur, born in Seattle in 1955. IBM handed the then 25-year-old the responsibility for developing the operating system on their "Personal Computers". The Harvard-educated William Gates along with his friend Paul Allen were far from freshmen in the world of IT, despite their youthful appearance. In 1975, they had provided Ed Roberts with a BASIC[13] program for the Altaïr. What already set them apart was their canny sales outlook: they deftly chose not to sell their program but instead demanded royalties. Ever the individualist, Bill Gates continued to separate himself from other IT developers, taking a major stand against a practice which had become commonplace amongst new IT users: software hacking, one of the symptoms of the new libertarian culture of the late 1970s. To rise to the challenge set by IBM, Bill Gates looked to Seattle Computer Products, a small Seattle firm, to provide him with a system for the modest sum of $50,000. Mystery surrounds the reasons why the most powerful company of the era should have felt the urgent need to call upon the young Bill Gates, who would go on to pose a serious threat to the "Empire". Much has been written about this curious incident in the history of IT. It must be recognized that Bill Gates" business acumen worked wonders from day one. IBM had initially contacted Gary Kildall to purchase the latter's new 16-bit version of CP/M. However, negotiations broke down, and IBM turned to Microsoft who were renowned for their version of BASIC. Tim Patterson, from Seattle Computer Products, spent two months developing his 86-DOS operating system for the Intel 8086 processor. 86-DOS went on to become MS-DOS. IBM's PC was an overnight success, and sold far more than the 250,000 units which had initially been forecast. The figure was reached within months, 50 million units eventually being sold over a ten-year period. With MS-DOS, Microsoft was propelled among the leading software industry players. In 1985, Microsoft released their first Excel spreadsheet program, which achieved immediate success on ... Macintosh!

3.2.3.4. *The world of games*

Ever since the beginning, the world of personal computing has gone hand-in-hand with games. Think back to those early black and white games of Pong, Tetris and Space Invaders! The games market was initially dominated by Atari, and was

---

[13] BASIC was created in 1964 for introductory IT, and soon went on to be taken on board, in its many forms, by the micro-computing development community, including Microsoft with Basic 80.

focused on arcade games before emerging on micro-computers and specialized games consoles, with companies like Nintendo (GameBoy, GameCube) and Sony (PlayStation) leading the field. Games were a way for programmers to explore new areas for freedom in the world of graphics. Starting out as a handful of programs designed by mischievous IT enthusiasts, the computer games sector has become one of the most dynamic within the IT programming industry, drawing in a lot of talented individuals and generating substantial turnover. The games market has become extremely large and competitive, and is estimated to be worth $17bn with cycles which follow the release of new consoles, hence, the level of speculation involved. Prone to fads and fashion, the computer games market closely resembles the cinema world, with its own writers, stars and symbols – such as Lara Croft who has even made the switch to the big screen. It is also the market which is the most prone to hacking. The online games market is likewise in full bloom, opposing players competing on the web. Computer games manufacturing, split between micro-computers and games consoles, is a high-yield sector. In 2001 alone, 60 million PC games were sold. Broken down into genres, strategy games accounted for 25% of sales, action for 11% and adventure 5%. In 2001, Microsoft, already a leading games software editor with successes such as Flight Simulator, moved into the games console market. "The Sims", created by Wim Wright and produced by leading US games manufacturers Electronic Arts, has become one of the seminal simulation games, with more than 4 million copies sold worldwide and spawning more than 200 websites. Its success can be attributed to its strong story-line featuring ordinary, everyday people. The Sims was the successful follow-up to SimCity, released in 1987. Electronic Arts have also gained the up-and-coming market for Harry Potter computer games. While Electronic Arts dominate the market, with a $650m turnover in 2000, followed by Activision, Europe has also entered the computer games sector with spectacular examples such as France's Ubisoft, Kalisto and Infogrames Entertainment (who manufactured Sid Meier's "Civilization"), the latter founded in 1983 by Bruno Bonnell and Christophe Sapet.

3.2.4. *A three-dimensional world*

IT has always sought to represent the "real" world as accurately as possible. Jim Clark believed that, as the world is three-dimensional, quite naturally, computers should also be able to show the world in three dimensions. In 1979, Clark was a research professor at Stanford, and invented a micro-processor – the Geometry Machine – which could deal with the real-time processing of the complex calculations needed to produce three-dimensional images. Some years later, he founded Silicon Graphics having attempted, in vain, to sell his invention to either IBM or Hewlett-Packard. While the commercial development of a computer capable of the industrial processing of images took a lot of time and money, it attracted a great deal of interest from the automotive and aerospace industries and from cinema producers. Come 1984, Clark and his team of brilliant engineers, having spent $17m, experienced the same fate as Eckert and Mauchly. Clark had to surrender the controlling power to Ed McCracken, a manager who had come from the more traditional world of Hewlett-Packard. Silicon Graphics had lost the leadership of their visionary founder, but with the backing of venture capitalists and under more conventional management, the firm began to soar and became one of the major successes of Silicon Valley. Within six years, the workforce grew from 200 to 6,000, and the share price rose from $3 to $30. The success of Silicon Graphics opened the door to the development of computer-aided design, which revolutionized the world of industrial design, particularly in the automotive and aerospace fields. Clark eventually parted company with Silicon Graphics and founded Netscape, which was taken over by Sun, Silicon Graphics" great rival on the workstation market. The development of computer-aided design software meant that the automotive and aerospace sectors, as well as other manufacturing industries, increased their performance potential considerably. Market leaders include Avions Marcel Dassault, a French company responsible for the development of Catia software, a 3D program that they later handed over to their subsidiary, Dassault Systems, who in turn were wise enough to sign a worldwide sales agreement with IBM.

3.2.5. Scientific instrumentation through servers: the story of HP

One company has played a unique role in the history of IT: Hewlett-Packard. The Hewlett-Packard group, negotiating the takeover of their competitor Dell at the time of writing, was founded in 1939 by two Stanford-educated engineers, Bill Hewlett and David Packard. They set up shop in a garage at number 367, Addison Avenue, Palo Alto. These beginnings have been used by CEO Carly Fiorina to trace the Silicon Valley legend back to the HP fairy tale. In fact, HP diversified into IT late in the day. A whole region – Silicon Valley – followed in HP's slipstream, its high-tech identity being molded by drawing on Stanford's intellectual assets. Hewlett and Packard's first product, a low-frequency oscillator used by Disney Studios for the animated feature Fantasia, was perfected as early as 1938. Oscilloscopes and electronic testing equipment then followed. Very early on, Hewlett and Packard used innovative management methods. In the 1940s, they were the first to set up private health insurance schemes for their employees. Company performance was driven by quality staff relations, profit-sharing and decentralized initiatives through streamlined hierarchical structures, all of which became known as the "HP Way", heavily influencing the Silicon Valley culture.

At the outset, the group was specialized in electronic measuring equipment and calculators, and only branched out into IT in the 1970s. In 1972, the first pocket calculator, the HP-35, was put on the market for $400 and was very successful. By

1975, 25,000 HP-65s – a programmable pocket calculator priced $795 – were already in circulation. HP's first computer was produced for internal purposes, but in 1972 they launched a more general mini-computer aimed at businesses. In 1974, an in-house engineer by the name of Stephen Wozniak designed a prototype personal computer, which failed to attract the company's attention. Wozniak left to join Steve Jobs, and founded Apple … It was not until the early 1990s that Hewlett-Packard gained a foothold on the PC market, where the company is now ranked third with a 7% market share. However, as early as the 1980s, the company thrived on the PC printer market, and also, ten years later, achieved considerable success with servers.

HP are renowned for the quality of their products, and are also an example of the American "citizen enterprise", attached to the idea of giving to charity, and avoiding redundancies. From 1945 onwards, David Packard took over management duties within the group, while Bill Hewlett supervised research activities. They passed away in March 1996 and January 2001 respectively. Their two families remain company shareholders. During the autumn of 2001, after an unsuccessful attempt to break into the services industry, HP began a new venture with the Compaq takeover bid, the Texan giant already having absorbed Digital in 1999. Successive concentrations such as this one are justified by the race to achieve critical mass and to generate large-scale savings, but mean more complex innovation, product line and brand management. Disorientated customers have not necessarily adhered to the Wall Street logic behind the move, while the descendants of HP's founders dispute the merger, which, they consider, goes against the company's original ethical basis.

3.3. The internet explosion

Is it a rebellion? No, milord, it's a revolution! Yet another one … The term "revolution" is wearing thin, but superlatives suit IT. In fact, as the drama unfolds in an ever-changing manner, superlatives *fuel* IT. Firmly rooted in the client-server world, IT had come to terms with the arrogant rise of micro-computing, and came to a temporary standstill in the period leading up to the year 2000. And then, as if by magic, the web sprang out of nowhere to change the world. The reality of the situation is less picturesque. The web is but the visible result of long-standing work which took root in the early 1960s, at the height of the Cold War. And the web is not the end of the story …

Who was at the forefront of the data-processing world in 1993? US magazine *Fortune*'s "Fortune 500" listing published the following standings in the field of IT and office equipment.

Company	Rank	Turnover $ (millions)	Profits
IBM	1	62,716	(8,101)
Toshiba	2	42,917	113
Fujitsu	3	29,094	(349)
Hewlett-Packard	4	20,317	1,177
Canon	5	16,507	190
Digital Equipment	6	14,371	(251)
Ricoh	7	8,974	88
Apple Computer	8	7,977	87
Unisys	9	7,743	565
Compaq Computers	10	7,191	462
Olivetti	11	5,479	(296)
Bull	12	4,987	(895)
Sun Microsystems	13	4,309	157
Casio Computers	14	3,557	49
Pitney Bowes	15	3,543	363
Seagate Technology	16	3,044	195
Minolta	17	2,976	(45)
Dell Computer	18	2,873	(40)

Source: Fortune, 25th July 1994 (numbers in brackets indicate deficits)

At the time, IBM was the seventh leading company in the world, but 1993 was a tough year for major traditional IT equipment manufacturers, all of whom recorded losses. Within 12 months, IBM lost $8bn, equivalent to the average annual profits generated between 1980 and 1990. Everyone was talking about the IT crisis.

3.3.1. *From ARPANET to the web*

As with many IT innovations, the origins of the internet can be traced back to the work carried out by the US army to face up to the threats of the Cold War, and to the fundamental research being carried out by academics. It is the fruit, not of one single source of inspiration, but the convergent result of research made by a relatively small number of experts, all of whom were used to high levels of exchange. It could even be claimed that the very need to exchange ideas across such a vast country led the researchers to implement the practical means needed to work together. Initially, the main aim was to share the valuable processing resources of central computers. The researchers, who were IT engineers, soon came up against communications-related constraints. These could only be solved by telecommunications experts, whose skill centers were far removed from the field of commutations. Their principal objective was that of effective voice data transmission, which is subject to different levels of fidelity and bandwidth than those of straightforward data, and is far more demanding. They did not believe in the development of digital telephony, and instead made use of analogue telephone exchanges, fine electro-mechanical constructions which were the source of much pride.

Researchers wondered how to get around the frustrating obstacles put in their path by the standard telephone network and the limits it placed on data transmission. With the Cold War gaining in intensity in the early 1960s, the necessary funds and motivation were forthcoming. The army was well aware of how vulnerable their communications systems were, and it was obvious that a system needed to be implemented that would enable communications to be maintained between the armed forces and the civil administration, if the US command centers came under nuclear attack. RAND, the strategic, military and technical research organization which was set up at the end of World War II, and financed by the US Air Force and other US agencies, was at the forefront of the thinking behind "survivable communications". Paul Baran, an engineer who had joined RAND in 1959, was working on the concept of a network which would allow the reliable transmission of voice, facsimiles and data during times of crisis. Simultaneously, ARPA considered that it was essential to link up the various university-based research centers it had financed, and appointed Lawrence Roberts, whose MIT background had included network projects, to manage the project which would lead to what became known as ARPANET. So, there were at least three varying channels of reflection, stimulated by different needs, all of which were working towards the creation of a data telecommunications network. Several scientists involved in the different projects exchanged information at a symposium held in the United States in October 1967. Issues addressed included the speed of such a network, and those present agreed that a 56-kilobyte bandwidth would be essential. This norm is still commonplace, but has hit hard times. In 1967, Roberts heard about the work being done by Paul Baran, and asked him to join the ARPANET project.

ARPANET began as a response to ARPA's desire to manage the financial resources allocated to the research centers across the US territory more efficiently. Material assets had to be optimized by pooling resources. Furthermore, a network would enable faster exchanges and speedier diffusion of knowledge. However, the technical stakes were high, and many were skeptical as to the feasibility of a network based on such a curious concept: split messages into packets, have them follow a random trajectory, and reconstruct them upon arrival. Telecommunications experts did not subscribe to this process, pouring scorn on the very ideas! Hostility continued to rage until the mid-1990s … For IT engineers, it was a utopian belief that resolutely incompatible machines might interact. However, Roberts stood firm in the face of criticism, ensuring, as early as 1969, that any conceivable IT object, whether hard- or software, would be linked up to the network. The network connection would be through an interface program known as IMP (Interface Message Processor). At the height of the Vietnam War, major resources were poured into the project by the university community and limited companies, including BBN to name but one. It was financed by the State, and indeed Congress periodically questioned the worth of the investment. In short, the very management of the project was in itself remarkable! At the end of 1971, the 15 centers involved in the project were linked up, as were US Air Force bases. However, not all the necessary software was either ready or set up, leading to disappointing operational results. At the first International Conference on Computer Communications, held in Washington in October 1972, a public demonstration was made of the potential of the network which convinced scientists and led to renew excitement across the IT community. In the wake of the conference, traffic on the network increased, and ARPANET became an integral element of university activities. Contributors to the project soon launched the first commercial services. Lawrence Roberts thus became CEO of Telenet Communications Corporation, who, in August 1975, opened sales departments in seven US cities.

The internet revolution was still, however, a long way off. Those who used the network complained about how complex they found it to be. It remained, above all, an expensive[14] IT tool which was difficult and slow to install and operate. Users sought to improve the system, and soon took things beyond the initial project framework. First of all, they made it into a management tool for local resources (LAN: Local Area Network), although it was later replaced by Ethernet, developed by MIT alumnus Robert Metcalfe at PARC. At MIT, Metcalfe had invented "Ping", the program used to check adequate network response, and which is still commonplace today. IT engineers illicitly connected ARPANET up to other networks, by creating a link with CERN (the European Laboratory for Particle Physics) in Geneva, via Cambridge University, and by ingeniously grafting secondary networks onto the main one. ARPANET also developed outside the IT community, as it began catering for military-financed research into climate and seismology. However, network resources were still not being fully used, as the initial principle of sharing valuable resources was no longer of paramount relevance with the development of cheaper local resources thanks to the rise of mini-computers. In fact, the network's lost *raison d'être* re-emerged with the unexpected emergence of electronic mail, which rapidly spread throughout the community. The no-frills, protocol-free, asynchronous tool was perfectly suited to researchers" needs. The application did not feature in the original project brief, and even though no initial assessment was made of the profitability of e-mail, it turned out to be a powerful factor, boosting the research community and promoting exchange, and taking things beyond the simple shared usage of IT resources.

---

[14] Installation costs for each location were between $55,000 and $100,000.

In 1975, ARPANET also experimented with radio transmission technology for military purposes with PRNET, the Pocket Radio NETwork. That same year, the SATNET project (Atlantic Packet SATellite NETwork) was set up between the United States, the United Kingdom and Norway.

In France, teams at the CNET (*Center National d'Etudes en Télécommunication*) were great believers in temporal switching, in direct conflict with their counterparts at INRIA, who subscribed to the ARPANET packet transmission philosophy. France was in the midst of a state telephony crisis, and the telecommunications sector solution became established as the norm, in the shape of the X.25 standard administered by Transpac, the company set up by the *Direction Générale des Télécommunications*. Nevertheless, the Cyclades packet switching project, launched by Louis Pizon under the aegis of the *Délégation à l'Informatique* (State IT Commission) and in conjunction with INRIA, led to 20 centers being linked up in 1974, before the project folded in 1978 due to lack of funds. Cyclades, which drew heavily on the ARPANET model (Louis Pouzin knew many of those involved in the American project), was an innovative and effective network, particularly as regards data flow control, but could never stand up to the power of the telecommunications players.

3.3.2. *1993: the official birth of the web*

ARPANET developed in an anarchic fashion, branching out in all directions but without the means for the different branches to communicate with each other. It was Vint Cerf at UCLA (University of California, Los Angeles) who came up with an elegant solution to the problem of how to go about linking up the various networks: each data flow would be split into packets according to a new standard, known as TCP (Transmission Control Protocol), and which enclosed packets in "datagrams", enabling them to be dispatched across gateways between networks and to their final destination. The protocol was later improved and split in two, with TCP for data and IP (Internet Protocol) for routing information, resulting in TCP/IP.

The concerns of the US army had not gone away, and in 1977, ARPA showed it was now possible to link up its three networks – ARPANET, SATNET and PRNET – within a single entity, attracting interest from the Strategic Air Command. If progress to an industrial level was to be achieved, an operator had to be found. The ARPA management team contacted AT&T, who declined the offer to purchase ARPA's equipment and to run the network. In 1975, responsibility for the network was finally handed over to the Defense Communications Agency, while the objectives of the network shifted. It was no longer focused on serving the research network, and instead was given over to the operational needs of the military. Under the leadership of Major Glynn Parker, the network was back on course. Access rights were monitored more closely, as were the innovative or overly laid-back habits of researchers. Such rigor did not prevent the military from continuing to innovate, or from implementing the TCP/IP protocol in 1983.

In a world where proprietary protocols had mushroomed throughout IT manufacturers (most notably IBM's SNA in 1974 and Digital's DECNET in 1975), ARPANET's TCP/IP standardization genuinely rendered matters more straightforward. However, intense discussions continued, each party aiming to impose their own closed commercial standard, and as TCP/IP only ultimately concerned a limited community of academic and military users, it had little chance of standing up to the economic challenges faced by IT manufacturers. At the time, the most powerful market players were the public telephony companies, and were members of the CCITT (*Comité Consultatif International Télégraphique et Téléphonique*)[15], the organization formed by the 1865-founded ITU (International Telecommunication Union). And yet, while voice telephony norms could be easily defined and adhered to by state-dependent telephony operators, CCITT only began looking into data transmission issues from 1973 onwards, in a totally new context, in which private corporations were dominant, including IBM vying to establish their SNA norm. To avoid this situation, CCITT deliberately ignored TCP/IP and opted to take the X.25 transmission norm on board, which was soon taken up by states and, somewhat reluctantly, by major IT firms. The two systems clashed, as far as guaranteed service quality was concerned. X.25 achieved this through the creation of virtual point-to-point circuits at the level of carrier-controlled communication nodes, while the internet policy was that monitoring would be handled by the respective computers of the sender and receiver without the carrier having to intervene. There was no rush from private companies to deliver X.25-compatible goods, slowing down the progress of the norm. Meanwhile, TCP/IP began its spectacular rise.

The number of computers linked up to the network increased rapidly: 2,000 in 1985, 30,000 in 1987 and 159,000 in 1989, as a consequence of the rising amount of local networks connected to networks between centers, which in turn was due to the generalization of local Ethernet architecture and TCP/IP. Problems with address systems then arose, leading to the idea of splitting the internet world into sub-sets, or domains, allowing the addresses of individuals and servers to be managed in a simple fashion. ARPA split the world into six domains: education (.edu), government (.gov), military (.mil), organization (.org), commercial (.com) and network resources (.net). During the 1980s, the National Science Foundation (NSF) began financing research into IT, and launched NSFNET, its own, more modern network. In December 1987, it was decided that NSFNET should take over from

---

15 Known as ITU (International Telecommunication Union, its parent organization) since 1993.

ARPANET, which by then was showing its age, and eventually ceased operations in February 1990. However, the internet remained under public control, continued to receive grants, and those in charge at NSF considered the implications of transferring the management of the network to the private sector. The decision was thus made to transfer network administration duties to private operators: Internet Service Providers (ISPs). But only in April 1995 did the US government abandon all formal control over the internet infrastructure. ISPs launched a host of commercial services, while university and research departments migrated to the faster, new generation internet, known as vBNS (very high speed Backbone Network Service), which was still funded by the US state authorities.

Back on the open marketplace, the internet did not have at its disposal the kinds of attractive services which were destined to enable it to break into whole layers of the population: data-classification systems, a user-friendly graphic interface and e-mail software. The first attempt came with the "gopher", a system for organizing and displaying files in rank order. However, while the ARPANET community had become accustomed to their cumbersome system, the application which would finally make the internet attractive and practical came from elsewhere. Tim Berners-Lee, a researcher at CERN in Geneva, had the bright idea of adding multimedia sound and image capabilities to the interface, as well as a system for navigating through data and documents, with "hypertext" linking them all together. Berners-Lee's ambition was to create a "reservoir of information". To achieve this, it was essential that technology provide a concrete means of linking data in a straightforward and attractive manner. This implied building, from scratch, several pieces of the technical jigsaw puzzle. In collaboration with his colleagues, he invented HTML (Hypertext Markup Language), a page description language enabling navigation between links, and HTTP (Hypertext Transfer Protocol), a tool for workstation-server data transfer. Finally, for the system to be complete, it was necessary to be able to identify the addresses of servers, hence URLs (Uniform Resource Locators), a standardized address format. In December 1990, the various tools were assembled and functioned for the first time within CERN. In 1991 and 1992, CERN distributed the tools, free-of-charge, across the university community. In November 1993, a team from Illinois University's NCSA (National Center for Supercomputing Applications) led by Marc Andreessen introduced a "browser", which made it possible to link text and images in color. This was Mosaic, which met with overnight success, 40,000 copies being downloaded in the first month alone. By April 1994, more than a million browsers were in service worldwide. Mosaic went on to become Netscape. After less than five years, 50 million people were using the internet. It had taken the radio 40 years to hit the same figure!

Chapter 4

Light and Shade in the Digital World

4.1. The family tree of the digital world

The digital world is complex. The family photo features converts from the field of conventional IT standing uncomfortably alongside the pioneers of networks and micro-computing, themselves pushed aside by the web generation. Many companies have gone missing in action, either because of their own mistakes, the whims of the market, or the gap between what they had to offer and what was fashionable at the time. It might, therefore, be suggested that the survivors of the IT odyssey have developed survival capabilities which deserve recognition. This is not necessarily good news for the end-customer, because, when innovators are taken out of the picture, ambitious routes are abandoned in favor of conformity, and, worse still, monopolies emerge on certain markets …

4.1.1. *Stalwarts undergoing change*

The IT world has its big names, the products of monopolistic situations as created either by public authorities or by technological success achieved in fields such as mainframes. These major league players have aroused tension and admiration in virtually equal measures, and have demonstrated their ability to sail through successive waves of technical innovations and to adapt, not always painlessly, to the surrounding market environment.

4.1.1.1. Honor to whom honor is due

IBM has been and will continue to be abundantly mentioned in this book. Not only is IBM the oldest of the IT companies, but it is the only one to have maintained its position in the ranks down through the years, and, therefore, deserves a particular standing here. With turnover of $88bn, IBM remains powerful and prosperous. Big Blue has been there from day one, and has taken on board the precious experience gained from successful ventures and tough setbacks alike. IBM got back on its feet in remarkable fashion in the 1990s, having flirted with death induced by self-satisfaction and obesity! IBM could have followed the path of a number of its competitors, who have either fallen by the wayside or have been reduced to stagnation in an oversized framework which trades on past glories. Had they lost any one of the many anti-trust cases brought against them in the 1960s, IBM would have disappeared completely, or suffered the same fate as AT&T, which was split into seven local companies in 1982. Today, IBM is an active player on all IT fronts, its strength residing in its patents, its commercial know-how and its *bona fide* international presence. Business success has been based on mainframe computers, the *savoir-faire* being handled with much commercial talent, and a fair degree of arrogance. Granted, the expansion of the IT market has led to a reduction in IBM's share, since IBM has not been able to, or known how to, claim the same market share levels on specific niche markets as on the mainframe market, where they are now the sole player. While at the end of the 1960s, IBM accounted for three quarters of the mainframe market, by 1976 the figure had dropped to 66% and IBM could only claim 50% of the worldwide IT market. By 1985, IBM's overall market share had fallen to 25%. But after a major crisis at the end of the 1980s, IBM's successful switch to the digital era was second to none. Under the firm leadership of Lou Gerstner, who, in 1993, put paid to long-standing managerial excess, IBM reinvented itself. The company tore apart its sluggish bureaucratic systems, downsized by cutting its workforce by 160,000, opted to resoundingly apply e-business techniques to company operations, and, despite its track-record and renowned industrial expertise, chose to refocus on services with IGS (IBM Global Services), a tool which now accounts for 50% of overall results. IBM nevertheless continues to invest in cutting-edge technologies. Other than its commercial and financial efficiency, IBM has continued to maintain a remarkable level of technical know-how, in the fields of both hard- and software. Turnover is well-balanced between equipment (45%), services (38%) and technical software (14%), the latter essential for e-business applications, such as Websphere and DB2 databases. IBM was already a past master in the proprietary world, and has now emerged as a major player in the open source software sector, having provided Linux with massive support.

In technological terms, much is owed to IBM. Yet, IBM is seldom spontaneously mentioned in such terms, perhaps because the company has not always chosen to, or known how to, exploit its scientific side. IBM's research division brings together eight laboratories worldwide. Three are in the US, while the others are in Japan, Switzerland (Zurich), India, Israel and China. The central laboratory is the Watson Research Center in the State of New York. With more than 3,000 top-level scientists, whose specialities encompass all fundamental disciplines, the structure is one of the most important research organizations in the world. IBM boasts no less than five Nobel prizes in Physics[16] and four Turing Awards. IBM can be credited with fundamental innovations in areas such as copper semiconductors, magnetic storage disks (1956) and high-density magnetic reading heads, voice recognition, token ring local area networks (1985), fractals (in 1967 – Benoît Mandelbrot, the father of fractal geometry, was an IBM researcher), Fortran language (1957), relational databases (1957) and RISC architecture (1980) to name but a few, etc.

4.1.1.2. Telephone companies

Long regarded as little more than voice carriers, come the 1990s, telephone companies – or telcos – re-emerged at the forefront of the technological scene. Other than mastering the familiar transmission of voice data across landline infrastructures, their duties have now incorporated the carrying of other types of data for both businesses and private individuals. They are therefore at the very heart of digital and internet issues. At the outset, telcos' contributions were not the most dynamic, as they were intent on safeguarding their heavy investments, the status of their extensive workforce, and their overcautious internal bureaucracy. Some even suspect them of putting a brake on progress. Companies such as France Telecom, many of which were state-owned before being privatized as late as the 1990s, are products of the stable world of mail and telecommunications corporations, from which most split in the 1980s. The liberalization of the telecommunications market has slowly made headway in Europe, having started in the United States with the Reagan administration's 1982 dismantling of AT&T, as the result of a lawsuit which began eight years earlier. The American Telephone and Telegraph Company was hitherto better known as Bell. Local networks, with their sprawling infrastructures, are the final strongholds of the former monopolies, whereas competition has taken root on long-distance lines since the 1980s, and the advent of the mobile phone has given rise to a whole host of audacious and greedy new market players.

Data carrying has been slow in gaining importance. As early as the 1930s, AT&T was experimenting with techniques enabling data to be dispatched over the telephone network, most notably the first faxes, but it was not until 1962 that AT&T introduced the first modem (for MOdulator/DEModulator). The very nature of telephony changed with Bell Laboratories" introduction of digital switching in 1969.

---

[16] 1973 Leo Esaki, 1986 Gerd K. Binning and Heinrich Rohrer, 1987 J. Georg Bednorz and K. Alex Müller.

From the mid-1970s, the complete digitalization of telephone exchanges enabled constant improvements for a low cost.

France Telecom picked up the mantle of French state-owned establishments, and only really began to exist as an autonomous public establishment in January 1991. For many years, the French telephony market had been overshadowed by the state monopoly, Alcatel and Thomson sharing state contracts. In 1995, headlines in the French newspaper *Libération* – and elsewhere – referred to France Telecom's "technological dictatorship", and accused them of taking too much time in boarding the internet vessel, so as to protect their beloved and highly lucrative Minitel system, and of pursuing an absurd technical approval policy for equipment. France Telecom's tariff policies continue to be called into question by the French telecommunications regulatory board (ART – *Autorité de Régulation des Télécommunications*). France Telecom has also been conspicuously slow in opening up the different branches of its activities to competitors, and furthermore has had to pay heavy fines for having granted lower rates to certain major customers. It was never going to be easy for the weighty French telecommunications machine to break free from the grasp of its monopolistic past, particularly as much of the workforce continued to be registered as civil servants. However, change is clearly underway. As has been the case for many counterparts elsewhere, France Telecom's acquisitions policy has meant heavy debts for the company, but it has led to substantial presence on the international mobile phone market thanks to the takeover of Orange, which has made them the number 2 European mobile phone operator behind Vodafone. Meanwhile, robust data-carrying services have been developed with Equant. Not all the formerly state-run telcos have fared so well. Holland's KPN is one of many to have encountered tremendous hardship. British Telecom, Deutsche Telekom and Telecom Italia have all experienced major teething troubles in their respective countries when adapting to the newly demanding, competitive markets. Telcos, like airlines, can no longer depend on a national base to stand up to international market concentration.

4.1.2. *How golden was my Valley!*

Silicon Valley, just a few miles of congested motorway from San Francisco, has been described by one of its founding fathers, venture capitalist John Doerr, as "the greatest concentration of (legal) riches in the history of the planet". This claim has been severely dented by Nasdaq's sudden downturn, but the wealth amassed by the barons of Silicon Valley remains impressive. Hyperbole is endemic in this area where, within just a few years, billions of dollars have been made by a handful of individuals. None of them have really been scientists or engineers, capitalists or entrepreneurs. Each of them has been a little bit of all of the above. Most importantly, they have utilized anti-conformity as a powerful engine to create collective riches, and, even more so, individual wealth. They started out by building machines which were more efficient, more effective and ever cheaper, with Fairchild's micro-processors, Hewlett-Packard, Silicon Graphics and Sun responsible for PCs and graphic workstations, and Apple keeping the dream alive. However, as equipment of this sort has a habit of becoming commonplace, so the profit margins melt away. Hence, the reasoning behind the emergence of concepts, which have come in the shape of software – such as Yahoo, Excite, eBay and Sun's Java – resulting in minimal risks and lower investment.

Of all the individuals who have built the modern-day image of IT, one category stands apart from all others, the gurus: Steve Jobs, Larry Ellison, Scott McNelly and John Chambers, all of whom are among the top experts in creative forecasting. By managing their personal image, at least as well as they have managed their companies, they have created the new archetypal boss who is wealthy, athletic and casually-dressed[17]. When Steve Jobs appears on stage, wearing his trademark round-rimmed glasses, customary black trousers and polo shirt, he is not selling his products, he is preaching. He is the ultimate TV evangelist, united with his followers live on the web, coming together to wage war against the evil enemy – the world of Intel PCs – with live demos on hand to save the day. Larry Ellison is also a graduate of the school of preaching, announcing that the end of the road had been reached with the web … before shamelessly altering the pricing policy of his database software. Scott McNelly has always sung the praises of open source software, in the hope that other companies will lose out on a valuable source of income, while Sun sells even more servers. Cisco's John Chambers is more focused on content, but his presentations are benchmark examples of pedagogical efficiency which never fail to make listeners feel guilty about not instantly scrambling for the nearest IP voice carrier solution …

The four pillars of Silicon Valley's mythical status are competency, reactivity, success and money. This astonishing microcosm has evolved in isolation, with the various experts flitting from one company to the next. Where do the customers fit in? On rare occasions, they have been allowed to penetrate the inner sanctum for a few short hours, or have been called to attend what might be termed "religious conventions". Granted, the *really* good customers have been allowed to travel – some might say go on a pilgrimage – to the heart of the Valley. More generally, it is not unusual for the CIO of a French client, say, to receive a phone call from a worried Domestic Sales Manager informing him of his CIO's exceptional decision to stop off in Paris on his way from Tokyo to New York, and how he would just love to meet a few French clients (less than 5% of the world market, but even so …).

---

[17] One of the distinguishing features of the internet era is the virtual disappearance of the tie from the IT world, which is still very much dominated by men.

The man in question, accompanied by a number of feverish press attachés – and sometimes even by bodyguards straight out of the latest CIA movie – then, grants you a 60-minute audience with him in a swish Parisian hotel, so that he can explain how the world is changing, how the web has now arrived, how he wants to be sure that his company really is entirely customer-driven, before slipping you his business card with his e-mail address and direct number, no less. "Don't hesitate to call me, night or day!" Then, with a charming smile, he is gone, in good time to catch his plane to London or Frankfurt. The "conventions" also have their rituals. Other than major conferences such as SAPHire – at which SAP present their view of the world – the Gartner Group brings together, once a year, several thousand IT professionals, on all three continents of the IT planet, to assess the state of play across technologies and the market. Gartner offer analysis of the situation which, while remaining prudent, is of vital worth to vendors, making use of the now famous "Magic Quadrant" strategic planning system, which ranks suppliers according to their vision and ability to deliver. This classification heavily influences users, and can help or hinder the expansion of a company.

4.1.3. *Integrated software editors*

The rise of integrated software is a relatively recent phenomenon in the history of IT, and was a by-product of the run-up to the year 2000. Companies were worried about the complexity and transformation costs of their systems and, urged on by consultants, turned *en masse* towards integrated business management software applications, now best known as ERP systems (Enterprise Resource Planning). Europe has carved out a respectable market share in the ERP sector. SAP has become the biggest name in ERP systems, now overshadowing its younger European rival Baan, who had shown signs of real talent. Although the latter's technical approach was more modern than the SAP system and its ageing sources, the Baan brothers" desire to expand whatever the cost – through an audacious external growth policy which went so far as to take certain liberties with some rules of accounting – bled the company dry and resulted in the acceptance of a takeover bid from British group Advensys in 2000. For a quarter of a century, SAP has been developing a global answer to companies" information system needs. SAP was founded by three IBM employees, each of whom had a background in programming. Dietmar Hopp, Claus Wellenreuther and Hasso Plattner had been working on a financial software application project, which was turned down by their then-employer. In 1972, they therefore decided to leave IBM and start up their own business. System R, their first software package was released in 1974, and by the end of the decade, it had been installed in 80 businesses. A second version was launched in the early 1980s. R/2 retained a mainframe system, and achieved major success, with more than 2,200 installations. With IBM prevaricating – their Systems Application Architecture (SAA) had been a failure, and OfficeVision had been abandoned – SAP opted to develop its third generation software under UNIX. The first version of R/3 was released in mid-1992. The conventional mainframe approach had made way for a client-server model, before later converting to web-based tools, and in the process SAP became synonymous with end-to-end systems. It was no longer a simple tertiary system, as it had gradually incorporated all corporate functions, stealing the thunder of specialized software editors. In the United States, the market for integrated management software applications was developed by Oracle, with their flagship database systems, and PeopleSoft, who had initially specialized in human resource management solutions. JD Edwards and SAA were similarly influential on the SME market. SAP currently leads the field, with 11,000 corporate clients, and lucrative bases installed in 30,000 locations[18], which provide funding for initiatives in the fields of supply chains and CRM (Customer Relationship Management). While these latest offerings have been less successful than SAP's core ERP activities, they are testament to the fact that the company is prepared to plough resources into achieving its ambitious aim of providing global solutions that encompass all corporate activities, and putting niche-market software editors in jeopardy.

4.1.4. *Microsoft: an entirely separate case*

When evoking Microsoft's part in the history of worldwide IT companies, a whole new category would need to be defined! Microsoft has always made its own way, and continues to do so, knowingly managing alliances in a manner which is subtle and carnivorous in equal measures. It has cost IBM dearly. By choosing to set up shop in the mild, rainy city of Seattle, far from the existing IT hotbeds – the East Coast and Silicon Valley – Microsoft broke the mould of American IT conventions. Indeed, the Seattle climate is very much in keeping with Microsoft's tribal culture, where company loyalty is cultivated more successfully than elsewhere. There is no room for exuberance in Microsoft's neat and tidy Redmond buildings. In a rigorous environment, the staff-members work hard for the company, as well as to make a living.

Microsoft's management team has remained stable for years, with Bill Gates – an outstanding and yet shy character – leaning heavily on the hardy figure of Steve Ballmer, who, since the early days, has kept the company on a faultlessly profitable straight and narrow. Such continuity can cause one to cringe! Users are constantly protesting about the bugs in Microsoft products, whether the bugs be real or imaginary. However much CIOs grumble, they have no choice other than to adhere to the *de facto* standards. Competitors take every available opportunity to burn the

---

[18] Maintenance programs are a guarantee of recurring income for software editors, and each year represent 17% of the initial cost of software licenses.

Redmond effigy at the stake, and all the while dream of signing a partnership deal. The federal state administration, in which the Democrats have a stronger position than the Republicans, has for years been on the lookout for Microsoft's antitrust practices, with a view to smashing its "monopoly". Microsoft, or Microsoft's boss – the two are often inextricably linked – may not be liked, but they are respected and, above all, feared.

Microsoft's success is undeniable. Bill Gates has a 12% stake in the company, making him one of the richest men in the world, currently worth around $54bn. A website even keeps track of his personal fortune, although at that kind of level fluctuations have little or no significance. Microsoft's economic record has been exemplary: turnover has increased constantly, from $140m in 1985 to $25bn in 2001, with profits of more than $7bn recorded in 2001 and market capitalization of $350bn in November 2001. All Microsoft employees have benefited from this extraordinarily long-standing and consistent success.

There is a simple formula behind Microsoft's success, and this formula is the dream of every self-respecting salesperson on earth: take an indispensable product, sell it at a high (but not too high!) price in large numbers, and issue replacement versions as often as possible. Microsoft's vocation is not to invent, innovate or explore new directions. They are quite content to let others pursue that particular path of intellectual pleasure. 92% of the world's micro-processors use a Microsoft operating system, alone representing 20% of overall company turnover. The Office suite, with its flagship products Word, Excel and PowerPoint, has left its competitors standing. Microsoft has even gone so far as to produce excellent software (Office X) for the rival Apple platform. Microsoft has moved in on the sector of Intel platform network servers, and gained almost 60% of the market with Windows NT and Windows 2000. Major corporate clients now account for 50% of Microsoft turnover, SMEs representing 35% and the general public just 15%.

When Microsoft senses a promising market is slipping out of reach, or that a competitor is encroaching on its territory, the reactions are immediate. This was notably the case on the PDA (Personal Digital Assistant) market, which was dominated first by Psion and then, even more so, by Palm OS, before Microsoft's powerful and large-scale counter-attack with Pocket PC, coming in the wake of the failure of Windows CE. The enormous wireless and mobile market is at stake. Bill Gates may not have invented the internet, but he knew how to make use of it at the right time. The fight for the control of the internet has been fierce. Netscape Navigator's supremacy was brushed aside by Internet Explorer, the former's market share falling from 75% in 1995 to less than 15% within a few short semesters. Windows XP is more than just the umpteenth new version of Windows. It is a veritable machine that facilitates access to online services, especially multimedia resources, thanks to a straightforward, unified product. As they frankly say in

Redmond, it comes in response to the needs expressed by customers for greater simplicity and comfort. And yet, access to multimedia content has given rise to niche-market specialist firms, such as RealPlayer and Apple with the Quicktime multimedia player. Their very survival on the market has been put in jeopardy by Windows Media Player. Is this desire to split from the "other" market standards – such as MP3 and Java – still a legitimate policy? With the launch of Microsoft's XBOX games console, is the need to compete with Sega, Nintendo and the Sony Playstation essential to the future of science? These offensives – some of which might fail – are driven by an understandable desire to gain a durable position across all entry points to the information society by targeting all types of audience. The same can be said about Microsoft's decision to change its software sales policy, switching to a rental model for clients, the updates going hand-in-hand with the clever "Software Assurance" mechanisms, in turn, leading to substantially increased costs. This is in line with any typical businessman's will to ensure future income.

However, given Microsoft's leadership position and the research and development teams the company boasts, we might have expected more attentiveness, a more thorough approach to services for businesses, a higher degree of product innovation, and more user-friendly interfaces. It can be tempting to dispute such overwhelming dominance, but it is difficult to uncover convincing evidence. In 1998, the US Justice Department filed an antitrust suit against Microsoft, leading to a first triumph for Microsoft's opponents in June 2000 as the company was ordered to break up into two smaller entities, split between operating systems on the one hand, and diverse products on the other. A Federal Appeals Court reversed the decision in June 2001 and Microsoft vowed to make amends. In fact, other than donating computers to disadvantaged US schools and informing the market about new products sooner than previously, nothing really changed. The European Union has also been tempted to demonstrate the ways in which Microsoft has taken unfair advantage of its overriding position on the operating systems market, with a view to dominating the entire market for internet-related communications and network products.

Clients, by their own choice, are responsible for the tremendous success of this outstanding firm, which, like it or not, can by no means be ignored ... but still remains difficult to love ...

4.1.5. *The web generation*

The meteoric rise of the internet has brought about the appearance of a new generation of entrepreneurs. They have seized the opportunities arising from the new techniques associated with the web, either by providing for essential infrastructure needs, by developing new types of software made necessary by the increased potential of technology, or by exploiting technology as a means of providing new services. The internet gold-rush led to many hopeful cases of get-rich-quick schemes, but the expansion of new companies far outpaced the market's ability to absorb new developments. Thus, many projects were botched affairs, taking a simple idea which was hurriedly put on the market by often youthful entrepreneurs whose blind faith in the potential for growth of their project led them to conceive, and find the funding for, audacious business plans which would long remain in the red! The most vulnerable quickly faded away, and the collapse gained pace towards the end of 2000. Nevertheless, the entrepreneurial effervescence of the period has enabled a number of promising start-ups to blossom, survivors of the merciless natural selection process. Most importantly, it has awakened wide-ranging interest in IT from key decision-makers who were hitherto largely indifferent or resistant to the sector. This is an essential factor for the future.

4.1.6. *The inescapable consultants and service providers*

IT products are not delivered ready-to-use. The more ambitious they are, the more they require support. If objectives are to be attained, such services are essential. These can be provided by specially trained in-house staff, but generally entail the use of external specialists, employed by software editors, IT equipment manufacturers or generalists. Support skills are needed in an ever-wider range of situations: assistance in diagnosing needs and recommending solutions, aid with information system or technical project management and implementation, design through deployment, and help with change management programs during deployment schemes. While organizational needs have long led specialized firms to develop specific skills that businesses are unable to develop and maintain at a reasonable level in-house, the development of large-scale IT projects has been responsible for the sky-rocketing expenditure on contracts with consultancies. We have now reached the point where it has become virtually unthinkable to launch an information system project without the support of one or more consultancies, whose role can go from simply providing strategic advice to taking charge of all aspects of the project. The vogue for ERP solutions has given birth – particularly as regards SAP – to an ecosystem of manifold companies overseeing the deployment of the software package at hand, and adapting it to specific company environments. By developing the unique skills needed to implement business management software packages, consultants and service providers have been able to put up their prices substantially. The tight market has sent salaries higher and higher, with a new peak of excess being reached in 2000.

In the early days of IT, hardware manufacturers provided these services themselves. Then, independent firms appeared, as did a wide spectrum of specialized companies, whose service offers were compartmentalized until the

1980s. The major consulting groups stemmed from the worlds of finance, auditing and strategic consulting, and cared little for IT realizations, which they left to IT service providers. Then, in the light of technological progress and globalization, they felt the essential need to build all-encompassing entities in which strategic and organizational consultants now worked alongside IT project managers, technical architects and developers. A whole wave of mergers followed, giving rise to a host of major international firms, capable of dealing with issues faced by multinational clients all over the world.

During the 20th century, the so-called "Big Five" built their worldwide reputation on their core auditing and accounting activities. Arthur Andersen (85,000 staff, $9.3bn turnover in 2001), Deloitte Touche Tohmatsu (95,000 staff, $12.4bn turnover), Ernst & Young (84,000 staff, $9.9bn), KPMG (108,000 staff, $13.5bn) and PriceWaterhouseCoopers (160,000 staff, $17bn) have all branched out into the information systems sector, as integrators and outsourcers. The Big Five thus employ 530,000 people, with combined turnover of $62bn. They have tremendous say in the direction the market takes, and heavily influence vendors, even though data-processing only accounts for a small fraction of their overall activities. But now, management and organizational consulting are closely intertwined with IT solutions, and major corporate clients tend to seek global solutions. Other major players have consolidated their position by building on their IT expertise. Cap Gemini's takeover of Ernst & Young Consulting in 2000 took the workforce to more 60,000, the US accounting for 35% of global activities, now worth $8.5bn. Andersen Consulting was founded in 1953 and became Accenture in 2001. With more than 75,000 staff, Accenture is directly involved in major IS projects and as an outsourcer. IBM is also heavily committed to this market with the IBM Global Services subsidiary. Computer Sciences Corporation was founded by a couple of young programmers in 1959, and now employs 68,000 staff, achieving a turnover of $11bn in 2001. CSC acquired the consultancy Peat Marwick. Together, these firms make up an impressive whole in terms of skills, resources and turnover, in a high value-added sector. As such, they have become major players in the world economy.

These firms may have gained in terms of the consistency of their service offers and their ability to attract large sums of money, but have had to sacrifice clear brand identity and their independence *vis-à-vis* IT solutions. Whatever, riding the successive waves of the year 2000 projects and e-business, they flourished throughout the 1990s and until 2001, hiring the best young engineers fresh out of college and on the job market, and offering them high salaries. However, their sheer size and structural costs have rendered them more sensitive to market fluctuations, the slowdown in technological innovations and to the international economic outlook than their smaller competitors, who remain focused on local markets such as the US, Japan or Europe, or on niche sectors of activity. Smaller, French-style IT service providers have, over recent years, launched external growth policies, but have still proved to be highly profitable and maintained generally high growth rates.

4.2. The slippery slope

IT continues to be referred to as a successful milieu in constant growth when, in fact, as in all sectors of economy, firms lose their footing and experience terrible hardship before finally disappearing completely. These include some famous names, who left their mark and played their part in the technical progress achieved, and in the process greatly satisfied their – sometimes unreasonably loyal – customers. Such companies, often the brainchild of talented individuals, showed how competitive they could be, and yet failed in a growing market. Why is that so? There are many reasons, but all suffered from their managers" over-confidence – if not to say blindness – and many were unable to find a second wind when faced with severe difficulties.

4.2.1. The victims of the second wave

Many major names from the 1970s IT aristocracy have disappeared. Digital, like Tandem, was acquired by Compaq, the arrogant Texan star of the 1990s. Prime Computer and Data General also faded into history, after being shining examples of efficiency, successful growth and a strong image. Compaq, founded in 1983, achieved a turnover of more than $100m during the first 12 months of operations. By 1987, the figure had hit $1.2bn, and Compaq's growth rate was second to none throughout the 1980s. Compaq's mythical founding president, Rod Canion, did not survive the company's first growth-related setback in 1991. IT is a pitiless world which devours its innovators. Mistakes are not allowed, competition is fierce and often even disloyal. The major IT manufacturers who followed IBM onto the market for high performance computers and those who sought to escape IBM's stranglehold on the minicomputer market all struggled to survive the 1980s. "Eat or be eaten" was the law in this most peculiar of ecosystems.

Seymour Cray was one such person who played a major part in the development of high performance computers, enabling significant progress in areas necessitating substantial calculating power, such as the military, meteorology, aerodynamics, crash tests, and prospecting for oil. In 1964, he designed the first-ever supercomputer for Control Data, the CDC 6600. In 1972, he went on to found Cray Research, who made his name in the 1970s, thanks to a range of compact and elegantly-designed super-computers which followed in the lineage of the CRAY-1, released in 1976. Eighty-three CRAY-1s were sold at $5m each. In 1989, he founded another company – Cray Computer Corporation – to work on the CRAY-3.

Come 1995, Seymour Cray filed for bankruptcy, shortly before his death, at the age of 71, in a car crash in 1996. That same year, Cray Research merged with Silicon Graphics, and was acquired by Tera Corporation in March 2000. After Cray's departure, Control Data had struggled to maintain the same high level of creativity. They then invested heavily in PLATO, an ambitious project for access to documents and archives which was, in its own way, a forerunner of the internet. As a result, CDC began making enormous losses in the early 1980s, which led to its founder Bill Norris leaving in 1986.

In 1970, Gene Amdahl left IBM at the height of its powers, and started up his own firm, Amdahl Corporation. The company delivered Model 470 V/6, its first IBM-compatible system in 1975. Amdahl was often technically in advance of IBM, as was the Japanese firm Hitachi, who specialized in IBM-compliant equipment. Both were able to compete with IBM in the top of the range market, but were never really in a position to give the giant serious cause for concern. Amdahl was eventually taken over by Fujitsu, and, like Hitachi, pulled out in 2000, leaving IBM with the entire mainframe market.

4.2.2. *Ousted leaders*

The IT world can be cruel for its losers … of which the list is long. Some had the right idea too soon and rested on their laurels, success causing their heads to spin and easy money making them lazy. It is often forgotten that while some players are reviled because of their monopoly, they have often reached that position because of the weakness of their competitors. Take WordPerfect, which was invented in 1976 by Bruce Bastian and Alan C. Ashton, a couple of music-loving computer engineers. Initially designed to run on Data General's mini-computers, by 1990 WordPerfect held a 46% share of the word processing market, and was being used on all micro-computing platforms. Today, WordPerfect's market share is insignificant. In the early 1990s, WordPerfect held out all of 16 months before integrating the Windows graphic interface, and was unable to deliver a competitive office suite. The firm was acquired by Canadian software company Corel, in 1996. Corel has now hit hard times as well …

CP/M was long the leading micro-computer operating system. It had been launched by Gary Kindall at Intel in 1974, and then manufactured by the company Kindall founded, Intergalactic Digital Research. CP/M suffered, because it was well-suited to 8-bit micro-processors, but commercially outclassed in the 16-bit world. CP/M 86 was launched as a response to MS-DOS, but was done so far too slowly, and the marketing campaign was poorly orchestrated!

In the world of software, Philippe Kahn's achievements deserve a special mention. In 1982, this talented French programmer arrived in the heart of Silicon Valley. He worked wonders with his firm Borland, which became a leader in the software market in the 1980s with a turnover of $500m. Borland's business products made the company famous. Many, like the Quattro spreadsheet program, Borland C++, the Delphi and Turbo Pascal languages, competed head-to-head with Microsoft products ... until the company found itself in a state of ruin, its founder was ousted and the decision was made to change the company's name, with disastrous effects on the firm's image. Since then, Kahn has pursued his career as an innovator with his companies Starfish and Lightsurf. The former was founded in 1994 and dedicated to tools for synchronizing wireless devices (using the TrueSync software program) and was sold to Motorola in 1998, while the latter specializes in the distribution of images on the web, regardless of format. He also spends much time enjoying his two favorite pastimes, playing the clarinet and yacht racing ...

Among the fallen equipment manufacturers, such as Atari and Commodore, the sad fate met by word-processing pioneers Wang merits attention. Wang, managed by Dr Wang, was one of the first companies to sense the central role to be played by IT in office automation. Wang produced a sophisticated, yet homely word-processor, with a cathode-ray screen displaying half a page of text, with an unprecedented degree of user-friendliness. The $30,000 machines were a success, and, by 1976, had propelled Wang among the top data-processing companies in the world. However, the death knell for dedicated machines came with the rise of generalist PCs, and in 1990, after a failed attempt to manufacture PCs, Wang filed for bankruptcy.

4.2.3. *Micro-computing* à la française

Many of the seminal players of the 1980s French micro-computing movement have faded into obscurity. Normerel, Micral, Thomson, Goupil, Léanord, R2E and Logabax are no more. There again, there were many reasons for this collective collapse. The lack of sound financial resources was a major factor, as were marketing shortfalls and daring alliances, such as that signed by Logabax and Olivetti. Technical errors (the belated switch to 16-bit technology, non-respect of recognized standards, Bull did not release its IBM-compliant Micral 30 until 1985 ...), blind faith in the backing of state authorities (in 1987, 34% of Léanord's production was for the French state) and the disproportionate ambitions of company directors also played their part. All these factors combined to put a premature end to the rise of these companies, and soon left the French market open to North American vendors alone.

However, failure of the like is not an *exception française*. In October 1994, Newsweek published an article which explained why Europe was trailing in the race for what was then known as the "information highway". History has since shown that the severe criticism leveled at Europe's industrial weakness in the field of basic technology was justified, with the complete collapse of all public IT solutions providers. Telecommunications, with the success of GSM, is the sole key sector in which Europe has managed to retain significant industrial and research capabilities.

4.2.4. Broken promises: could do better!

Although much hope was pinned on so-called "artificial intelligence" in the 1980s, AI proved far more difficult to exploit than was at first believed. On the one hand, the knowledge to be formalized requires high levels of natural intelligence, and sometimes more than we have at our disposal, while on the other, the tools which *have* been implemented, far from having become more democratic, require high-level specialists to operate them. These specialists sometimes feel undervalued, reduced as they are to operating as lowly "programmers". Artificial intelligence was very fashionable in the 1980s, although it now has a much lower profile in the media. The effective applications of associated concepts and tools are now concealed within black box systems which are – by their very nature – opaque, or within software packages designed for CRM, knowledge management, artefact design, plan administration and resource management purposes. Generally speaking, they only re-emerge once the packages begin attracting attention, and the intelligence is no longer visible through its abstract capacity but through its concrete ability when applied to a given trade or business area. Some success achieved in tangible and profitable business applications should be highlighted. Take, for example, steel giant Usinor's Sachem project, aimed at providing accompanying measures for operating blast furnaces. ILOG is one of many companies who now sell more solutions based on artificial intelligence to end-user-oriented software package editors than to major contractors.

The development of Enterprise Resource Planning applications has raised hopes of unique, seamless, integrated information systems which can be purchased as seen, and easily tailored to the user company's specific needs. However, implementation has proved to be a long and costly – sometimes extremely costly – business. Maintenance is tricky, as illustrated by how difficult it is to upgrade versions in order to keep in line with the software editors" offerings. They remain difficult to master when being used not only to draft project briefs but also to cater for other practices. It can also sometimes be awkward to identify the fields or processes in which it is in the company's interest to take best practices on board – which then turn out to be nothing more than the average performance results obtained from the pool of businesses used to design the software package – and tell them apart from the areas in which expertise gained in core activities remains an essential element of any genuine competitive advantage, thus justifying specific developments. Globally speaking, the total ERP-based integration of an information system is still an unattainable dream for most, regardless of the current attempts made by ERP software editors to provide a full range of trade-based vertical solutions, and of horizontal solutions incorporating supply chain and CRM tools. However appealing such increased consistency might appear on paper, it fails to live up to the actual complexity of companies or to the difficulties associated with steering such changes on a long-term basis.

Other domains in which promises have not been fully kept include optimization techniques, the old-fashioned "operational research". The internet revolution, with its promises and advantages, has also brought about a new generation of complex problems of architecture, performance and security that IT engineers have had to tackle.

4.3. The engines powering progress in the digital era

The success stories of the digital era have been the result of the infinite number of possible ways of combining technology and uses, and the happy union between "useful products" and their users, who seize the said products, in order to create the accompanying lifestyle! In this world of alleged innovation, few of the change release mechanisms can in fact be identified. Granted, the industry is constantly pushing a mass of products which enhance the basic layer of "usable technology", users then making choices and implementing products, often for only a short period of time and with an intensity that falls short of their potential. The second layer of "utilized technology" is in turn explored, assessed and transformed to be broken down through applications into a limited sub-set of "useful technology", which provides the services expected with a satisfactory cost to value ratio. The frontline role of CIOs has been to transform utilized technology into useful technology, by seeking to achieve yield levels that should ideally be as close as possible to 100% …

Among the plethora of fake and genuine innovations which have shown the technological, commercial and marketing creativity of vendors, some ideas have favored the emergence of new practices which have taken firm root in the organizational landscape of businesses, by providing real services for users. But, all in all, the list is still short.

4.3.1. *Human/machine interface*

If one is to tap into the full potential of the computer or electronic device being used, a means of communication is essential. This is referred to in generic terms as the "human/machine interface", and it enables the user to enter the commands to be executed by the machine, and to monitor the subsequent operations and results. The properties of the interface being used can be directly linked with the quality of the work which the user aims to produce, the time taken and the mistakes made. This has become one of the most complex IT issues, as it involves taking human input – which is by its very nature analogue and blurred – and converting it into a digital signal which can be recognized by the machine. The whole process must be as fast, reliable and user-friendly as possible. Likewise, the results must be returned in a format which the user can exploit.

Enormous progress has been made over the past 30 years, and, today, it would be inconceivable to revert to the passive green and amber monitors of bygone years, which were, in fact, still commonplace in companies, up until the early 1990s. Exchanges with machines have been rendered far more comfortable with the arrival of the mouse, graphic interfaces, drop-down menus and dialog boxes. These developments can be traced back to PARC and the Mac, and have become part of everyday life, although they have evolved little, since Microsoft belatedly took to the Macintosh approach.

The simplification of user interface remains at the heart of research being carried out by IT manufacturers and software editors, just as in the past it was a central concern of those who invented typewriters and calculators. Users soon get used to new performance thresholds, and their desire for greater ease of use goes hand in hand with the need for increased productivity. This is another area where a technical approach alone does not suffice, given the fact that human/machine interface issues have a direct consequence on each individual's personal experience and sensitivity. It is not simply a case of dealing with isolated functions such as inputting or restoring data, but it involves creating a global environment conducive to work – or leisure – needs, in which the user feels both comfortable and confident. Factors such as noise levels, cluttered design, aesthetics, keyboard ergonomics, reliability and reaction speed all contribute to the intrinsic qualities of a given interface being strengthened or weakened. If, when combined, these various components satisfy the user and lead to greater acceptance of the inherent constraints of the task at hand, the quality of the interface has a far more critical role to play in the case, say, of the controls for an aeroplane cockpit or on an industrial machine, or even in a car, where the slightest misunderstanding of data can lead to a fatal error.

Complex problems continue to be raised by the design of a "good" interface. Designers are faced with a wide spectrum of possibilities within which they must make their choices. The best-received systems are those that place emphasis on certain factors, such as on intuition rather than on explanations, explicit symbols rather than written instructions (the vocabulary of which is invariably difficult to understand or translate), simplicity rather than sophistication, and speed rather than exhaustiveness. It remains difficult to control and ensure accuracy with sound and voice data, given the interference of background noise and the quality of reaction speed and reproduction.

That is why the subject generates so much hope and passion, as well as much frustration and disillusion. In an article published by *Science & Vie* in July 1985, Bruno Lussatto, a lecturer at CNAM (*Conservatoire National des Arts et Métiers, the French National School of Engineering and Technology*) and widely regarded as an "*éminence grise* of the industrial world", wrote that it was futile to teach children in France to type because "in ten years" time, this ability will be of no use whatsoever, but if anything will hold them back because by then every computer will have a touch screen monitor and a mouse or, even better, will be voice-controlled, demanding that thoughts be formalized before speaking". He concluded by saying that "children who have not learnt to type will be better-equipped to confront a computer than those who are currently being taught how to handle a machine". Although these predictions have proved to be erroneous, the same cannot be said of his vision, in 1985, of the tuition of computer programming, which he thought to be totally without purpose since "henceforth engineers and even company directors will be able to use a micro-computer to deal with highly complex management problems, without any particular IT qualifications".

The whole human/machine interface issue is thus perfectly illustrated: how does one communicate with the machine, and for what purpose? While it has been thrilling to witness the constant increase in the power of micro-processors, it goes without saying that it is frustrating how little progress has been achieved in the field of human/machine interfaces. Machines may be ultra-powerful, but are not instantly accessible, and use has been thwarted by the complexity, instability and slowness of programs. The promises of voice command are but slowly being realized, and handwriting recognition tools have yet to become reliable. Therefore, the keyboard, despite all its constraints, remains indispensable.

In his book, *The Unfinished Revolution*, Michael Dertouzos cried out against everything faced by ordinary IT users on a daily basis. Even as Director of the MIT Laboratory for Computer Science, he was not immune to the thousand and one mishaps that we all have to put up with when using our beloved machines. He writes: "We are surrounded by these creatures – the personal computers, laptops, handheld assistants, printers, internet-savvy phones, music storage drives, and other digital wonders. They are everywhere and multiplying fast. Yet instead of serving us, we are serving them. We wait endlessly for our computers to boot up, and for bulky Web pages to paint themselves on our screens. We stand perplexed in front of incomprehensible system messages, and wait in frustration on the phone for computerized assistance. We constantly add software upgrades, enter odd instructions, fix glitches, only to sit in maddening silence when our machines crash, forcing us to start all over again, hoping against hope that they did not take a piece of our intellectual hide with them." The tools of this menagerie take all our time and energy, imprisoning us when they should be setting us free. Dertouzos" book is a plea for our freedom!

And yet, the history of progress achieved as regards human/machine interface has been full of promising innovations. Some have enabled us happily to move forward. It is now our right to demand more!

4.3.2. *The laws in the new world*

The computerization of society can be measured by the simultaneous increase in the power of micro-processors, the development of networks and the growth of digital data storage capacity. We have entered an age of plenty, thanks to the development of basic technologies with ever higher performance levels. Since the 1970s, these technological engines have been powering progress in the IT industry, which, in turn, has drawn on its new achievements to fuel continued growth. This is done by speeding up the renewal of hardware and software equipment and by pushing the limits of the tools" potential ever further back. The industry does not make the best possible use of its new abilities, weighed down as it is by the source code of new applications, which are written without any size limits and which take up substantial capacities of space and speed. Nevertheless, net gains have been forthcoming, adding gradually but unspectacularly to the overall perception of ease of use. Each technical achievement feeds an unsteady system which is then distorted, its ramifications extending into all domains of activity. As each component of the system develops in a manner which is consistent only with itself, it is hard to imagine the global impact of the transformations at hand. However, the outcome of these developments promises to be an infinite combination of powerful, miniaturized and interconnected tools associated with increasingly refined software. When applied to the numerous problems of the economic, cultural and social worlds, the results will bring their own potential.

The IT world has always been fond of powerful symbols, and it has personalized developments by defining "laws" which have been given the names of those who initially formulated them, all of whom were not only eminent specialists but also key players personally committed to the development of the IT sector and of the companies who benefit from the market.

4.3.2.1. *Moore's Law*

The most famous is undoubtedly Moore's Law. In an article published by *Electronics Magazine* on 19th April 1965, Gordon Moore, then Director of Research at Fairchild before co-founding Intel in 1968, analyzed the situation after four years" development of integrated circuits. His forecasts were soon dubbed "Moore's Law" by the press. He predicted that the number of transistors per square inch on integrated circuits would double every 18 months, and would continue to do so until 1975, although it now transpires the rate will be maintained until 2015 thanks to the progress since achieved in design- and circuit-technology.

Some authors, like Ray Kurzweil in his 1999 book *Age of Spiritual Machines*, have considered that the cycles of Moore's Law are closer to 12 than to 18 months, and, more importantly, that the law has been applicable to 100 years of developments across all data-processing-related domains, whether mechanics, electro-mechanics, vacuum valves, transistors or integrated circuits. Kurzweil, a specialist in voice-recognition issues and an authority on artificial intelligence, has deduced that such exponential growth will mean that, come 2020, a $1,000 computer will have greater capacity than the human brain.

	Year of introduction	Transistors
4004	1971	2,250
8008	1972	2,500
8080	1974	5,000
8086	1978	29,000
286	1982	120,000
386™ processor	1985	275,000
486™ processor	1989	1,180,000
Pentium® processor	1993	3,100,000
Pentium II processor	1997	7,500,000
Pentium III processor	1999	24,000,000
Pentium 4 processor	2000	42,000,000

Source: http://www.intel.com/research/silicon/mooreslaw.htm, May 2001.

4.3.2.2. *Metcalfe's Law*

Harvard graduate Robert Metcalfe was an inventor who designed Ethernet, currently the most prominent local area network protocol. In 1981, in Santa Clara, California, he founded 3Com Corporation, a pioneering network solutions firm. Metcalfe highlighted the power of network interconnections, stating that the usefulness, or utility, of a network is proportional to the square of the number of machines connected (computers, telephones, cars, etc.).

4.3.2.3. *Ruettger's Law*

Mike Ruettger, CEO of EMC, now firmly established as the worldwide leader in software and hardware data storage solutions, forecast that storage requirements for companies would double every year. Obviously, the highly imaginative EMC have fully benefited from this "law".

4.3.2.4. *Gilder's Law*

According to author and journalist George Gilder, one of the great American technology visionaries, bandwidth trebles every year. Traffic in bytes doubles every hundred days. More data can be carried by a simple 2001-vintage cable in one second than the total amount of internet communications over one month in 1997. In Gilder's words, we have evolved from the micro-computer world, or "Microcosm", the title of his 1989 book, to the telecommunications world, or "Telecosm".

4.3.2.5. *Shannon's Law*

Shannon's Law states that the performance of digital communications decreases as power increases, and conversely performance increases as power decreases. Indeed, a rise in electric power causes fiber dispersion and nonlinearity, and greater interference in Hertzian communications. The rise of digital communications has therefore meant reducing the electrical consumption of each component of the infrastructure. Miniaturization has thus brought about improved performance.

4.3.3. Machine diversification and interoperability

The IT market was long a compartmentalized collection of specialities and product ranges. The major characteristic of the digital era is that it is grounded on continuity of service between the various components. Progress has not been as fast as forecast or hoped, but the trend towards standardization today seems stronger than the move towards diversification, given the fact that no single market player can impose their law on others, however tempted they might be to do so! On top of these foundations, the mechanisms of which have already fuelled previous technical revolutions, many additional elements have taken root, such as increased autonomy, more lightweight systems, improved human/machine interface, high quality devices, etc.

These parameters have combined to give birth to a host of new types of generic or usage-specific tools. The traditional computer has led to a large family of devices which are interconnected by the network, and whose users soon forgot that the micro-processor-driven devices in their hands were in fact IT tools. New, improved, "intelligent" versions of bygone analogue and mechanical machines such as cars and telephones have subsequently appeared, along with radically new devices such as electronic books and GPS watches.

Faced with such a wealth of prospects, the market may have to choose between the two trends currently taking shape. On the one hand, manufacturers will seek to simplify use by conceiving machines which incorporate several functions (combined digital telephones and PDAs with internet access), while, on the other, some products will continue to be dedicated to a single function (wide-screen television sets, cameras and digital camcorders). However, the interconnections between these various tools will be facilitated by broadband exchange protocols which will soon do without cables by using radio frequencies (the Bluetooth norm) or infrared signals, and through the use of interchangeable high-capacity memory banks. One of the most spectacular aspects of these changes will be the development of direct links between machines themselves. Thus, a drinks dispenser can already monitor consumption and place long-distance orders for the necessary supplies. Vehicles will be able to provide a complete diagnosis of their working order, and suggest appropriate solutions.

The diversification of "intelligent machines" will also benefit from the normalization of software. To be able to exchange over the internet, trouble-free deciphering is essential. This implies decoding incoming data instantly and with no need for technical knowledge. Software editors have thus had to make use of recognized standards such as Java, JPEG, MPEG and MP3. The improved quality of compression algorithms – coupled with increased bandwidth – will enable complex data to be exchanged, including broadcast-quality video files and voice telephony. Enhanced media will allow high levels of creativity to be applied to content, rendering electronic commerce and activities such as education and in-service training even more attractive. However, if promises are to be kept, technical leverage will not suffice. Instead, they must be a consistent, controlled and integral element of overall practices. The implementation of changes is the most important factor behind technical potential being transformed into measurable progress.

Chapter 5

The Promise and Reality of New Technology

5.1. IT effectiveness called into question

More than 50 years down the line, the Information Technology gamble has paid off. It has been deployed across all sectors of activity in developed countries all over the world. Automated systems now cater for all main collective and trade-related functions. Large companies worldwide are fully computerized. Few businesses or governmental organizations, regardless of size or sector, still operate without resorting, at least partially, to IT tools. The message is coming in loud and clear: the IT industry has achieved what it set out to do. No-one would even think of reverting to typewriters, manual telephones or mechanical processing tools. Why then does "IT" – a generic term if ever there was one, encompassing a wide range of products and situations – continue to be such a big issue?

Whilst visible IT tools such as machines, PCs and programs have become an integral part of most corporate functions, understanding of their actual role remains fragmented, superficial and debatable. IT generates cloaks of doubt or even suspicion. The messages expressed by all sorts of consultants have yet to be backed up by hard factual analyzes, and whilst computerization may now be accepted in principle, it has yet to become a simple and risk-free process. Companies may use the same tools, but the benefits gained differ substantially. There have been many cases of major projects failing, but more importantly the repeated micro-breakdowns or large-scale failures of major networks lead to irritation, frustration and lost time. Faced with the triumphant attitude of technology and the accompanying industry, one soon becomes aware of the fact that a corporate information system is not a utility which can be bought off the peg, but rather a fragile, complex and living whole, of which technology is but one component. Just because authors all use

Word does not mean that they will all win the Nobel Prize for Literature. It is exactly the same for businesses. Software packages are such loose entities that they alone cannot effortlessly shape an ideal high-performance business, as was so hastily believed. It is so easy to blame everything on IT, or to claim that IT is both incomprehensible and too expensive. And yet, efforts must be made to understand technology in order to construct a realistic and controlled way of utilizing this marvelous tool, which successive generations of scientists – whose dreams and ambitions have been detailed in the preceding chapters of this book – have intelligently shaped over the years.

5.2. The value of IT

The overall image of IT has changed. The IT world is no longer a closed shop inhabited by specialists, as the use of IT tools now concerns all active individuals, as well as more and more people from outside professional circles. Those in power traditionally kept their distance from "manual" tools, but, come the mid-1990s, they also began to take an active interest in what was on offer, if only to be able to send e-mails to their offspring studying at universities overseas and who spread the news about how modern the web was. The internet has indeed made IT far more attractive and practical. However, behind this pleasant façade, the reality of data processing – opportunities and constraints alike – has not changed. It is still a question of structuring processes, ideas and information generated by business activities in order to be more reactive and enable decision-making. This is still the ultimate aim of IT in business circles. It is nothing more than a tool to be able to act, perform and synthesize. And yet, there is still a tendency to confuse investment in equipment, software and consultants with improved performance.

It is obviously in the best interests of technology providers to promote the use of IT tools within businesses, but it is more difficult to understand why some corridors of power have become so fascinated by new information and communications technologies. The craze has given rise to a mass of official reports, followed by recommendations which have been as peremptory as they have amusing. Opinions about IT innovation go back as far as the techniques themselves. And yet, innovation is a slow process. When a given innovation emerges, it attracts huge media interest, which then dies down as soon as the innovation is either assimilated or abandoned. From then on, no-one pays it any more attention. Who, today, could imagine producing industrial goods without the omnipresent support of IT, as was the case in the 1950s? Do you know of anyone who still goes up to the bank clerk to withdraw cash rather than making use of the ubiquitous cash dispenser? Do you know of any dentists, plumbers, hotel directors or takeaway pizza parlors who do not use a computer to manage their client portfolios, invoices or even their knowledge? However, these undeniable long-term transformations cannot be instantly measured on a company's performance or quarterly results, apart from those in the business of selling IT solutions. If company directors are to oversee the permanent transformation of their organizations, a number of qualities are essential: an informational culture, the ability to think up new working processes, and the kind of managerial energy which, in time, breeds the persistence without which success cannot be achieved. We can no longer imagine that change can be managed without the use of IT. Finally, before making the indispensable tools their own, and using them both as a vehicle for their own ambitions and as an instrument for their tempered power, the directors themselves have to take the culture on board. The overly technical vision of bygone years – which has left so many directors with nothing but bad memories – is long gone. Company directors must cease to shelter behind a pathetic "you know, I'm not a computer scientist", which they claimed in order to shirk any kind of responsibility in this vital domain. As early as 1968, Pierre Lhermitte wrote: "The interaction between the organization and the introduction of an integrated management system within businesses represents one of the fundamental difficulties associated with the implementation of computerized management systems (…). It is therefore important to be reminded of the essential role to be played by company directors in the setting up of an information technology system and in the definition of the company's information technology policy". It is high time things changed.

5.2.1. IT and economic savings: can the case be closed?

The short-lived reign of the so-called New Economy re-ignited the time-honored debate about the economic value of IT. In a report submitted to the French Economic and Social Council[19] by Pierre Lhermitte, the following word of warning was expressed: "The introduction of IT within a company is indisputably the result of an act of faith in the potential renewal that can be brought about by new techniques… The economic appraisal of an IT system only becomes distinctly positive at the end of the transitional period, during which the cohabitation of old and new methods generates additional expenditure". This rings as true for us today as it did then. IT is by no means an overnight miracle cure! Later, in an article published in 1993 by management consultants Arthur D. Little[20], the author highlighted the frustrations of managers faced with their inability to obtain reasonable returns on their increasing investments in Information Technology. He

---

[19] *"Conséquences prévisibles du développement de l'automatisation de la gestion des enterprises"* ('The predictable consequences of the development of automated business management systems'), position paper published by the French Economic and Social Council, 14th March 1968.

[20] "Getting a return on your information technology investment", Edward T. Choate, Prism, 1993.

concluded by saying that despite technical innovation itself promising an easier way to make future savings (a definite constant!), it was still up to the directors themselves to show enthusiasm for the ways in which new technology could enable transformations, by promoting change. In other words, if you yourself are not convinced, show just how determined you are all the same! Bill Gates recommends nothing else, writing in 2000[21] that the initial financial outlay for an IT infrastructure is high and that the CEO should shoulder the responsibility for IT expenditure. Gates adds that rather than attempting to contain IT costs, it is best to assess them in terms of efficiency in relation to the end results, and that in this digital age, the secret of success lies in the success of IT. This is a recurring theme among consultants, which is very frustrating because it reinforces the theory of the inevitability of technological investment, and shows the ideological nature of its character.

Despite the consistently declamatory style used, IT spending is considered virtuous even though there is a lack of norms with which to set targets. It remains an act of faith. From a macroeconomic point of view, countries are now being ranked according to the amounts invested in information and communications technology. In businesses – where chief executives are invariably anxious to know whether they are spending enough or too much on IT (such an expensive commodity in their opinion) – considerations as regards the relationship between performance and levels of investment evolved with the New Economy, resulting in overcautious companies extravagantly launching into major e-business investments.

Ever since the 1980s, when the inexorable rise of IT expenditure began to get company directors worried, academics and experts have examined the link between the level of IT expenditure and that of growth and increased productivity. They have sought to draw up convincing links between levels of IT expenditure and economic results, from both macro- and microeconomic viewpoints. It might intuitively be believed that IT has brought about profound changes in the ways goods and services are designed, manufactured and distributed, when in fact research has never delivered convincing evidence! The gurus of the New Economy have accused official figures of not accounting for the intangible reality of using old tools initially designed to measure the value of material things. Recently, software spending has come to be considered as investment – particularly in the US and in France – although this justified change in accounting rules has failed to bring about any major changes in the demonstration of returns on investment. When handling the IT productivity issue, the question should be simultaneously approached from a global perspective and through a company-focused analysis.

---

[21] *Business @ the Speed of Thought*, Bill Gates, Warner Business Books, 2000, New York.

5.2.1.1. *The macroeconomic approach*

Understanding the information economy is essential for the transformation of businesses – and, for that matter, of the functioning of society as a whole – to be properly controlled. The theoretical basis of the debate can be traced back to a 1957 article by Robert Solow, which explained that growth in a country's gross national product depends on capital and work, but also on a third residual factor: technical progress. This global factor encompasses various types of innovation related to research and development, the implementation of new processes, materials and components, alongside the innovative use of capital goods. Information Yechnologies have not been identified as a specific category, but contribute to the dynamics of progress on several levels.

There are, unfortunately, still no clear-cut macroeconomic measurements of the impact of information technologies. According to research, carried out by Daniel Sichel and based solely on US data, the money spent by businesses on office IT equipment (PCs, workstations, mini-computers, mainframes and peripheral equipment) played a secondary role in growth over the period from 1970 to 1993. OECD researchers reached the same conclusion: the 4% per annum growth in the US economy between 1950 and 1973 was fuelled by an increase in productivity, which rose by 2.8% per annum. From 1913 to 1973, the combined productivity of work and capital increased by 1.6% per annum. Between 1973 and 1995, work productivity rose by 1.4% per annum. The OECD researchers have deduced that there is "insufficient evidence to support the theory of a new economy that might enable the benefits gained by new technology manufacturers to be distributed among users". Several factors have been suggested to explain the counter-performance. Integrating new technology is an extremely costly business, as it involves highly-qualified (and therefore expensive) labor. Any subsequent software developments within the company necessitate the construction of interfaces with existing systems, another costly process, which causes disturbance and undermines the positive effect of incorporating new features. Equipment becomes obsolete far too quickly, meaning that the agreed investments fail to become profitable. In the 1980s, the technological cycle of a typical mainframe computer was seven years. Depreciation costs could be forecast, and replacements planned. But technological cycles have gained pace and it has become impossible to obtain stable products with predictable life cycles. In the case of fully operational software programs, it has been known for editors to hastily render them obsolete, ceasing investments in previous versions before putting an end to maintenance schemes overnight. There have been only too many failed projects, which have been on such a large scale and so well publicized that the very notion of "project" has been discredited. Finally, for the lackluster inventory to be complete, the negative impact of the failure to take the Y2K issue into account – despite the fact that it was so predictable – must be highlighted. This straightforward technical rightsizing operation mobilized enormous resources, and while the offers on the market often lacked consistency and performance could not be measured, executive boards were drawn to the problem, before the whole affair was ultimately suspected of having been blown out of all proportion, for the benefit of the IT community as a whole!

However, renewed growth has been measured over a very short period in the US sectors such as banking and insurance, and has been linked to new technologies. Indeed, productivity rose by 2.5% per annum between 1995 and 2000, against 1.4% between 1972 and 1995. Rigorous economists consider this phenomenon to be far too recent and incomplete to be able to come to any kind of conclusion.

On the other hand, those who observe the impact of investment in computers, software and communications equipment across the sectors which manufacture the said goods, and then carefully pinpoint the impact on the sectors which actually utilize them, will note that productivity has risen considerably in the IT manufacturing sector. This phenomenon was analyzed in research carried out by McKinsey[22], and the ensuing report was published in the fall of 2001. It showed that recent growth in the US can be put down to leaps made by just 6 sectors of activity, while the remaining 53 sectors failed to register any significant progress (0.3% per annum). Over the period studied, investment in IT doubled. Of the six sectors in question, three were directly related to IT: telecommunications, semiconductors and computer manufacturing. The others were retail, wholesale distribution and finance. The report explains how the rapid transformation of retail in the US can be attributed to the Wal-Mart phenomenon. As competitors have followed Wal-Mart's successful lead (by using the same EDI and radio barcode tools, as well as by increasing the size of stores and rationalizing warehouses), the sector has been completely restructured. Levels of productivity rose by 48% at Wal-Mart, competitors achieving 28%. In 2000, online trade only accounted for 0.01% of overall productivity, against 0.9% of retail turnover. In the technological sectors, productivity is due to the soaring PC market and to the increased efficiency of products themselves and of their components, particularly micro-processors and the soaring PC market.

It has been in the field of stock market trading that the most spectacular internet-related profits have been made, the sector accounting for 40% of transactions made in 2000. In a scenario that mirrored that of Wal-Mart, it was the success achieved by Charles Schwab on the online transactions market – with productivity levels ten times higher than traditional transactions – that forced competitors to follow suit. But the financial bubble also explains the apparent growth in productivity by incorporating the market value of transactions within the denominator. During what was a euphoric period for information technologies, McKinsey noted that changing processes, dynamic competitiveness within the sector and managerial innovation all

---

22 *US Productivity Growth 1995-2000*, McKinsey Global Institute, October 2001.

enabled new departures in terms of productivity, and IT provided an essential but insufficient backbone. Money invested in the Y2K issue, the renewal of PCs and the improvement of network bandwidth have not brought about increased productivity, but have simply enabled businesses to keep up with the pack. Furthermore, breakeven points will not be reached for many years as far as many investments are concerned. These are often infrastructure-related, such as improved telecommunications network capacities or increased numbers of PCs (two per capita in retail banking!). If gains in productivity have been largely limited to businesses from within the sector, who then are the real victors in the race for IT investment, and what are the prospects for the future? The answer lies in the ability of other sectors to take on board and develop the innovations that have been behind the dynamic rise of the winning sectors, particularly in the fields of manufacturing industries, tertiary and public services. It is obvious that the potential of the internet for commerce – both B2B and B2C – and that of intranet systems for internal corporate processes come to fruition when investments have been judiciously gauged, and that management teams have reaped the rewards by breaking away from previous practices. Less should be invested, and products and services should be cheaper! It might also be considered that the immediate reactions to the events in September 2001 will cause productivity to increase through massive job cuts, forcing the straight technical impact on productivity into the background.

5.2.1.2. *The microeconomic approach*

IT spending remains a controversial subject which has been thoroughly debated, but has yet to be properly formalized. Research analysts and consultants Gartner have drawn up three groups in which businesses can be categorized. Group A houses the companies who wish to lean on information technology in order to develop their activities and who are prepared to take risks. Group B features the companies who follow and keep up with technical developments while keeping a firm rein on their technological processes, who are well aware of the value of information systems, and who have the ability to make lucid choices. Group C is made up of the companies who consider IT as simple costs which must be cut, and who turn to the market to get rid of the problem. Managerial attitudes of the like lead to highly contrasting results from the deployment of information technology, and thus in the benefits obtained.

Historically, the first information processing tools (calculating machines and then calculators, and typewriters) were introduced in order to improve the efficiency of stable and recognized tertiary production processes such as accounting, calculating tables, mail and paper documents. Their implementation led to an immediate increase in productivity without any changes being made to the actual processes, with a measurable qualitative impact on data accuracy, and the ability to retrieve and analyze it. However, much of the benefit gained from automating previously manual processes was absorbed by economic growth, which generated higher volumes of activity. IT was then gradually introduced to companies in the early 1960s, replacing the mechanical data processing systems used for basic tasks. With industrial automation, IT was also exploited for the purposes of production processes. However, even with electromechanical machines gradually making way for computers from the 1960s onwards, uses remained much the same. Pioneering companies made considerable efforts in terms of the massive investments that had to be made, along with the sheer complexity of implementing the new systems, and yet the much-vaunted breaks with the past failed to materialize in the spectacular fashion that had been envisaged. IT was slow to spread, and for a long time its use was confined to corporate departments far-removed from production and sales. The computerization of IT back-office systems, which was at the root of the first wave of ERP set-ups, was ultimately a response to concerns which barely differed from those catered for by Burroughs and Hollerith amongst others. It was a far cry from the ambitious vision of society as dreamt up by the pioneers of computer science.

However, IT is present in the fields of research, production and retail, where innovations are nurtured and then circulated. In actual fact, IT is not an innovation as such for a given user company. It contributes to all performance factors in place, whether industrial or commercial investments, new working processes or new products. To further hone the analysis, the following classification[23] could serve as a starting point. It distinguishes two types of innovation:

– Incremental innovation:
- The significant improvement of an existing product.
- The introduction of a product which is new to the firm but not to the market.
- The significant improvement of a production process.

– Radical innovation:
- The introduction of a product which is new to both the market and the company.
- The introduction of a major shift in the production process.

Precisely how does IT contribute to the development of innovations in the corporate world?

Instances of incremental innovation encompass a large number of products and processes. Let us take some examples from the automotive industry, beginning with upstream processes before moving downstream. Through market analysis, IT has enabled customer requirements to be more accurately identified. By receiving direct

---

[23] As proposed by Emmanuel Duguet in a report drafted for the French Industry Ministry.

feedback from customers as to incidents which have occurred, correction cycles are shortened. With computer-assisted design, IT has enabled product development cycles to be shortened, and has linked up designers and sub-contractors. In factories, the precise monitoring of production has made finer product quality analysis possible, and made it easier to react when malfunctions occur in order to achieve high levels of quality. In the past, new vehicles were developed over five-year periods on average. Nowadays, a 36-month development period has become commonplace, and a 12-month threshold is the target for 2005. Finally, by collecting data relative to incidents affecting customers (such as malfunctions and breakdowns), it is now possible to obtain precise information about the ways vehicles are being used on the road. Even though, for historical reasons, each system contributing to the aforementioned missions has been designed using differing techniques and objectives, convergence towards a single system will bring about even more finely-tuned analysis and, consequently, increased reactivity between downstream and upstream operations. All the major companies who have heavily invested in separate systems over the past 30 years are now working on the implementation of integrated technical and functional platforms with a view to drawing full benefit from the data they are collecting but currently failing to exploit to the full.

As far as a given company's support services – accounts, wages, human resources, supplies and everyday purchases – are concerned, the use of IT to carry out a familiar and unchanging task (like drawing up an employee's payslip) instantly generates savings of time spent per unit, cuts the number of people needed for the task, and renders operations faster to correct in case of error, and more flexible and simpler to keep in line with changes in the law. Furthermore, within an integrated software package, the links between different support activities are automated, providing an integrated overview of those activities. Tasks which, in the early 20th century, would have utilized countless clerks and were at the very heart of businesses are now being handled by limited numbers of individuals, who can easily be brought together in centers housing shared departments.

However, players in the fields of both management and production have not automatically regarded the impact of computerization as having brought about substantially improved performance levels. Indeed, rationalized work processes have directly resulted in increased productivity, which in turn have been exploited in such a manner as to redistribute skills across higher value-added sectors. Thus, gains in productivity circulate constantly, and general re-appropriation is more evident than immediate net gains. The scattering of the benefits of computerization highlights a common phenomenon in our tertiary society: the confusion between one's "work" and one's "occupation". Work represents the energy needed to carry out an identified task, and this energy can easily be measured. This was the mission of the first organizers. Whereas an occupation represents duty, status and one's actual or imagined position within an organization. Although it might be possible to measure the impact of automation on work, there is nothing to provoke – or in many cases to justify – the measurement of how relevant a given occupation is, other than as part of organizational decision-making. That is why IT can contribute to the very destruction of work, by diverting the energy needed to achieve stable objectives, but without allowing a reduction in personnel, the only way to improve productivity.

If companies are to be more proactive, transparent and consistent, and obtain greater means of monitoring their operations, the availability and integrity of their data must be ensured. IT is the essential tool for all of the above, and yet the associated performances have become so familiar and natural that no-one attributes them to IT … except when problems arise. Without such a firm framework in which to work, managers would be unable to diagnose situations and thus to make decisions! Progress cannot be achieved without formalization or measurement! Cutting back on the time it takes to publish accounts is no longer a mere technical feat, it has become a veritable financial obligation in order to make key strategic decisions at the right time and, quite simply, to be worthy of existing in an economic world which loathes dissimulation and a lack of precision.

Information technologies have also fuelled radical innovation, and were vital to a host of otherwise inconceivable feats: the decoding of the human genome, the invention of new, life-saving molecules, the space conquest, the democratization of air travel, and the ability to venture inside the human body with the aid of medical imaging techniques. Thus, the internet has revolutionized the world of biological research. Gene sequencing data is available online. In 2000, five million sequences were published on the GenBank database. When researchers successfully clone a gene, they can immediately compare results with previously identified sequences. As for less specialized domains, IT has transformed areas such as industrial manufacturing, logistics and air travel. In each of these sectors, programming and real-time production monitoring have raised output levels by optimizing capacity investments, and have therefore generated reachable service levels in excellent economic conditions. Today's financial markets owe their very existence to the complete virtualization of products and exchanges. The stock exchange would grind to a halt without the network. Take away telecommunications and the powerful IT systems, and there would be no financial products left.

The simultaneous quest for cost cuts, increased reactivity and improved performance has constantly led entrepreneurs to seek to exploit the potential of information technology as a tool for transforming organizations. It no longer appears possible for a complex organization to innovate and grow without large-scale and versatile input from IT across each and every phase of its everyday operations. But the IT sphere has expanded in successive thrusts without any form of global method, overall plan or tools for evaluation. When drawing up company accounts, it therefore remains difficult to demonstrate the individual impact of investment in IT. Consider the fact that IT is a vast domain, and brings together a wide spectrum of different types of expenditure, in terms of both operations and investment. Data processing must be handled with great care so as to avoid coming to erroneous conclusions. But this complexity must not breed complacency. As IT is still regarded as innovative and immature, it is also subject to an unusual form of tolerance. A number of factors are behind this preferential treatment *vis-à-vis* other forms of expenditure and investment, which are subject to stricter controls. The most common reason for the lack of inquisitorial intensity is primarily the lack of understanding of the sheer scale and of the objects at hand. There is no such thing as a registered unit to measure IT work. Putting figures on technical data – such as the power of machines, network bandwidth and storage capacity – does not make the information any more legible for managers, who remain unable to make decisions on such a basis, particularly with IT engineers generally presenting developments as inevitable. The second reason is probably ignorance as to what is best practice. It remains extremely difficult to find one's bearings in the quagmire of IT policy-related data. This situation remains unchanged, and is maintained by the absence of a universal measurement system and the lack of public statistics, as well as by the relative confidence of decision-makers in the benchmarking research commissioned by their CIOs and carried out by specialized entities who, they too, are part of the IT ecosystem, with its own language and beliefs. Finally, there is a reliance on the weariness of managers when faced with such a whimsical subject, the consequences of which are so unpredictable that even business analysts are often knocked off course!

On the other hand, any kind of cost which has to be shouldered by users is income for the manufacturers. The latter are perfectly well organized to manage their income levels with great foresight, and have been ever since the birth of the profession. Hence their forceful explanations that investment in IT is a benefit in itself, and one which is not prone to the somewhat vulgar necessity of having to be justified. And should this visionary argument not suffice, they do not hesitate to brandish products obsolete or even totally *passé*. To this end, manufacturers have put extremely powerful marketing networks in place, and are now making good use of the general public and the generalist press to go beyond those professionals who remain overly demanding and skeptical as to the wonderful promises of hitherto unparalleled profits to be gained from the *latest* version of such and such a software package. Creative forecasting has become the dominant means of expression: heralding change so as to render it inevitable. Meanwhile, the top bosses of IT corporations do not hesitate to shout their ideas from the rooftops with a view to championing the cause. If they say it, then it will happen! That great man of marketing William H. Gates has written two books to explain the ways of the new world: *The Road Ahead* published in 1995 and *Business @ the Speed of Thought* in 2000. The latter featured a number of pearls of wisdom, including the claim that the more consumers take the internet lifestyle on board, the nearer all business sectors of the economy will edge towards economist Adam Smith's vision of the perfect market. There is nothing left to prove: the internet is the key to prosperity. This ongoing and discouraging gap between promises and operational reality damages the credibility of IT.

5.3. The IT sector set up as a model

The democratization of information processing tools gathered pace throughout the 1990s with the PC boom. From then on the industry rallied together to tap fully into the potential for growth and was behind successive waves of "progress" designed to maintain the high rate of expansion. The IT barons took center stage to sell not only their products but also, and above all, a whole new economic model which belatedly became known as the "New Economy". In 2001, with so many New Economy star players having fallen by the wayside, SAP traded on their longstanding experience with their ironic "The *New* New Economy" slogan, this being founded on the true values of web-friendly ERP systems. This commercial one-upmanship was both fed and broadcast by the media, and even in political circles there was a sense that this ode to technological modernity was a concept with high potential for growth. The short-lived fashion in 1999 was to welcome Bill Gates with the kind of pomp usually reserved for heads of state. This was very much indicative of how helpless decision-makers had become faced with the rise of this rich and powerful *élite* of IT tycoons. Company presidents and directors were advised by hybrid entrepreneur-gurus, whose emergence was, by no means, an historical shift, but rather the high-tech version of the system of influence operated by barons during France's Second Empire[24] and by American steel and railroad magnates, who would lobby politicians to obtain the state authorizations and investment needed for the success of their ventures. Political powers have traditionally held prestigious "captains of industry" in high esteem, and quite naturally this kind of attention has been paid to the IT sector ever since its inception. In 1949, France awarded Thomas J. Watson one of the country's highest accolades when Councilor Robert Schumann made him *Grand Officier de la Légion d'Honneur*. Watson was also received by Vincent Auriol, then President of the French Republic. Bill Gates is still a regular at ministerial functions and at the World Economic Forum in Davos, as is his rival, Lou Gerstner, President of IBM until 2001. What makes today's situation so original is that all these *nouveaux* sales reps are running under a single flag: the Star-Spangled Banner. Nationalism is no longer an appropriate element on the IT agenda; it has been replaced by the recognition of total US supremacy. Indeed, even the most successful European businesses must gain a bridgehead across the Atlantic if they are to have any hope of

---

[24] During the reign of Napoleon III, 1852-1870.

accessing the enormous US market. Companies have to adapt to the American scheme of things if they are to gain any form of recognition. French market players such as the software components supplier Ilog, and business intelligence software editor Business Objects have gone down that road. Even ERP software giant SAP underwent Americanization in order to gain credibility.

Beyond these mercenary games which are part and parcel of any market economy, the reality of IT is a far cry from the glamorous image of such supposedly unselfish individuals. Entrepreneurs are not intent on changing the world, but aim to dominate the market and successfully handle their infamous quarterly results, which provide the short-term overviews which, in turn, affect the value of stock options, essential bait in the hunt for new talent. If sales figures are on the wane, businesses react quickly and sometimes violently, so that the profit levels announced in front of shareholders are maintained, whatever the cost. In this context, prices serve as a variable for adjustment. This entrepreneurial thinking is grounded in US culture, and is a powerful enabler of strong economic and technological performance. Social and ethical virtues have no need to be part of the equation.

However, the IT sector's desired claim to be the new model for successful businesses has true worth. Indeed, the sector promotes values and behavioral practices that favor the development of dynamic processes and individual talents. Another "natural" consequence has been to promote the tools and services produced by a mere handful of companies. Nevertheless, beyond the self-interest-motivated promotion of the virtues of new technologies, it is possible to pinpoint the five major trends which have been brought about by technology-sector businesses and which, sometimes later, have inexorably led to major evolutions as regards practices in companies: staff mobility, knowledge management, extended companies, one-to-one marketing and the paean to speed.

Autonomy has been imposed both by the developing nature of workers" cultural backgrounds and by the necessity to provide frontline players with the means to respond to customers" requests. It campaigns for the atomization of structures in combination with the strengthened sharing of information, knowledge and corporate values. Modern-day companies, focused on processes and results rather than territorial presence and activities, are founded on swift decision-making at all levels, and the pooling not only of both problems and solutions, but also of profits and losses.

Knowledge is now at the heart of performance, whether knowledge of customers, knowledge of the market or knowledge shared between colleagues. But the extension of company boundaries has also meant businesses sharing their knowledge with suppliers and, increasingly, with clients. The development of networked companies has been grounded on the exchange and sharing of knowledge.

Customers will no longer accept being under-informed or deliberately left in the dark, as Mitsubishi and Firestone recently discovered to their cost. They want to understand products and services, and suppliers" sites are providing ever more elaborate – and sometimes deliberately technical – information about the products they sell. Demands for internal and external sharing were initially catered for through the innovative use of IT by the very companies responsible for producing the technology. The first web portals were thus installed at Digital, Cisco, Microsoft, Hewlett-Packard and IBM. With more lightweight procedures and the worldwide standardization of norms for internal controls, administrative constraints within companies have been rendered less taxing, thus enabling staff to focus on the essentials, such as sales, customer relations and product development. The major achievement of these companies has been to refocus staff on their key missions, the source of much pride for the firms in question who, following in the footsteps of Patterson and Watson, have even set up organizations to advise their clients.

Corporate *frontiers* are now shifting. The value chain between customers and suppliers is irrigated by information, which alone enables logistical processes to be set in motion, and allows all involved to focus on the best-controlled high value-added content. The technological world is made up of a number of complementary and/or competing businesses who work alongside each other in the name of "co-opetition", a neologism which illustrates the joint existence of co-operation and competition within a given alliance. These companies have sought to build effective relational flows with counterparts whilst retaining the means of breaking them off swiftly. The process is one of progress, combining concerns for high performance with effective collaborative working. Firms like Cisco and Dell have led the way towards lighter production structures, thus concentrating on service and product quality. Some more traditional businesses, such as Boeing and General Electric, have adhered to this model and been faster and more effective than their competitors in tapping into the potential offered by information technologies when applied to logistics chains.

One-to-one marketing has resulted in the development of goods and services that are highly adapted to customer needs and profiles. As such, it demands the implementation of flexible production systems that will keep stocks down, and limited production runs that go completely against the grain of industrial production processes that still owe a great deal to Ford-style factory assembly lines. Dell were the first to reap the rewards of one-to-one services. The main benefit expected to be gained from e-commerce, as much for the customer as for the supplier, lies in the fine-tuning of the offer, which in technical terms is best suited to minimum cost demands. Contrary to far-reaching marketing campaigns which send out general messages and are randomly received by target audiences, online marketing allows precise work to be carried out, generating levels of productivity that are far superior to traditional sales approaches. The Amazon example provides a highly-accomplished example of what can be achieved. When customers log on, they are greeted with offers, which are consistent with their usual interests, and have the means, over time, of monitoring their orders and spending.

Finally, *speed* has now become an ever-present element in the corporate world: the speed of information, speed of design, speed of execution and speed of decision-making. Technological firms were the first to publish their accounts virtually instantly (one of IBM's administrative feats), the first to have permanent access to the state of sales and profits, and the first to manage time as a strategic factor when dealing with announcements and deliveries, for better and for worse. Cisco CEO John Chambers keeps track of his company's results on a daily basis. Apple product launches are case studies in the mastery of events, marketing and communications. Microsoft have followed suit: the New York launch of Windows XP was a telling example. Lastly, it must be recognized that technological firms were the first to exploit the full power of e-mail, linking directors, managers, experts and sales forces across a dense relational network, allowing the asynchronous pooling of elements for analysis and decision-making on a worldwide scale. This intense use of e-mail facilitated the early adoption of intranet systems and B-to-E (Business to Employee) tools, which firms use extensively in order to cut back on decision-making processes, consequently bringing administrative costs down.

5.4. Telecommunications in the eye of the storm

In order to exploit technology to the full and develop the value-generating services that the information revolution has promised, a dynamic network infrastructure which can develop economical and reliable services is essential. Without it, the information society becomes stifled. However, the telecommunications industry, manufacturers and service providers alike, has been badly hit by the crisis in the information society, after having been the first to reap the rewards of its unreasonably meteoric rise. This deep-seated crisis poses a threat to growth across the sector as a whole for the foreseeable future.

After being worlds apart for many years, IT and telecommunications are now inextricably linked. Developments within information systems now depend totally on the progress achieved in the field of telecommunications networks. It is now virtually taken for granted that micro-computers, even home computers, are linked up to the network. Moreover, the internet has been responsible for the rise of the home computer market. Progress achieved in the field of telecommunications has mirrored that achieved by IT, following a similar course. Moore's Law enabled IT to lead the way over a long period, leaving telecoms lagging unenthusiastically behind, burdened with state monopolies (or private monopolies, in cases such as that of Bell) and the cash cows that were the local loop networks. Everything changed with the advent of deregulation, the appearance of mobile telephony and the emergence of new and voraciously-minded competitors. Technical innovation has also led to a major reshuffle. With the progress achieved in fiber optics and signal compression algorithms, increased bandwidth has enabled unlimited throughput at a reasonable price.

Competition is now fierce on the long-distance and data communications markets. However, the infamous "last mile", which has to be traveled in order to get data to the end-user, is still a veritable bottleneck situation in technical terms and as regards tariffs. Longstanding carriers have sought to retain control of the end-client by jealously keeping tabs on those last meters of copper wire that keep them apart from the fiber optic communications network, which has been opened up to the competition. In 2001, in the country which is the standard-bearer for deregulation, and five years on from the 1996 Telecommunications Act, 86% of the US's high-speed ADSL connections and 96% of the home telephony market remain in the hands of the so-called Baby Bells, the companies that resulted from the re-organization instigated by President Reagan. In France, the frequent disputes between the regulatory authority and the longstanding carrier – France Telecom – have had little or no effect on FT's unwavering position on the home telephony market. If anything, their position has been strengthened by the collapse of firms operating local loops, despite the technology having been backed by the French regulatory board. This situation has been mirrored in all industrialized countries. The five main historic carriers have maintained strong positions in their national markets: AT&T in the US, France Telecom, Deutsche Telekom and British Telecom in Europe, and NTT in Japan. Competition is limited to emerging markets and mobile telephony.

But of course, the dramatic rise of the mobile phone market has turned the tightly-controlled sector upside down by calling monopolies into question and, most importantly, by radically overhauling uses and pricing practices.

Within just a few years, GSM swept aside the first attempts at developing wireless communication services, such as pagers, which could be used to receive short written messages, and which met with great success in professional circles and among teenagers. Another example was Pointel, which France Telecom commercialized as Bi-Bop in 1991, a unidirectional system enabling calls to be made when within a short distance from a terminal, and which its supporters claimed would replace traditional pay-phones. The tremendous success of mobile telephony in Europe, with the GSM standard, can be credited to the excellent ratio between service value and cost. It is easy to use, devices are cheap, audio quality high, total geographical coverage has rapidly been achieved, and, with ever more special offers and formulae on the market, rates have become as attractive as they have become incomprehensible.

Completely different factors were at play with the arrival of the next generation of mobile telephones: WAP was complex, the services provided were poor, and access was far too slow. The success which had been expected failed to materialize, thus putting the rise of third generation (3G) mobile telephony standards GPRS and UMTS in jeopardy, through a combination of customer skepticism and caution on the part of operators. 3G standards should enable telephone services to benefit from broadband data access. NTT subsidiary DoCoMo, which operates iMode services in Japan, is the only carrier currently earning money from broadband technology. In an innovation-hungry society, the company has prompted customers, particularly teenagers, to use their telephones more often and for longer by exchanging messages, ringtones (!) and now photos. More than 30 million people signed up to DoCoMo over a three-year period, and the company now brings together the lion's share of NTT mobile phone subscribers.

However, the fact that the mobile telephony market is no longer achieving the 45% annual growth rates achieved in 2000 – when 415 million phones were sold around the world – does not mean we should come to bury it. The market slow-down is a direct consequence of the saturated demand for services currently on offer. When customers have been equipped, they no longer need to change devices any more frequently than the usual renewal rate, and, as regards uses, a plateau has been reached as far as asynchronous voice communication is concerned. New uses need to be invented in order to stimulate creditworthy demand.

Victims of the crisis have included telecom service providers, who have in turn brought down their network component and software providers. The decline was as brutal as previous growth-rates had been impressive. US telecom firms increased investment by 25% per annum between 1996 and 2000, injecting some $124bn dollars into the upstream equipment sector. During the first half of 2001, more than 170,000 jobs were cut by the industry, which overnight had found itself lacking in liquid assets. Even a company as powerful as Lucent Technologies found itself on the brink of bankruptcy and was forced to make half of its workforce redundant (45,000 staff). Nortel was also badly hit, laying off 30,000 employees. Meanwhile, 2001 also saw Alcatel announce 25,000 job-cuts and JDS Uniphase Corp. declare losses of $50bn for the financial year! Even the untouchable Cisco Systems had no choice but to slow down operations and rapidly make substantial internal changes.

In France, when the carriers – albeit belatedly – spoke out against the tyrannically imposed amounts to be bid for UMTS licenses, and which had sent accounts spiraling $100bn into the red, the French government did sit up and take notice, subsequently accepting to divide the previously approved amounts by six, meaning a drop from €3.59bn to €619m. Although the damage had been done, the gesture is liable to be re-enacted by other governments in an attempt to get the telecommunications industry out of the corner into which carriers and manufacturers alike have rashly and greedily painted themselves. Not only have licenses been acquired for disconcertingly large amounts of money, but it now transpires that the UMTS standard will take much longer to fine-tune than was initially forecast. Numerous technical difficulties have arisen. The much-vaunted 384 kilobyte per second target – far superior to GSM's 9.6 kilobyte per second rate and which is essential for top range broadband uses – can only be achieved in highly limited situations, and would require a costly increase in the number of transceivers.

Indeed, on a short-term basis, cost control is the sole option that remains open to the industry. It has been forecast that investment programs will remain out of line for several years, and business models founded on "new service"-related income are now seriously in doubt. Production must be reorganized, whatever the cost. Offers must be rationalized, the number of market players must be reduced in order to generate large-scale savings, and international coverage must be broadened. Telecoms manufacturers and carriers will continue to suffer from a lack of liquid assets, inevitably leading to often hastily-arranged mergers and a period of major turbulence for the sector which was triumphant as recently as late 2000. It is obvious that it will take some time before high value-added services bring a second wind to the sector. In all likelihood, the market will not be back on its feet before 2005 and beyond.

5.5. Shifting boundaries and extended companies

From a strictly legal point of view, companies are clearly defined entities, with a business name, assets, directors, structures and brands. When combined, the various elements make up a whole which is specific to each company, comprising brand identity and scope of action. From the very outset, information systems were designed in order to bring operational consistency to the whole, by means of kingly and operational functions. Thus, accounting was the first area in which pre-IT information systems were automated.

Information systems have gradually come to encompass all in-house corporate functions, contributing to the monetary structuring of data flows. Before all else, IT was a means of counting, classifying and sorting, and precious and costly IT energy was given over to managing the enterprise as a closed structure. Systems were aimed at guaranteeing the book-keeping value of corporate assets and operations. However, companies are no longer closed shops. They are links in an increasingly complex value chain. Inter-company relations founded on the exchange of paper documents – now that the documents themselves are drafted using electronic tools and media – have been rendered obsolete by the development of regular customer-supplier relations, the rise of outsourced corporate functions in partnership with specialized firms, and increased co-operation in the field of design and conception. It is estimated that documentation and procedures account for 10% of overall assets. Automated exchanges bring these costs down by half. Hence, the extensive research into the ways in which IT can simplify exchanges, as carried out since the 1990s on an international level by the United Nations[25] and by other sector-based societies, most notably in the automotive and retail industries.

Ever since the 1980s, the notion of "extended company" has developed hand-in-hand with EDI (Electronic Data Interchange), which was the source of considerable progress in the field of inter-company relations. EDI is based on the definition of a standard message structure by standardization boards. These can either be international – as in the case of EDIFACT (Electronic Data Interchange for Administration, Commerce and Transport) – or sector-based, such as Odette for the European automotive industry and Gencod-EAN for retail. These organizations draw up the message structure which is then used by all member companies, as well as norms such as those pertaining to barcodes. Odette's ranks include the 420-member strong GALIA (*Groupement Pour l'Amélioration des Liaisons dans l'Industrie Automobile* – Association for Improved Links within the Automotive Industry), which has published 150 recommendations in the fields of logistics, engineering and e-commerce. In international terms, since 1986 the highest-level norm has been drawn up by the United Nations. They publish the Trade Data Elements Directory (UNTDET) which acts as a basis for all transactional systems.

EDI's sphere of activity is limited to certain sectors (automotive, food distribution and transport industries) because of the relative complexity of the messages and the high cost of equipment and transactions involved. The use of PC network connections has been simplified and generalized by the internet, the latter having thus generated enormous potential for the electronic development of customer-supplier relations, and destabilized the relatively hemmed-in EDI world by offering a more straightforward and cheaper alternative. However, the shortcomings of the internet in terms of reliability and security have led major corporations to come together in order to define and then implement, sector by sector, secure IP services and a privacy-friendly internet that ensures quality services. The automotive industry was thus behind the founding of the ANX network in the US, ENX in Europe and JNX in Japan.

---

[25] "United Nations Working Party on the Simplification and Standardization of External Trade Documents", founded in 1960 before becoming the "Working Party on Facilitation of International Trade Procedures" in 1972: www.unece.org/trade.

5.6. Corporate network players

5.6.1. *The customer is always right!*

In today's modern economy, the immense power of customers is even more influential than that of shareholders. This has arisen because customers now make their own choices in an open economy, and are in charge of making arbitrary decisions on a daily basis as to which types of spending to opt for, and which products to purchase from selected categories. Of course, the sovereignty of customers is not devoid of outside influence from marketing and fashion, but, on the whole, freedom of choice is lethal and unquestionable. The more information is freely available and the more channels for exchange are open, the more consumers will be able to express their choices unreservedly. Today's era is characterized by this new order. The actual contribution of IT to this widening scope of knowledge remains to be measured. Indeed, the hopes pinned on the meteoric rise of consumer-centric e-commerce proved to be in vain. E-commerce accounts for but a marginal percentage of overall worldwide trade volumes. Worse still, US e-commerce figures in 2001 were down 20% on 2000[26], albeit for global reasons directly linked with the economic climate rather than the intrinsic shortfalls of the sector itself. It goes to show just how "normal" e-commerce really is, equally prone to the ups and downs of the economy as other forms of trade.

In France, the Economy and Finance Ministry has set up a Digital Economy task force which regularly publishes its "Innovation Scoreboard". This tool is made up of indicators used to measure the e-commerce market. The task force has recognized how powerless it is to put a figure on transactions between companies, with so little information being available. It has pointed out that virtually all data describes the internet alone, despite EDI accounting for more than 80% of total flows. Despite the difficulties encountered in attempting to measure the market, France is reportedly the third leading online retail market in Europe, with estimated year 2000 sales figures between €380m and €960m, to which can be added approximately €550m worth of purchases made using the Minitel system, which remains actively used, particularly by traditional mail-order companies. The task force has also sought to identify potential flows on the basis of data relative to the behavior of households and the equipment they own. It has thus been established that at the end of 2000, 27% of French households owned a PC and 12% had internet access, and of these between 12 and 23% had made an online purchase. At the end of 2000, with 8.5m internet users, France was catching up on her main European counterparts. However, only 15% of France's industrial companies were placing orders over the internet, compared with between 30 and 60% in the most advanced European countries (the UK, Sweden and the Netherlands).

---

[26] Forrester Research estimates: $8bn in 2001 against $10bn in 2000.

If the gurus were to be believed, sectors such as book publishing, food and the automotive industry were destined to be hardest hit by the tidal wave of e-commerce. Instead they have succeeded in adapting to what ultimately turned out to be a lackluster threat, and, more importantly, have drawn benefit from the new distribution vector. Companies unanimously regard the internet medium as a huge opportunity, but difficult to tame. It takes more than just an online shop to provide convincing services. Businesses must strive to understand the needs of internet users, cater to their habits, and provide attractive, renewed and lively websites that are more than just electronic versions of paper documents, as was the case with the first generation of sites. It soon became clear that it was a mistake to reproduce existing practices, and that instead new processes had to be invented, along with a whole new way of presenting companies and their products. Excellent services backed up by seamless logistics are also vital. Change is a slow process, corporate information systems are not designed to incorporate the end-customer, and working methods have proved to be unsuitable for maintaining direct contact with knowledgeable and demanding customers 24 hours a day.

The recognition of the core role played by customers enabled a new branch of IT products to blossom in the late 1990s: CRM tools (Customer Relationship Management). Once again, the products disappointed. This was predictable: how could CRM tools be imposed on a sales force unfamiliar with formal constraints, unless there had been thorough upstream analysis of customer and product portfolios and the sales practices in place? Without it, failure was inevitable. Research carried out by CIO Magazine has shown that 70% of American CRM projects ultimately broke down. And yet, projects of the like cost on average $10m, much to the delight of consultancies and specialized software editors!

E-commerce was to have sealed the fate of conventional distribution channels. However, on the contrary, the resistance and versatility of traditional circuits has been nothing short of remarkable. The "clicks and mortar" era has cemented the reconciliation between net technology and the robust virtues of "bricks and mortar" trade. The example of food distribution is indicative of changes in the market. Pioneering start-ups have all disappeared, overtaken by the major league retail specialists with long track records in logistics and purchasing. Peopod, the figurehead start-up founded by brothers Andrew and Thomas Parkinson in Chicago in 1989, achieved a turnover of $93m in 2000 before being taken over by the Dutch group Royal Ahold, which already boasted 8,500 stores and a $50bn turnover. In France, online food stores are in the hands of the major retail groups. Ooshop is Carrefour's online supermarket, Houra belongs to Cora and Auchanland, as the name suggests, to Auchan. Galerie Lafayette's Telemarket was up for sale at the time of writing (November 2001), as the online supermarket is inconsistent with the group's targets. However, over 15 years, Telemarket has failed to make money. These companies have all moved in on the internet through loss-making exercises that have generated extremely low levels of turnover. In 2001, French online supermarkets achieved a turnover of around €200m, which represents around 1% of annual food sales achieved in the greater Paris region alone. However, the potential for growth justifies the money invested in warehouse automation, a key factor if the cost of order picking, currently estimated at around €20 per order and involuntarily shouldered by conventional supermarket shoppers, is to be brought down. Such additional costs have directly led to these activities remaining unprofitable.

The example of record and bookstore FNAC has been more promising. FNAC rapidly put the lion's share of its catalogue online whilst maintaining its network of conventional outlets, banking on the complementary nature of the different approaches. While many "100% digital" competitors have thrown in the towel, FNAC has become the leading book and recorded music "e-tailer" in France. The figures remain humble: 870,000 unique visitors and a €13m turnover for the first half of 2001. In the US, the fight between Barnes & Noble's traditional bookstore network and Amazon.com, the flamboyant symbol of the New Economy, resulted in neither the much-expected technical failure of the former nor the all-out triumph of the latter, who, despite comfortable levels of turnover, has yet to generate the sort of profits that will ensure longevity. There is enough room for two types of retail, each providing complementary means of either obtaining information or of purchasing books.

The travel agency sector is another area in which online trade has quite naturally been on the increase. Travel-related transactions account for 30% of online trade, although again the actual statistics remain unspectacular. In 2000, €300m was turned over by online French travel agencies. Major success stories include the national railway corporation's website, sncf.fr. However, the sector is highly competitive, with failures aplenty. The US companies at the forefront of the sector are backed by powerful shareholders. In 1996, Sabre – the worldwide leader in electronic booking systems for airlines and founded in 1960 by American Airlines – started Travelocity, which has gone on to become the market leader with sales of $2.5bn. Microsoft launched Expedia, which achieved a $1.8bn turnover in 2000. Recent developments include Expedia and SNCF collaborating on projects.

In the automotive industry, static product ranges were initially put online by manufacturers, although some now propose an increasingly enhanced range of services. Renault, for one, now enable online customers to specify their desired vehicles down to the last detail, to simulate the cost of their credit and to get in touch with the dealer of their choice. The links between the brand, the dealer and online customers – who have proved to be demanding consumers – still need to be thoroughly reorganized and transformed into firm sales before the internet can come to be regarded as a *bona fide* sales channel. The coming together of "clicks" and "mortar" was ultimately quite a surprise for the market. Contrary to what e-business gurus might have predicted, physical contact with the object is still in most cases essential. Rather than eliminating physical sales infrastructures, web tools enhance the purchasing process. The intrinsically complementary nature of the different channels has developed, with the web providing a means of obtaining information prior to a purchase being made, but physical networks are resorted to in order to, quite literally, have a better "feel" of what is on offer. Obviously, across domains where products are conceived, distributed and consumed in their digital format, the web has virtually entirely taken the place of physical networks, such as in the software field where downloading is by far the fastest method available, provided network throughput is sufficiently high. In the worlds of cinema and music, a true multimedia approach will remain on the agenda for some time yet, with material devices remaining necessary in many situations such as vehicles. But when it comes to flowers and clothes, physical *in situ* choice will continue to offer unparalleled advantages for the foreseeable future.

5.6.2. *Marketplaces*

An extremely appealing concept if ever there was one: to widen competitive scope by facilitating the exchange of information and decision-making in a virtually pure and perfect competitive environment. Digital marketplaces are the modern-day equivalent – on a planetary scale – of Medieval fairs. All parties are present in the same place at the same time, and prompt supply and demand to fluctuate instantaneously and transparently. The objective is not only that of speeding up exchanges, but of offering a complete range of services that facilitate commercial links and openness. Marketplaces are the beating hearts of networks, putting upstream players in touch with their downstream counterparts. As such, the dynamics of what they provide are far stronger than EDI systems. That is why, the expectations of marketplace customers are so much higher, with huge potential savings theoretically at stake for all parties. The total pooling of data and free-flowing physical exchanges should lead to lower stocks, precise knowledge of delivery dates, standards being boosted, logistical processes being optimized and increased reactivity. In an ecosystem such as that surrounding the major car manufacturers, a marketplace should enable thousands of market players to link up with each other, whether systems and integrated systems providers or component suppliers, each acting as both customer and supplier within such a complex set of intersecting relations.

However watertight the idea may seem, and despite the simplicity of the concept, actual deployment is far slower and more complex than might be expected. The tools on offer theoretically encompass a wide range of services, such as online catalogues, bidding and invoicing. However, many obstacles lie in the way. Communications between corporate information systems had already been explored in the 1990s with EDI, analyzed earlier in the book. Originating in industrial circles, developments of the like were relatively slow and costly for businesses, but were very successful, particularly in the automotive and retail sectors. EDI flows are now firmly in place, and businesses are seeking cost-effectiveness across shared vocabularies, interchange norms and contracts, and technical investments. Marketplaces aim far higher, and are by no means limited to simplifying the flow of logistical and material exchanges as successfully achieved by EDI. Instead, a more global approach towards inter-company relations is targeted, with a view to generating substantial savings on services provided and transactions handled. Marketplaces like the automotive industry's Covisint[27] aim to provide a range of products and services that cover not only procurement – with most notably online bidding tools – but the supply chain as a whole along with product quality and development. They aim to cater for the full spectrum of manufacturers and suppliers, not only first level suppliers, who had already been integrated by EDI systems, but also second and third level suppliers. The ideal marketplace is more than just a tool to facilitate purchases and sales, and is in fact a value-added knowledge and information system that enables players from a given profession to share information either collectively or bilaterally.

However, if marketplaces are to live up to their value-creating potential, the companies that look to them must be able to integrate them within in-house operational procedures in a straightforward and effective manner. Major marketplaces, both vertical (like Covisint, and food and beverage marketplace CPGmarket, which brings together Danone, Nestlé, Pernod Ricard and Coca-Cola amongst others) and horizontal (including Answork, co-financed by Banque Nationale de Paris, Crédit Agricole and Société Générale), have come up against many difficulties in their quest to live up to their ambitious promises. The troubles encountered can be cultural or of a technical nature: system continuity and consistency, reliability and availability of the tools being implemented. And it is not easy for a professional purchaser to recognize that 30 minutes spent bidding online can bring about far greater savings than the results hitherto gained from patient canvassing and negotiations.

Hence, the failure of digital marketplaces to hit the expected levels of income or market value, other than during their often chaotic start-up periods, which coincided with the crazy dot-com years. Indeed, costly technological offers had to be built from scratch, the ensuing lucrative and attractive services only being made possible with the aid of partnerships which were as fragile as they were numerous, drawn up with suppliers who were equally unsteady on their feet. There are just short of a thousand marketplaces currently operating in the US. Only 50 will make it as far as

---

[27] Covisint was initially launched by General Motors, Ford and Daimler-Chrysler. Renault, Nissan and PSA Peugeot-Citroën have since joined.

2005, according to Forrester Research, who see substantially reviewed business models as an essential key to a marketplace's survival. The others will either have been taken over or will have simply disappeared from the scene. In France, marketplaces – of which there were around 150 as of December 2001 – will suffer the same fate. Philippe Nieuwbourg, President of the European Marketplace Association (AEPDM, *Association Européenne des Places de Marché*) went on record as saying that marketplaces may revolutionize purchasing policies throughout businesses … but not before 2008-2010. He added that expectations had been running too high as regards the success of marketplaces, which target the invariably conservative world of industry, and whose leaders are unlikely to overhaul processes in order to add a percentage point to company turnover[28]. To add to the confusion, vertical and horizontal marketplaces have sought to justify their ambitious business models by fighting over the same territory. This has made it increasingly difficult to choose which suppliers and customers to work with, and as such no single marketplace has been able to lay claim to bringing together all the players from a given sector. In late 2001, automotive industry marketplace Covisint announced that 4,600 businesses had joined its ranks, but was being challenged by the arrival of marketplaces for car parts manufacturers. One such digital marketplace, Supply On, has targeted a community of 5,000 businesses. Of the 30 European car parts manufacturers who turn over more than €1bn, 18 have already signed up, and four were in advanced discussions at the end of 2001. Supply On's main stakeholders are Bosch (36%), three German parts manufacturers (Continental, INA and ZF, with 18% each) and SAP, the technological partner (with 10%). Siemens is also set to become a Supply On stakeholder.

There is enough room for several marketplaces, given the fact that no single marketplace could possible claim to satisfy a company's every need. Furthermore, e-business solution providers such as CommerceOne (now backed by SAP), I2 and Ariba posted such disappointing results for 2001 that the market doubted their ability to remain independent or indeed their chances of survival. While the concept is undeniably an attractive one, marketplaces take time to take off, many are destined to fail, consolidation is essential, and years will pass before a limited number strike the right balance between the relevance of what they have to offer in technological terms, the quality of the services they provide, and the levels charged.

5.6.3. *Employee-centric*

Let's get back to basics! Information has one single ultimate purpose that of enabling each and every corporate player to become increasingly effective by making the right decisions in the right place at the right time. To be able to do this,

---

[28] As told to *Décision Micro* Magazine, May 2001.

each individual must be given the most efficient and cost effective means of accessing company information and knowledge, regardless of where they are. The real information revolution has involved empowering employees, giving them the ability to act locally by exploiting relevant information and making them instantly accountable for their actions. This new corporate model, based on the autonomy of employees, who have themselves been trained and linked up by an effective information system, enables high levels of reactivity by, in principle, eliminating the need for external validation. A number of sectors and companies have gone down that particular road without prior redevelopment of their information systems, managerial logic taking precedence. However, bringing systems up to standard allows new levels of performance. This has been the case in the loan and mortgage sector, where tools have enabled rapid risk analysis and made it possible to accept or reject applications virtually instantly. Industrial player Renault, for instance, has introduced a customer guarantee management system that provides an immediate and precise overview of how much repairs will cost and what the manufacturer will contribute, enabling staff at local dealers to react appropriately and instantaneously in front of the end-customer.

The management values of networked companies call on practices, norms and behavioral patterns that are a far cry from traditional pyramid-shaped hierarchical models (inspired by military systems and religious orders), which proved to be effective during the early decades of the industrial revolution but showed their limitations as early as the 1960s.

Old World	New World
Hierarchy	Coaching
Certainty	Problem-raising and solving
Authority	Involvement
Orders	Negotiated objectives and advice
Power	Competency
Sanctions	Recognition
Rigidity	Openness
Manual labor	Intellectual labor
Control	Empowerment

The new paradigm of organization and behavior

IT is also a means of strengthening the quality of the relationship between employee and employer … wide-ranging B-to-E (Business to Employee) systems enable staff to have personalized working environments that provide the professional services needed to do what is required of them, along with a number of additional more personal features that create comfortable surroundings conducive to overall efficiency. The "portal" concept has brought the two dimensions together.

Instead of a highly heterogeneous collection of intranet sites, with varying presentations and content, portals are unifying tools which provide a single vision of corporate services, erasing the multiplicity of interfaces from previous generations of IT applications.

Finally, the pooling of information and knowledge within a business enhances the overall level of skills across the workforce, and contributes to the development of a learning culture. The idea of Business Intelligence is at the heart of this transformation, although we are still in the early days of its conscious deployment. It is still a concept, and has yet to become a single product, even though software editors are keen to make it into a lucrative market. The Business Intelligence concept is caught in a whirlpool of complex forces. Companies need to generate powerful corporate cultures which will guarantee their identity, image and identifiable presence *vis-à-vis* their customers. At the same time, the pooling of essential knowledge demands the full involvement of individuals, which is difficult to combine with flexible forms of human resource management, in line with the economic situation. If it is considered that the collective appropriation of knowledge enables a more even distribution of power within a company, it is evident that such "information democracy" will take various forms and work on different levels. Each and every worker will nevertheless be concerned by the irreversible move towards the use of grey matter as the essential primary resource for competitiveness. As regards information systems, corporations will seek returns on investments by building on evolutive structures, thus refusing to accept the expense and constraints brought about by changing systems and instead looking to adapt smoothly and permanently to external environments and internal organizations that are changing. Portals should provide a durable response to demands of this type.

5.7. New opportunities and new competition

Surviving in the digital jungle[29] demands whole new skills. Whilst taking digital tools on board still causes problems, it is even more dangerous to ignore or underestimate them than it is to recognize and deal with them in a professional manner. Lower costs and increased user-friendliness are the engines that drive the acceptance of technical change. In the world of large-scale businesses, introducing new systems is a highly complex – and therefore expensive – process. This does not apply to small companies, not-for-profit associations, local authorities or other miscellaneous groupings of individuals. The most modern, cutting-edge tools are now within the reach of the smallest companies. Economic and technical barriers are weakening, and companies will be able to take new tools on board more quickly,

---

[29] As coined by Jack Shaw in his book *Surviving in the Digital Jungle*, published by eCommerce Strategies, 1999.

thus reaping the rewards in their organizations. The internet has opened up enormous potential for faster deployment of new developments than conventional IT. The internet took four years to reach out to 50 million users, compared with 38 years for radio and 15 years for television. Whilst the internet has not expanded quite at the rate forecast by some wildly optimistic analysts – if anything it has reached a plateau – the medium still offers exceptional levels of performance which must not be wasted. But, to be properly exploited, the internet must be properly mastered, and not be regarded as a miraculous source of instant profit.

Granted, online trading does not require sharp technical skills or costly resources, which has meant that even the most humble organizations can have their own internet showcase displays, and can generate levels of brand awareness that are second-to-none. If the company is so small that in-house investments cannot be justified, a competent, reliable and – above all – durable partner must be found. Many independent consultants, designers and IT engineers, devoid of any specific skills, gained a foothold on the then-rising local web agency market, before struggling to survive as the environment became increasingly professional, given the technical constraints at play. Of course, before rushing into the provision of technological solutions, entrepreneurs tempted by the web adventure must first have the relevant products at their disposal, along with sound knowledge of the market and genuine skills. By no means can the internet correct the genetic shortcomings of a commercial project that has been poorly-conceived. The internet does, however, open doors towards a potentially worldwide market for a host of small and medium-sized enterprises. For SMEs, new solutions – provided they respect professional norms – can be more effective and less expensive than having to maintain longstanding systems and equipment. The very existence of an enormous world market enables software industry players to provide appropriate solutions that encompass a wide range of businesses and sectors. Whatever, it has become clear that a given company's corporate and product information can no longer bypass the web, which has become an unavoidable distribution channel, and looks set to stay with us!

Website	Number of unique visitors (millions)	Length of visit per individual (in minutes)
Yahoo!	105	47
AOL Time Warner	88	31
MSN	86	44
Lycos Network	60	21
Microsoft	56	9

January 2001 (source: Nielsen/Net Ratings)

5.8. The new time/space framework

The history of world economy has been driven by the unceasing conquest of distance and time. Space and time have always been barriers against the interpenetration of cultures and the exchange of goods. The creative imagination of humankind has systematically sought to reduce distance and compress time. This permanent quest made it possible to save precious weeks (with the arrival of sailing ships), before the weeks became days (steamboats) and then hours (jet planes), constantly compacting the time/distance ratio, culminating in today's instant transport of information, sound, image and data. "Anywhere, anytime" has become the motto of a minority of Westerners. Fact: capitalist economy is speeding up. However, it must not be forgotten that more than a billion human beings will never make a phone call as long as they live.

For businesses, the internet economy has been a remarkable factor, calling the years to come into question. Nevertheless, it was soon acknowledged that they could only achieve their full potential if there had been deep prior thought about the key products, markets and processes at stake. The internet by no means operates in mysteriously magical ways, but, like any other major innovation, it implies a complete rethink as to the traditional design of sales and industrial processes, as well as in-house management processes. The major wave of ERP-based re-engineering in the 1990s needs to be kick-started, because few consultants or directors had imagined the sheer scale of the technology-fed revolution that lay ahead. The ensuing mass of mergers and reorganizations was justified by claims of generating value, although this process failed to tap into the mass of skills, autonomy and creativity revealed by the extraordinary ease with which it was now possible to communicate within and between businesses. ERP systems were initially exploited as a vector for the normalization of corporate practices, but they can no longer cater for companies" every performance-related requirement. Today, they are nothing more than a basis in need of being enhanced by complementary business management tools which handle logistics and complex relations with suppliers and customers. What is more, knowledge management is now emerging as a major boardroom priority, with a view to developing a dynamic of perpetual progress that might become a hotbed of creativity, thus giving rise to a competitive edge. "E-business" may have become the electronic facet of a global and systemic vision of corporations, but it is much more than the straightforward setting-up of a showcase site online. It implies exploring completely new business models that call on the full involvement of companies as a whole, and delve deep into their fundamental processes.

Chapter 6

IT Policies in Efficient Enterprises

6.1. Reduce the shortfall between promises and reality

Data-processing techniques, which, as we have already discovered, have been in constant growth since their inception, remain ineffective unless they have been thoroughly and methodically integrated within the organizational, cultural and social make-up of organizations. In order to transform their potential into operational reality, the processes involved encompass a set of often complex but essential steps. These cover aspects ranging from the resolution of technical problems to the management of cultural and sociological changes. Parameters of the like are absolute pre-requisites if projects are to fulfill their theoretical potential, and if work content and processes are to be successfully transformed.

IT and information systems policies are characterized by these actions as a whole.

The techniques used to build corporate information systems have undergone tremendous change since the pioneering days, when everything had to be invented from scratch using whatever could be found. The complex and opaque image of IT can be traced back to the period when machines had to be physically harnessed and computer scientists were at one with their tools. The more machines became sophisticated, the more those direct links faded. Today's IT is an industry that assembles hard- and software components of various origins, all of which have desynchronized life cycles. It is the quality and originality of the assembly of components that makes for consistency in the end-product and confers specific spheres of activity on businesses.

The *raison d'être* of corporate IT departments is to provide their companies with added value that goes beyond that conceivably offered by software editors, consultants and outsourcers. To ensure their durability, IT departments must have thorough knowledge of their companies" business lines, and then inject the types of IT skills necessary to achieve the strategic objectives at stake, in order to tap into the full transformation potential.

At the heart of issues faced by modern businesses lies the selection of informational products and services that they are to deploy in order to manage activities. The solutions market is prone to fads and fashions, and considerably darkened by overly invasive marketing drives. It is by no means possible for companies, regardless of their size, to keep track of the trends and ploys on the market. It is no longer enough simply to come away with the best price deal. One must know how to make astute choices, and therefore be strong enough to say "No" to the tempting promises made late in the financial year.

IT departments therefore have to face up to whole new constraints, far-removed from the technical challenges they had been trained to deal with. The decision-making power of corporate IT departments is on the decline with the increase in working in a networked environment. Exchanges between companies can only be achieved when working on a shared and open basis, which implies the mutual respect of exchange norms and, going even further, common practices. The general consumer market has become a determining factor for manufacturers and software editors, in terms both of their sales policies and of the ergonomic design of the user-application interface. The web has made its mark in the home as well as in the corporate world, generating substantial savings in the acceptance of new solutions and in learning how to use them, but bringing about problems of consistency between home and corporate use which were hitherto unknown by IT engineers.

For industrial reasons, and because of the aforementioned user-friendliness and training issues, machines and software being used in the corporate world are increasingly similar to those being used at home. Products from the internet field have rapidly achieved high levels of distribution. Internet and intranet sites work on the same principles and have the same design. There is little or no difference between effective corporate portals and those run by consumer market internet service providers. In terms of the sheer volume of users, e-mail has definitively won the battle against proprietary mailing systems, because it has become second nature to millions of users around the world. Company workers are now demanding to use the same tools at work as those they use at home, just as customers are now seeking to gain access to their suppliers using the same products as they themselves use.

Such major developments have led to a major wave of software normalization, along with rationalized data structure formats.

Many companies have pointed to Internet security issues as the reason why they have not openly committed themselves to the e-commerce credo. Security problems will, in all likelihood, be resolved by improved encryption and personal identification tools (Secure Electronic Transaction standards). The widespread use of smartcards, which have at last come to be recognized by the IT world in the US (slow to acknowledge this non-US invention), has brought about flexible and personal means of reinforcing security. However, the unending fight between cops and robbers is bound to continue on the web, necessitating increased police and legal powers and improved public security measures.

IT departments need to keep in line with internet solution-based developments of the like by constructing appropriate infrastructures and methodologies. As solutions converge, IT of the future will become simultaneously ubiquitous and invisible, in homes, businesses and society. As components become commonplace, whether hardware, software or accompanying norms, creative energy will be released, leading to product and service diversification across all fields. However, for most of those players who have to face up to the operational malfunctions generated by the shortcomings of IT at large, the brave new world of efficiency, simplicity and openness seems a long way off. To avoid what might often be deemed to be a misleading marketing message, conditions must immediately but patiently be created to render IT credible once again, by resolving issues one by one in a taboo-free manner, thus constructing a coherent and calm vision of the real assets of IT. It is necessary to get back to the roots of a rational and professional approach to IT that delivers, keeps tabs on costs, and manages to achieve ambitions and bring projects to fruition, without being blown in different directions by the winds of false innovation.

This is the ultimate aim of an IT and information systems policy, which should encompass the complete spectrum of situations and solutions.

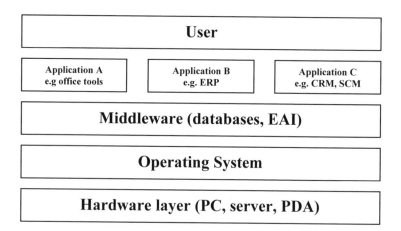

A stable multi-layer model

6.2. Shedding light on IT and information systems

For company directors, the IT world is still obscure and coded. When they do venture into the field, their guards are up because they remember only too well the failure of large-scale IT projects, and because they are privy to the frustrated qualms of their closest staff on a daily basis. And yet, directors dislike being up against problems which they cannot explain, let alone resolve. However now that they are fully aware of the fact that the manner in which they deal with knowledge is a major performance indicator, they can no longer feign disinterest. The attitude of directors in France wavers between two extremes and, in either case, the direct influence of consultants, software editors and high-level service providers is obvious. First, those who claim they do not understand a thing, the less they hear about IT the better and … "it's all too expensive, anyway!". Here, IT is viewed as a costly and cumbersome commodity which needs to be brushed aside, leading to outsourcing agreements. And then those who support the development of e-business as part of a whole re-engineering scheme to break away from the limits of traditional IT. This invariably leads to fantastic projects that are sub-contracted end-to-end to top consultancies. Proof then that, only too often, the attitude of company directors to IT still lacks consistency and stability.

IT engineers themselves can be held largely responsible for the highly uncomfortable position in which they have found themselves. The IT tribes are not renowned for their desire to explain the complex workings of their profession. And yet, it is essential that company directors understand the importance of current upheavals. That is why they no longer need to be talked to about technology, but rather about the company and its business. In 2001, Gartner carried out research into the subjects that kept company directors awake at night. They are, in order of importance, brand strength and growth, stock market values, legal issues, cost management, technological breakthroughs, competencies, strategic planning, the customer's position and information systems have a direct impact on each and every one of these concerns, since each can be linked with an administration tool. Whatever, it is seldom easy to awaken company directors" interests by talking to them about CRM (Customer Relationship Management). It is best to talk market share and customer satisfaction! Similarly, SCM (Supply Chain Management) should be avoided in favor of operating margins and return on capital employed.

To develop understanding of what is at stake and who is accountable for what within companies, the difference between "Information System" and "IT" must imperatively, at long last, be clarified. The former carries a company's knowledge and structure, while the latter represents the hardware, software and technical dimensions. The hard-pressed ambiguity between the two is harmful. It carries the seed of incomprehension and failure. Technical choices are no longer at the heart of strategy. The offer is wide-ranging and, despite its limits, can resolve most problems encountered in the life of a company or organization. It is often tempting to attribute managerial and structural mishaps to technical problems. Poison arrows are often aimed at even more precise targets, meaning that IT at large is no longer the culprit, and instead the buck is passed to SAP, the corporate portal, the network or the e-mail system. If one night, when logging on from a hotel in Johannesburg, the connection is poor, the company's whole remote communications system finds itself in the hot seat! Indeed, without clear pointers, norms or continuity between tools and practices, there can be no gospel truth in the world of data processing. At any given time, there can be right and wrong choices, and right and wrong policies. Further down the line, judgments have been known to be reversed. This unsteady complexity does not mean IT bosses can shun their responsibilities. If anything, it makes it even more difficult to assume them!

The Chief Information Officer's job is to steer the IT vessel through seas strewn with coral reefs … in bad weather. This can only be achieved with a good radar, a map, and a certain *sangfroid*. The quality of the crew is by no means a secondary factor either.

6.3. Information governance

IT is no longer simply the business of IT engineers, but of companies as a whole, and naturally, above all, of their directors. In the words of Paul Strassmann: "Computerization is the conduct of management by other means". This explains why decisions purporting to information processing must be made with the same care and rigor as other formative decisions affecting the company or organization, whatever its type. Decisional process, progress and procedure all make up what has become known as "information governance". Decision-making rules have brought IT out of its technical ghetto and have made it possible for all involved to contribute. This brings us to back to where there is conscious knowledge of what is possible. A CIO's first objective must be to give directors the means to make clear-headed, well-informed decisions. To do so, it is necessary to swim against the tide, and dispel the temptation of directors to hide behind the technical nature of IT, thus avoiding the very company policy decision-making that is their responsibility and passing on the responsibility to technicians alone – albeit without actually giving them any kind of backing – or to external consultants. Bringing middle managers and users into the picture is the CIO's second objective, so that they gain understanding of the decisions which will affect them. It has now become inconceivable that solutions be designed unless decisions affecting the very nature and content of work have been made as the result of close collaboration between the IT experts and those concerned at the end of the day. This however should not be achieved through informal meetings, but emerge from a thorough process of system co-production.

Yet, system development methods have only too often put greatest emphasis on the technical and functional aspects of projects, ignoring their organizational impact and the cultural transformation which is an unavoidable element of new processes. Therefore, even though decisions made throughout the duration of a project often have a major impact on system performance for end-users, the legitimate decision-makers are generally elsewhere. It is necessary to urge those in charge to get heavily involved in project elaboration processes, and to an even greater degree in defining underlying structural principles. Obviously, this level of involvement demands the full agreement of those concerned, within a context that goes way beyond projects alone. The objective of establishing a consistent and durable framework for governance has been met with the setting up of domain-based committees for each major sector within companies, and corporate-level information system committees providing stimulating awareness, training and decision-making programs.

6.4. Making choices

The IT world has been totally intoxicated by the constant focus on change. Software editors and IT manufacturers have been urged on by technological issues to put under-developed products on the market. Businesses must find a way of coping with the technologically sufficient "desired innovation renewal" cycle, ranging from four to seven years according to components, and generally speaking longer than the technology firms" two to three-year "imposed innovation renewal" cycle, in line with the development of their new offerings. Regulating the distribution of innovations across information systems is one of the major issues faced by those in charge of steering information system policies. It is possible to continue operating using relatively old systems, but the pressure exerted by both suppliers and users has a tendency to wear down those barriers put up by IS departments with a view to being free enough to maintain the pace of modernization at the correct rate. The scope of computerization is constantly growing, interface complexity is ever-increasing, and the risk of failure is on the rise. Therefore, in order to control the cost and quality of services provided, it is essential to fight against the perpetual hard sell of providers, which systematically seeks to discredit existing systems in order to knock them off course. All decisions thus involve taking calculated risks. The four following characteristics must therefore be sought when choosing an information system component: interoperability, scalability, reversibility and predictability.

6.4.1. *Interoperability*

Interoperability is the property that enables a given system component to operate in conjunction with others ... without affecting the others and without any need for major re-developments. Interoperability is a more realistic interpretation of what might previously have been termed "systems integration". The best way of attaining this essential goal would be normalization, drawn up on the basis of public norms. This has been successfully achieved in the telecommunications sector with the ITU, enabling all fixed-line communications equipment and protocols to operate together. No equivalent has yet made its mark in the IT world. Instead, the market itself has made its own choices, resulting in *de facto* standards. This is a random and costly process given the unstable nature of software editors. Microsoft's Office suite is the most accomplished example of a *de facto* standard. Obviously, editors automatically present their own solutions as being the most complete, and are constantly looking to widen the functional scope they cover. However, such ambitions are rarely realistic, and when branching out beyond the basic core functions that they have already mastered, attempting to take the full complex workings of a company on board, the solutions provided often prove to be extremely limited. We, and this is especially true of large-scale corporations, are then compelled to oversee the costly business of making incompatible tools function together.

6.4.2. *Scalability*

The notion of scalability applies to both hardware and software. It involves being capable of adapting the size of the solution provided to the changing mass of data being processed and to the increased complexity of transactions being handled. Scalability is a prerequisite if sound investments are to be made. It implies that after the implementation of a system, and with a limited configuration up and running, performance levels can be increased without having to resort to reviewing the initial architecture. In innovative fields, it has become particularly important to make sound investments. This is especially true of systems for e-commerce transactions, where forecast volumes are difficult to establish, and which lead either to over-investment in a project that is subsequently discontinued, or to under-investment to the detriment of the performance levels needed. Black box-type solutions must be avoided at all costs, since it is impossible to identify how scalable they can be. Ultimately, scalability implies initial levels of design quality which have become more and more difficult to attain.

6.4.3. *Reversibility and independence* vis-à-vis *suppliers*

Suppliers – and their products – are by no means eternal. According to the Gartner Group, 50% of those firms operating at the end of 2001 will have folded by the end of 2004. The volatility of the market has become a constant, and innovation brings wave after wave of new solutions which start out with neither the financial clout nor the technical stability needed to reassure those businesses daring to head into such uncharted territory. IT teams are therefore compelled to opt for tried and tested solutions which provide recognized levels of performance rather than new solutions with their aforementioned unproven durability and technical worth, but this practice does not favor shake-ups in the competitive environment. It must be emphasized that such choices have to be made between market newcomers and longstanding players, and even between well-established vendors who have no qualms about halting, without any prior warning, the development of the very products they had been praising just months earlier. A classic example would be the rate at which Microsoft puts new operating systems and office suites on the market, but all software editors and hardware manufacturers are now in the same situation where unstable versions are made available in order to push the market upwards or thwart attempts being made by competitors. The temptation is then to opt for market-led standards, with the risk of abandoning more appropriate responses to the problem at hand.

Minimizing risks associated with a given choice has therefore become one of the key variables in IT decision-making. The life expectancy of a product is dependent on its level – from major infrastructures right down to sharp applications aimed at a handful of users – and varies from around two years (the minimum threshold as far as most situations are concerned) to more than ten when dealing with major investments in infrastructures such as fiber optic networks. Obviously, the ability to reverse a decision depends on the hypothetical economic and technical breakeven points. Experience has shown that the life expectancy of an IT solution is in most cases longer than initially forecast, since the get-out costs are underestimated. The risk is that of extending precariousness over time, since solutions that can be disposed of without causing any collateral damage are few and far between.

6.4.4. *Predictability of performance*

IT investment should not be regarded as some kind of lottery! The stakes are considerable because it is a question of enabling a company to operate, and companies are complex and fragile set-ups whose performance depends on the capacity of each sub-unit to communicate and collaborate in a consistent fashion and in acceptable economic conditions. The first challenge on the agenda is to build and run a system – made up of generally unstable components – in the way envisaged in the original project brief. This can be achieved by mobilizing internal resources as well as vendors" teams, who, in general, have the means of correcting the initial shortfalls of their products by calling on their highly competent development laboratory colleagues. If further system developments follow – such as changing hardware or software components – without involving any interruption to the system or causing operations to suffer, this can be regarded as a major feat. Indeed, the conditions in which companies operate are ever more demanding for IT. The periods during which services are interrupted, even if they have been scheduled, are reluctantly accepted and difficult to plan in busy agendas in which globalization has been the death knell for night-time, Sunday or public holiday shut-downs. It is a little like performing brain surgery on a patient without being able to resort to anesthetic. All of which explains why it has become increasingly difficult to intervene while work is in progress. It is also the reason why IT is not allowed the slightest slip-up, with the slightest deviation from business as usual being regarded as an extremely poor showing. The road is still long, as the sheer complexity of technical and software layers makes performance levels extremely difficult to predict in normal conditions, and, naturally, even less so during the transitional phases during which components are being changed. Furthermore, the older the product being used, the weaker the vendor's interest. On the contrary, it presents an excellent opportunity to urge the customer to switch to the next generation of products. Modern IT must achieve the same degree of legitimacy as industrial systems, providing the ability to forecast, plan and attain pre-defined performance levels.

6.5. Structuring

Corporate information systems have progressed in successive thrusts to the tunes being played by executive boards and business line managers, and above all in line with technical opportunities or constraints. What has always been lacking is a clear global overview, as the laborious attempts to piece together development plans have generally been in vain, either because such complex and under-funded tasks never reach completion or because the context in which the company is operating evolves more rapidly than the development plan! In most companies, functional coverage has risen to a satisfactory level, and the time has come to take an active break rather than racing ahead in unbridled fashion. Fundamental developments in IT for the years to come will see movement away from exhausting, groundbreaking projects worked on in random order, and movement towards policies of continual improvement. In the corporate world, those genuinely interested in projects tend to be those working on conception and design, rather than end users. For users, a large-scale project is a long, dark tunnel that represents constraints, upheavals and a loss of energy and effectiveness. Therefore, if the benefits of information system investments are to be truly reaped, one must limit oneself to the bare essentials. The secret of a project's success lies in the elegance of its solutions, the simplicity of its concepts, the legibility of its applications and the cross-fertilized education of both users and programmers. The essential virtues of an information system policy lie in its consistency, its straightforward nature and its intelligent use of resources. This three-tiered approach is entirely in tune with the actual situation faced by systems in corporations.

In actual fact and in pragmatic terms, from the users" standpoint, IT encompasses three varying types of services, each of which needs to be handled differently.

As built

- Objectives: ensure that the existing systems necessary to the daily running of the company continue to operate by tightening the number of systems and reducing the cost of increased quality operations.
- Means: applications roadmap, technical inventory, evaluation of the actual number of end-users, systems stoppages and functions.

Actions: quality of productivity, synergy, technical simplification.

Better than built

- Objectives: increase the benefits brought about by existing systems through marginal investments offering rapid returns.

Actions: use and usability diagnosis, systems audit, training, delivery of complementary functions, generic tools, re-use, implementation of indicators, data analysis tools, portals.

Other than built

- Objectives: seek competitive breakthroughs by splitting from process and business models, major changes as regards user behavior.

Actions: technological innovation (and risks) selective choice of project teams, managerial commitment, small-scale units.

The first level is that of everyday service. The first cardinal virtue expected of IT is that it should work in just the manner it was designed to work, the *as built* category. It has become difficult to achieve reasonable levels of everyday service, with operating constraints constantly on the increase. Granted, when looking at single units, equipment is on the whole more reliable than before. But technical complexity has led to heightened risks by combining different generations of technical layers. Meanwhile, the merest interruption in e-mail service brings everyone's work to a complete standstill ... thus service reliability is the prime objective of IT departments. Using mainframe techniques, a 99% level of availability had become the common norm, but achieving comparable levels is a far more complex affair when using decentralized servers and internet standard architecture, which are less stringent than proprietary norms. And yet, users have come to expect and need continuous service. References are now made to the "five nines", corresponding to 99.999% levels of availability, which implies architecture that is hardened, superfluous and thus more costly. Rates such as these represent six minutes of stoppage per year 99.99% leaves room for 53 minutes of stoppage. 99.9% brings performance levels down to 426 minutes, a little over 7 hours. Ultimately, the apparently high 99% availability level represents 87 hours of stoppage, equivalent to more than an hour each week.

The second level is that of perpetually improving the operations of existing systems. This *better than built* category can be mistaken for the wider notion of general maintenance which covers both the correction of problems resulting from the "as built" category and major functional and technical improvements which can sometimes result in complete systems overhauls. The objective must remain clear, simple and be shared: to build on the application legacy in order to gain the highest possible levels of efficiency with limited levels of investment. Two methods are used to contain the demand for change: by looking to online training and support technologies on the one hand, and making use of generic tools and in-house norms or standards on the other.

The third level is more innovative. It is aimed at exploring and developing new business processes supported by new information systems, and referred to here as *other than built*. Change is no longer linear or reasonably predictable. Its interest is that of being part of a groundbreaking approach in relation to conventional processes, and, with the aid of technology, of seeking out new areas of performance hitherto inaccessible by any other means. Very few people are involved throughout the project phase. Indeed, with the use of intranet and workflow-styled tools, it has become possible to improve quality without having to spend considerable amounts of money, while obtaining extremely fast returns on investment. Particular attention must nevertheless be paid to the quality of software application development. When things are done too quickly and carelessly, the problems that arise are often of far greater proportion than their beginnings would first suggest.

The base layer of a corporate information system is built around a company-wide core made up of an ERP system and widespread communications and office suite products. The web has now imposed itself as the leading wide-scale mass deployment platform, and has turned the economic order upside down. Offerings have been knocked off course. It has now become necessary to break away from the traditional vertical approach of IT applications in order to define – on the basis of corporate processes – architecture and working methods that take the different components of informational architecture into account: data, information and knowledge.

A data repository is a major factor behind the effectiveness of a corporate information system, and must be constructed if consistency is to be targeted and attained. This is a tall order because, in the past, data had gradually been sorted during the course of projects, without any prior planning. Data must therefore be reorganized in order to render it legible for each system.

Data warehouses are strictly defined: they are collections of integrated, non-volatile, time-connected data, designed to back up decisions made by the management. Data becomes information when it becomes familiar and trustworthy. It no longer belongs to whoever produced it, but to the present company. As such, data in a data warehouse must be coherent, organized, complete and sound, but not necessarily exhaustive. A "datamart" is a data warehouse subset dedicated to a specific activity. In order to begin building such tools, it is necessary to choose a sector suffering from a lack of information but endowed with powerful management. It is also generally wise to begin things on a small scale.

This forms the basis of the market, split between low-level products (readers and search tools), characterized by massive volumes and low margins, and high-level products which are more lucrative for their editors. However, there is every chance the market will revert towards input, infrastructure and component-type products, and vertically integrated products. Business Intelligence suites will appear and be managed at corporate level, as will many open source software products, available on the internet and devoid of any kind of support. However, despite promises made, development in the sector has slowed down, with a number of minor players fighting to survive in the slipstream of the two leaders on the decisional product market – Cognos and Business Objects.

Companies must now have a vision that takes on board both technical and service architecture issues, encompassing the major components on the market in order to achieve durable levels of coherence:

– Definition, measurement and maintenance of the quality of primary information and data present in the data warehouse: dictionary of data, storage and library rules.

– Definition, measurement and maintenance of the data delivery architecture: dealing with mobile and traveling users, complexity management, shared objects, scalability.

– Definition, measurement and maintenance of technical layers: allocating code management rules.

– Definition of a standard architecture that segments levels of access to information, and consequently the very nature of services rendered: types of users (directors, analysts, administrators, specialists, experts, occasional users), frequency of use (constant, daily, monthly), level of training required (occasional user, input/output data user, regular user, constant user, seasoned regular), construction and use of tools providing contextual aid.

– Definition of a methodology for use: drawing up models, collecting data, developing tools for decision-making, sharing and collaboration.

When classifying services, it is a case of concentrating on the logical components of the company's global system in order, on the one hand, to ensure interoperability (rather than coherence, which has become a utopian pipe-dream), and, on the other, to be free from the limits of the products.

6.6. Realization

Information system project realization, whether handled in-house or outsourced – partially or totally – is one of the key responsibilities of the IS department, even if it is no longer regarded as the most essential of its missions. And yet, project realization, or carrying out maintenance work, is and continues to be a random venture that must be handled with care in order to respect the levels of cost and quality and the deadlines agreed with clients. The essential elements of an IS department include a "Project Bureau", totally given over to the realization and professional monitoring of projects. Its mission is that of applying total quality policies to project processes, bringing together those projects of particular significance because of their scale or their economic or technical impact.

Examples of difficulties encountered when managing information system projects have been multiple. Canada's Federal Government was particularly worried by the situation, and, in 1997, published a report outlining the corrective measures they had taken by implementing a reviewed project management model: "Recent research carried out across 8,380 projects in US state institutions and private corporations has shown that 31% of information technology projects were abandoned prior to their completion, and that 53% of those projects that were completed overshot their initial budgets by an average of 189% and included just 42% of the characteristics and features that had been proposed at the outset. Only 9% of projects were finished on time and respected budgetary thresholds. While it is impossible to quantify the cost of opportunities missed due to delayed operations and project cancellations, it is safe to say that billions of dollars are at stake. For instance, the delayed production of the luggage processing software for Denver airport cost the city $1.1 million dollars per day." The Canadian government therefore decided to impose the Enhanced Management Framework (EMF) for Information Management and Information Technology (IM/IT)[30] which is "an integrated management model comprised of principles, best practices, methodologies, tools and templates, designed to improve the capability to manage its IM/IT investments, successfully deliver IM/IT projects, and minimize risks". This type of textbook approach, inspired by the Capability Maturity Model developed by Carnegie Mellon University, must become an integral part of corporate practices, even if it implies high levels of initial investment in skills and methodology which sometimes leaves IT departments disheartened.

Indeed, we must today draw on the benefits of all the experience and disillusionment gained in this field. IT projects remain ambitious, difficult and complex. The responsibilities and powers delegated to all parties involved must be clearly defined and specified. Problems must be resolved in timely fashion so that

---

[30] http://www.cio-dpi.gc.ca/emf-cag/index_e.asp

they do not compromise the success of the project or the realization of the expected benefits. This is the reason why projects are major events in the management of a company, and demand extreme care and monitoring from the highest quarters. Wisdom would dictate that what is best is to do less, but to do it better and more cheaply. Those in charge must be the *élite* IT engineers, working in symbiosis with those overseeing project implementation as and when the systems become administration and management systems, and who can be regarded as veritable change managers.

Until now, IT engineers, and particularly project teams working to tight deadlines, have felt that they are little more than IT masons, with no clear overall vision of what they are working on. Today, they have to become *bona fide* architects, which takes time. It is also necessary to federate – within a department in charge of IT landscaping and functional architecture – the IT architecture skills which will define the overall corporate model and ensure interoperability between information systems. This high-level team then constructs a global vision, and guarantees coherence between the various system components through direct involvement in making important, formative decisions such as drawing up benchmark reference systems and defining projects.

Although still in their early stages, information systems make up a complex geological system. The plate tectonics theory is in evidence: IT is becoming more complex because successive layers are being constantly added, without, for essentially economic reasons, any being removed. Indeed, investments are generally required if an information system is to be refined, and businesses do not want this kind of additional expenditure when it does not generate tangible profits.

The construction of information systems implies the implementation of a host of stringent techniques which are all part of systems engineering. France did well in this field from the early days of major IT developments, with the fine-tuning and large-scale distribution of Merise, a method which met with a great deal of success. Despite IT developments in user companies being called into question, since they are regarded as activities which are not part of the core business, specialized IT development engineers continue to fight for greater professionalization in the field. This back to basics approach for IT engineers has been justified by the failure of so many major projects, despite specialized firms having been entrusted with their implementation, and the back-firing of numerous so-called "new technology projects", such as those involving the web. In 1999, a number of major French companies[31] set up the French Association of Systems Engineering (AFIS: *l'Association Française d'Ingénierie Système*). Its members are companies, public

---

[31] Alcatel, Thalès, PSA Peugeot Citroën, Dassault, EADS, France Telecom, EDF, Giat Industrie, RATP, Alstom, Snecma, Technicatome.

organizations and individuals, and its aim is that of developing a qualitative approach to IT development by looking at many tried and tested concepts which are only too often ignored by businesses and IT service professionals alike. Systems engineering is a key discipline which concerns a set of activities within the development of a system, equipment or a product. The "system" is defined as a set of equipment, software and human resources (organization, procedure and services) and of the environment in which the systems are to be deployed. The promotion of systems engineering, through the presentation and explanation of its principles and its multidisciplinary approach, with a view to the successful realization of complex systems, must incorporate training, use of tools, exchanges between users and professionals, and the recognition of the specific nature of the trade. The development of a system consists of several phases, from its inception (how to define context, relationships between different players and objectives) to architecture, development, integration and ultimately the start of the system's life cycle. Each stage demands methodologies, tools, measurement indicators and monitoring tools in order to ensure the system's consistency, successful integration and durability.

French thinking on the subject is certainly far from isolated, and the development and promotion of principles of the like is handled by other organizations, most notably INCOSE (INternational Council On Systems Engineering). These initiatives deserve to be mentioned in the name of the apparent simplification of IT which is now, more than ever, a demanding and complex multidisciplinary subject that calls on many types of know-how.

The mission of an IT department is to offer end-to-end services that provide a predictable response to criteria for corporate use: availability, reliability and reactivity. However, performance comes at a price.

6.7. Measurements and monitoring

The time has come to resign ourselves to a simple fact: IT is an activity like any other! And within a business, IT should not receive preferential treatment. Instead it must obey the same rules and be subject to the same restrictions as other activities converging towards the company's overall results. Such humility should lead IT engineers to be much more demanding when it comes to respecting rules for profitable investment, which they had flippantly played with for years on end. The economic monitoring of IT activities must become a central function incorporating both the definition of performance metrics that are an intrinsic part of the IT production line and the steering of project profit levels which, like any other form of investment, must achieve the targeted levels. Purchasing processes must integrate management control features as far upstream as possible. The success of the control systems will be the result of their coherence with the general management control systems used by the company. Indeed, as with other everyday corporate activities, IT must respect the same decision-making processes, operate at the same pace and use terms which are as similar as possible, and the same management control and auditing teams. Everything must be done in order to avoid IT becoming culturally isolated from the very company it is meant to serve.

The nature of IT can only be sensed by going back to its underlying principles, which are often ignored, forgotten or misunderstood. Businesses cannot regard IT expenditure as an exogenous set cost that has inevitably to be endured, when in fact it represents monetary compensation for the functionality that has either been delivered (operations up and running) or is planned (projects in progress).

Said functionality is then utilized within corporate operational processes:

– It plays an essential part in the accomplishment of corporate tasks (e.g. wages, pay authorizations, invoices, orders, etc.). In these fields, the impact of IT's effectiveness is instantly measurable.

– It contributes to user effectiveness (as an aid to decision-making, information, training, knowledge of the market and customers, etc.). It is far more difficult to measure return on investment in these areas, where, urged on by fads and vendors, demands are increasingly misled by consumerist behavior.

It must be acknowledged that there is a measurable link between what IT "manufactures" and delivers, and a company's results. It must be accepted that there can be measurably negative short- and mid-term effects on performance if features deteriorate or remain undelivered. On the other hand, IT products cannot exist without work and investment. The delivery of functionality implies the combining of means which are technical (infrastructure) and functional (applications, support), the money thus being spent on equipment and internal or external human resources, both IT and non-IT (training, re-definition of processes, etc.).

IT budgets incorporate different types of costs:
– Day-to-day operational expenses (running and maintenance)
– Investments in infrastructure and new systems (projects)
  – Equipment
  – Software
  – Services provided

Spending on operations is considered to be recurring as and when the activities being supported so require. However, it is necessary periodically to review the full range of applications being run, in order to check that they are all still being used. Investments are either in line with capacity levels (as regards equipment), generated by voluntary changes (new features) or endured through a change in scope. It must also be underlined that projects bring about delays in the triggering of investments, given the fact that production launches often lead to further unplanned investments.

As IT encompasses a heterogeneous range of activities, performance parameters are obviously equally varied. As long as it is a case of maintaining an installed software base on a stable infrastructure, the main aim of the administrators is to develop quality services for the lowest possible cost. Productivity is achieved by systematically renegotiating the individual prices of units at play (processing power, storage capacity, cost of communications), achieved through pitting vendors against each other. It is also necessary to reduce the number of objects administered by systematically implementing a policy of technical and functional simplification. This means crusading among users so that they uninstall applications and features which they do not use. If this delicate pruning task is to lead to tangible results, a reliable inventory of hardware and software applications is needed ... and yet this minimum requirement is often sadly lacking! Obviously, this should be an automated process and is a fundamental area in the management of IT assets, which also demands the monitoring of procurement sources. There should be a strict ban on individual users buying their own printers, scanners and even lightweight applications, bringing them to the workplace, and then claiming on expenses!

In order to achieve targeted results, it is generally necessary for line managers to trigger and monitor new practices and organizational set-ups.

To bring down the estimated cost of a project, project managers have at their disposal a range of tools which they can use according to circumstances and objectives:

1) Having no effect on contractual issues or expected profit levels:
    – pressure on unit prices: the negotiation factor,
    – switching between vendors providing same services: the substitution factor,
    – improved efficiency (e.g. less man-days): the productivity factor.

2) Necessitating the acceptance of lower profit levels:
    – lowering the level of services expected (less features and thus lower potential gains, slower response times, lower degree of user-friendliness, etc.),
    – decreasing the number of users (reduced geographical coverage, less workstations),
    – increasing the risk of not achieving the expected results (too much pressure on vendor, unproven technical choices, etc.).

Mastering project costs is a complex exercise that encompasses a whole host of situations and actions that the project team must be able to handle and manage in an often irrational context. Such periods are often tense and call constantly on the tactfulness, communication skills and pedagogical ability of those involved. The proposed decisions can be as follows:

– Straightforward and spectacular, choosing to halt all projects which fail to generate enough value. Clear decision-making processes must be implemented that draw up precise measurement criteria to assess the success of the project, and that enable those, who are ultimately to draw benefits from the investment (the department due to use the application, or better still the designated operational manager and authorized signatory) to choose whether or not to proceed and to assume the economic – and even social – consequences of the investment.

– Complex, by keeping a tight rein on project teams and functionality delivery in order to avoid the habitual drifts in terms of cost, deadlines and functional coverage. The rehabilitation of strict project steering methods is essential, including Internet technology projects which have too often managed to escape such elementary notions of rigor. It is also vital that decisions made during the course of a project be thoroughly documented and that they integrate the future impact on the operating costs and conditions for use of the resulting system. Experience has shown that operating costs should be mastered as far upstream as possible. Particular attention must be paid to the often overly optimistic decisions made by totally committed project teams. Decisions of the like can prove to be totally impractical in the field once deployment is in progress, can be rejected by end-users, and can result in painful and costly back-pedaling under pressure.

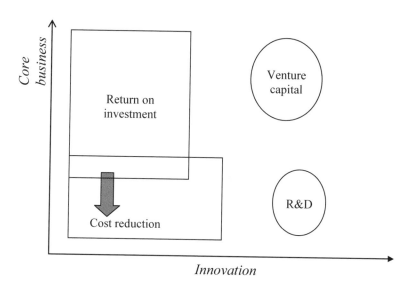

The drivers of cost and value management

The heterogeneous nature of activities within an IT department means that the performance measurement system needs to be adapted to each type of activity and to the associated risks. As far as stable activities are concerned, planned cost cuts and guaranteed service quality must be targeted. As regards core business projects, return on investment must be favored and measured on the basis of clear criteria shared between project contractors and owners. As for innovative activities, if they can be regarded as experiments, research and development-type criteria should be opted for (upper limits on budgets, cost per work unit) without seeking short-term profits. Finally, as far as activities which are new to the core business (and therefore impossible to benchmark) are concerned, projects must be steered using methods and criteria from the world of venture capital.

6.7.1. *Keys to IT operations*

Ensuring the faultless running of IT applications across all sectors of an enterprise is no longer regarded as being worthy of any particular praise. However, the merest failure can provoke storms of indignation, and every interruption of service immediately works its way up to the corridors of power. The everyday life of businesses at large is conditioned by the smooth running of the "IT factory". Critical applications are no longer solely those that handle traditional functions such as orders, production management and wages, but are branching out to the edge of companies and to aspects which are still condescendingly referred to as "office IT". When an internet server breaks down, the company's brand identity, in the eyes of customers, takes a serious knock. Within businesses, whenever the messaging system is momentarily down, the network is partially cut or response time is slower than usual, users immediately become incensed because they are being deprived of the tools they use to work. The price to pay for the success of computerization has been the constant expansion of the sphere of critical applications, often strongly advocated by IT engineers.

And yet, it is no longer the responsibility of IT people to say what is right for users. Quality of service on a daily basis has become imperative, and is a non-negotiable clause in the "contract of confidence" between businesses and IT. Turning in clear rounds is no mean feat when, far from becoming more simple, IT operations have become considerably more complex in recent years. Successive layers have been added to traditional mainframe applications. First client-server applications and then intranet or internet web applications brought their own supply of technical complexity and more or less complete administration tools, within a heterogeneous environment.

6.7.2. *Monitoring maintenance programs and new projects*

IT departments have only too often found themselves lit up by the lone spotlights of projects. Projects remain the flagship activity for many players including, naturally, vendors. Projects symbolize the hope that previous endeavors can be improved upon and that new channels for performance can be discovered. Nevertheless, projects also come with a number of worries in tow. They can be risky, and failures are commonplace, as are dissatisfied reactions. An information system project is indeed a delicate occupation. Sharp and subtle steering techniques are required to oversee quality, cost and deadline issues.

It is, has always been and remains difficult to know exactly how a project is progressing. Teams and management systems alike are used to measuring progress on the basis of resources and their use, which means that the state of advancement of a project is assessed according to the number of man-days consumed compared with the initial budget. The forecast budget is realigned according to the actual levels of consumption and to estimates of what remains to be done in order to reach the objectives outlined in the initial contract. These methods remain extremely rudimentary, and all the more so because in the magic triangle made up of cost, deadlines and quality, arbitration often works to the detriment of quality levels drawn up at the outset, and still considered to be "alterable". Furthermore, in a fixed fee framework, it is the supplier's responsibility to spend money on resources, and this can in no way be an indicator of a project's progress. Other monitoring methodologies – based on cross analysis between deliverables and a "baseline", on the benchmark scorecard method or on residual risk convergence plans – demand major cultural changes within IT teams. As a result, the mastering of progress can deteriorate when switching to a fixed fee system if the former method, based on studying the use of resources, has been stopped without a genuine project production measurement system coming in to replace it.

6.8. To do it oneself or ask someone else to do it?

In all fields, IT continues to carry the weight of its origins. As such, large companies still find it quite natural to have a department given over to information processing, when in fact such tasks are an integral part of business lines themselves, and more and more mature service solutions are available on the market. It could therefore be considered that the information processing function, just like electricity or telephone communications, is now perfectly mastered, and can thus be outsourced without fear. This is far from being the case, even though IT in these early years of the 21st century is far removed from what it was at its inception. The frontier which has been formed by the technical evolution between that which remains specifically "IT" and that which is part of a company's natural operations is constantly shifting, albeit in a mostly latent and unspectacular fashion. Internal IT is gradually migrating towards high-level functions, leaving specialists on the market with the task of solving operational problems. This transformation does not always take the shape of major outsourcing contracts.

The first generation computer languages were close to the machine, with electronic openings ("and" and "or" instructions and memories), before evolving towards basic elementary functions and then application needs. Today, talk is of business objects that enable ever more sophisticated behavior. With these developments, IT engineers have been able to distance themselves from having to intervene physically on their machines. In the 1960s, there was nothing unusual about accessing chains of bytes on a hard drive. Then came sequential access, hierarchically-managed databases and relational databases – which increasingly handled their own optimization – and more intelligent behavior in the footsteps of an object-oriented approach.

On the whole, we have witnessed growth in the ability of tools to express themselves, meaning that we no longer need to worry so much about the bottom layers and can instead concentrate on services that need to be rendered and corporate problems that need to be solved. Thus, with each successive generation of product, attention has been drawn away from instructions to data, from data to objects, and from objects to processes ... without totally abandoning layers which had hitherto been a central concern, and looking instead to off-the-shelf tools or external vendors to handle them. This slow and often painstaking transformation has left its mark on successive generations of IT engineers and has brought profound changes to the way they operate within companies.

6.8.1. *The rise of purchased tools*

Over the course of several decades, the rising performance levels of tools – bred by conceptual innovations that have been rendered operational by technological progress (particularly processing power) – have meant that things that, in the past, had to be handmade can now be acquired ready-to-use from suppliers of tools. The term "tools" is used in its generic sense. Tools are also referred to when talking about increasingly ambitious quality products: languages, data management, information (particularly content) and even knowledge, components that tackle generic or abstract problems, and object components that tackle trade and business issues.

Progress has undeniably been achieved, but has not always been completely mastered, nor has it always garnered the success expected either by vendors (intent on benefiting from the value generated by such lucrative tools) or by managers (intent on not getting caught up in incomprehensible, costly technical issues any more than is strictly necessary). In the IT family, the shortfall between promises and reality has led to frustration because the ongoing desire to rise above technical layers and to be more capable of providing appropriate means of handling business and process issues has been demolished by the irritatingly persistent basic technical constraints.

The myth of total information system integration around an ERP set-up – a strong and simplifying notion in the 1990s – has shown its limits. It is now part of another approach to integration, which recognizes the need consciously to reconfigure processes and reference systems, and is founded on Enterprise Application Integration techniques (portals, workflow and message-driven processing), with a view to incorporating several generations of legacy systems across process and business lines. ERP systems are present alongside other applications – particularly in-house applications – but do not have a dominant position. This approach is characterized by systems architecture principles where surface segmentation (which is visible to users) is no longer identical to underlying IT systems segmentation (which is often focused on data). The two levels are articulated by an intermediary integration layer which creates the transfer matrix between the two divisions. This movement has made life much simpler for users – enabling, most notably, unified web browser-based interfaces – while complicating that of IT engineers. The resulting change of perspective has not called the notion of project-focused organization into question, but throws doubt on the practice of identifying projects one by one according to their associated single-customer or single-functionality applications.

6.8.2. *The transformation of in-house IT*

Numerous questions have been raised by the shift from an in-house IT organization – where for decades on end it was a case of inventing and building specific solutions to make up for the shortfalls of market solutions – towards a policy of purchasing off-the-shelf solutions. It is not simply a case of looking elsewhere to buy things that were previously done more or less well in-house, but of entrusting external partners with major – and perhaps even exclusive – responsibility for the development and running of vital company data. The choice should not be made lightly! These are decisions that will affect the central nervous system of the company at large, and cannot be approached as though one were sub-contracting a cleaning service or appointing a staff canteen manager.

6.8.2.1. *Purchasing logic*

A corporate IT department is a veritable machine, programmed to purchase products and transform them into services rendered. This purchasing ability, responsibilities for which are shared at the purchase marketing and vendor negotiation levels, represents one of the important and highly sensitive functions of the IT department. The responsibility is heavy, because mistakes concerning the types of products purchased, their cost of purchase and total cost of ownership can profoundly damage the quality of the end-services provided. The field covered by purchasing is wide, and incorporates all tools, products and services needed to perform any type of service required in-house. A purchasing policy should feature multiple and often contradictory qualities which swing between thoughts of durability and the need to seize opportunities in an ever-changing market. The latter implies taking advantage of the increased numbers of offerings put on the market by vendors who, lacking in solid experience and ability, have no qualms about selling incomplete concepts rather than reliable products that actually exist. Types of purchases can be categorized thus:

– Development means in the strictest sense of the term (languages, personal- or collective-level software engineering tools).

– Widely distributed software components (such as database management systems) or more specialized components (computer-assisted engineering, CRM, accounting, etc.). Many such components may be large whilst others, such as those with high algorithmic content, may be small. Some may be focused on a company's business line and others independent.

– One or more wide-ranging systems aimed at the partial integration of a whole area of needs (ERP).

– Tools focused on integration issues (from portals to file transfer through integration workflow and message-driven processing), all of which are referred to as "middleware".

– Work and skills intended to implement, realize and transform the specific services which are of use to extended companies.

Once again, several sorts of purchasable services must be distinguished, regardless of contract type and project steering methods (fixed fee or time and materials). It is thus possible to draw up an equally quantitative and qualitative diagnosis of the comparison between internal resources and the ability of the market to respond to identified needs, and of the management means and legal framework to be implemented:

– The purchase of services which are unavailable in-house, but regarded as an integral part of the company's core business. If so, what is being purchased is more than just a result, it is also expertise that is to be transferred to within the company. These are purchases in typical sectors identified as being strategic.

– The purchase of services which focus on specialist areas which are unavailable in-house, and which are not regarded as part of the core business if, for economic reasons, it has been decided not to cater for such skills in-house. These are purchases of specialized external services.

– The purchase of services which focus on specialist areas which are available, but regarded as non-strategic, and which the company wishes to brush aside in order to concentrate on core issues. Specialist areas of the like can be widely available on the market. These are purchases of basic services such as technical assistance, wiring, installation of micro-computers and everyday programming.

– The purchase of services of a global nature, such as work to be performed or a project (or project batch) to be realized. A realization or position is then outsourced, while retaining levels of steering that can vary, but which must of course be pre-defined. This can involve remaining at the level of overall aims and the definition of expected results, or can involve taking on the task of drafting, in-house, a detailed project brief, complete with methodological constraints and quality assurance demands. These can be regarded as end-to-end realizations or services.

6.8.2.2. *The informed decision not to purchase*

The decision to do things in-house rather than to sub-contract or outsource is often met with criticism, primarily from vendors who are disappointed to observe valuable resources slipping through their fingers, and occasionally by top managers who reproach IT for not wanting to give up its allocated territory. The decision not to seek the backing of specialized suppliers must be properly orchestrated and not tacit, and must take corporate strategy and, obviously, economic thinking into account. Wherever the internal/external cursor is positioned, the ability to make and justify clear-sighted decisions must be maintained. Corporations must continue to develop their own expertise in order to retain full control over choices being made, and consequently over expenditure. They should be directly responsible for tasks such as needs analysis, the assessment of the cost to benefit ratio and overall planning (management guidance systems, architecture). Whilst outside help can be of value, full outsourcing should not be envisaged.

On a less macroscopic scale and equally applicable to projects, developments and systems operations, those phases which feature open reflection with a view to determining, refining and regulating the task at hand cannot be part of a contract-based approach. Indeed, this fails to satisfy the primary fundamental prerequisite of a contract-based approach, namely that of being able to express what is desired in clear terms. Pre-project phases are notable examples of items that can only be marginally outsourced, by batches of extremely precise and limited packages.

It is unreasonable to consider that steering duties associated with contracted projects should themselves be sub-contracted. The practice which involves looking to one vendor to steer the work being done by another should be avoided. With projects being sub-contracted both by their owners and their contractors, their very fate – and consequently that of the system destined to become an integral part of a company's set-up – is then in the hands of total strangers!

Some specialized tasks, including development work in the widest sense, take longer to outline than they do to be realized. Another question which can potentially result in a decision whether to sub-contract is more open, and demands a more qualified position: is it necessary to be competent within a given field to be able to sub-contract successfully? The answer is not clear-cut: it is possible to sub-contract in fields in which one is not an expert, and if anything this is a reason to sub-contract. However, sub-contracting agreements are handled more effectively when there is clear understanding of what is at stake ... provided one's position as principal contractor is properly maintained throughout. It is therefore generally recognized that it can nevertheless be useful to maintain adequate levels of skills – and the ability to handle adjustment variables – in a line or field where sub-contracting plays a predominant role.

On the whole, there is a slow but inexorable shift from doing to purchasing, which does not necessarily imply that we are doing less but rather that what we are doing is moving upwards towards what IT people might call "high-level tasks". These often bring new facets – and sometimes whole new areas – to their work. This transformation must occur, and sound judgment must be a part of its implementation, in order to properly manage the aforementioned risks, which are often linked to an over-optimistic understanding of the new practices at play and how well staff and managers alike will handle them.

We are therefore increasingly purchasing skills and services that we performed ourselves in the past. A thumbnail sketch of how the situation breaks down shows a move from 80% tailor-made solutions and 20% off-the-shelf to 80% off-the-shelf and 20% tailor-made. However, an overly naïve vision of what is available on the shelves can lead to rashly giving up the in-house capacity to conceive reference systems, draw up processes and integrate sub-systems, all of which can potentially generate competitive added value. Purchasing rates may be on the increase, but this does not mean that IT engineers should be transformed into purchasers or mediators between project owners and vendors. A more positive and realistic approach is to transfer skills, while taking into account the collective difficulties and individual risks that this implies.

Formalization by contract has a number of advantages, which have been identified here within the context of sub-contracting agreements. These assets should also apply to in-house agreements between those who indicate the way forward and those who put things into practice. In-house contracts can be productive if it means avoiding the pitfalls of formalism or even legalism, which can lead zealous minds to be even more demanding with their in-house suppliers than with external vendors.

6.8.3. *The merciless world of contracts*

An in-house IT system cannot do everything. For decades, there has been no doubt about the merits of IT hardware, but software applications have come up against a wide spectrum of situations which are dependent on a given company's background, the skill levels of its IT teams, their reluctance to call on external suppliers (counter-balanced by the stubborn selling prowess of the latter's sales forces) and ultimately on the desires of the management. Whatever the combination of internal and external forces at play, contracts should be formulated in order to define the conditions governing the implementation of external resources. This is a highly complex domain, and many legal specialists have emerged, working on both sides of the client/vendor divide, and therefore always on the winning side! Specialized books have also been published. I will therefore limit myself to providing pointers as to what might be considered and giving general words of advice.

When sub-contracting work, why opt for a fixed fee agreement? It implies the prior signature of a contract that stipulates the results to be achieved along the three axes of quality, costs and deadlines. Accordingly, substantial room for maneuver is granted as regards the means to be implemented. What advantages can be expected of this set-up?

Formalization by contract is a means of detailing what is expected, thus obliging the two partners to think before acting. This should have a number of virtuous effects:

1) It should prevent poorly-identified operations from being launched, thus also avoiding subsequent risks of failure.

2) Delaying operations can have a positive effective which is immediate, but can, in return, bring about lower rates of reactivity; in most cases, poor management can result in benefits being reversed, and this eventuality goes to show that the conditions are not conducive to formalization by contract.

3) Results can be rendered more predictable and monitoring procedures improved if there is prior knowledge of the technicalities of how work will be given the go-ahead (for fixed-period projects) and how service levels will be assessed (for both fixed-period projects and ongoing time and materials projects).

4) In the case of outsourcing agreements with pluriannual contracts, a clause must cover the possibility of splitting from the other contracting party in the event of major failures. Reversibility must be made possible by preserving the necessary

skills and through meticulous control of performance parameters. Precise monitoring is the essential key to the success of these contracts, which can rapidly turn into an outright catastrophe for clients if the projects are not firmly steered.

Preliminary consultations and negotiations can urge concerned partners to bring out the most productive combination of factors and to produce more innovative and effective ideas than in the framework of a time and materials agreement.

In all cases, including internal agreements, formalization by contract gives suppliers a sense of responsibility as they are judged – and paid, in sub-contracting agreements – on the basis of results achieved, thus obliging them to be more demanding when mobilizing their teams. When formalization by contract is done properly, it implies the compulsory advance clarification of the constraints which must be catered for by the services expected, in terms of methodology (quality assurance plan), integration within the surrounding environment and future maintainability. Such elements may at first sight seem secondary in relation to basic requirements, and yet can prove to be decisive in raising the level of demands in organizational and life cycle terms (in space or time). Whatever, these elements must not be sacrificed through a sense of urgency or by an accommodating attitude towards vendors, often fuelled by overconfidence when faced by a display of professionalism.

Formalization by contract is also a means of avoiding a bout of tunnel vision by demanding the vendor's work be subject to reinforced visibility, whether in terms of progress, methodologies or quality.

Finally, by projecting into the future of partnerships, contracts demand that the difficulties that will inevitably arise be dealt with accordingly. It is thus essential to carefully distinguish between what can be deemed to be a more precise request, and what, in fact, entails the contract being modified. The consequences of a modified trajectory are far less significant than those resulting from altered objectives. Anticipation of the like facilitates more constructive relationships with vendors, whose natural tendency – if such questions are not dealt with at the outset – will always be to make abusive use of additional clauses as an opportunity to dissolve responsibility.

The conversion of a sub-contracting agreement into a fixed fee arrangement can only be achieved if the foundations have been properly laid and if the transfer is accompanied by appropriate measures. It can often lead to a painful overhaul of working methods. IT departments have, for the most part, formalized their development methods, adopting market practices with varying degrees of flexibility. And yet, the codification of development schemes – a long and laborious process – has mainly been applicable to work being carried out within companies, or with ongoing external time and maintenance programs. Even when tools have been amended to pave the way for a fixed fee sub-contracting project or software package developments, some basic facts remain very much in evidence: the responsibilities of the principal contractor and those of the sub-contractor are highly interdependent. As a consequence, either the sub-contractors turn down their clients" methods lock, stock and barrel – including those that professional practice dictates they should respect – or the IT teams fail to fully sense the freedom of movement which invariably goes hand in hand with fixed fee sub-contracting agreements. The latter then throw in additional demands as regards how to proceed in relation to their backgrounds, and are disturbed when the overall attitude of the vendor veers away, and sometimes annoyingly so, from in-house standards judged to be too limiting or even outdated.

This is particularly applicable to developments in the internet world, where *nouveaux* specialists place greater emphasis on speed, trial and error than on methodology. There is, therefore, an essential and urgent need to distinguish between that which can be imposed on a fixed fee sub-contractor and that which can be requested to keep in line with in-house practices. In addition, operating constraints must, without fail, be stipulated in contracts, and those in charge of operations (whether internal or external) can then establish precise norms in relation to the quality of work to be accomplished.

The lay observer may find these precautions to be highly complex, and may feel that they pay excessive attention to detail, but it must be acknowledged that the formalization by contract of IT services is a dense field that perpetually generates conflicts, delays and over-expenditure, and even leads to disputes. Setbacks of the like always have disastrous consequences for the company in question, but can be avoided by developing high levels of precision. As in all fields of activity, a well-drafted contract that is entirely suited to the assignment is a fine safeguard against a lack of rigor from either party. It is in any case very much preferable to conform to market norms and standards, or at the very least to be inspired by them. Many have been developed in Anglo-Saxon countries, such as those initially worked on by the British Government as part of its outsourcing policy[32] (covering the ten areas that contribute to the delivery of IT services) and the work done by the Institute of Electrical and Electronics Engineers (IEEE)[33]. Reports published by France's IT and telecoms user association CIGREF have also pinpointed best practices in this field.

---

[32] ITIL: IT Infrastructure Library (http://www.itil-itsm-world.com).
[33] The IEEE Standards Activities Board (http://www.computer.org/standards).

6.9. Sisyphus and security

Businesses have become so dependent on the smooth running of their information systems that security issues – if not to say safety issues – are as crucial as they are complex. Every time the media reveal news of the latest bug to be working its way across the internet, managers worry about the state of their companies" defense systems. On a more serious note, it was clear on September 11th 2001 how much companies" survival rested on their ability to continue operations despite the destruction of key installations. Cyber-crime is now a fashionable subject because it houses a murky cast of spies and more or less manipulated deviants. Scriptwriters and tabloid editors can but be drawn to its *mélange* of technical skill and corruption, which is so conducive to inspiring storybook-like fantasies. In spite of everything, no-one truly bothers about security on a daily basis other than during periods when emotions are running high. The subject is uninspiring and unrewarding, and hardly enables those involved to shine or to carve out a dazzling career for themselves. It is also devoid of a natural patron, who might be capable of arbitrating decisions and of finding the necessary funds from within companies … and yet, there is no shortage of priorities.

As information is one of the raw materials of competitiveness, it is only natural that it should be coveted … and therefore, defended using appropriate means. This is now one of the major IT policy issues and as such concerns the protection of critical systems, infrastructure and data, alongside elementary security awareness programs for users.

The security of a company's material and non-material heritage must be an absolute priority, and constantly brought back to the top of the agenda since it has a tendency to be forgotten. What should be protected? All corporate data is now digitally stored and can be accessed far more easily than when it was buried away in any number of binders filed in as many different places. A company's legacy of knowledge must be protected, as it represents the said company's most precious and vulnerable asset: its image. In more conventional terms, material assets should also be protected. From whom are we protecting ourselves? The threats are wide-ranging, from harmless mistakes made by clumsy staff to business intelligence specialists working independently or for a potential customer, and who could be located absolutely anywhere. And yet men are far more vulnerable even than systems. The acronym MICES is used by security (and intelligence) experts as a symbol of the palette of means that can be used to obtain the more or less voluntary co-operation of an individual in the quest for information: "M" for money (anyone will give in if enough money is on the table), "I" for ideology (a wide range of possibilities), "C" for compromise (a classic method), "E" for ego (a common Achilles heel among hackers) and "S" for security (threatening the physical security of an individual and their associates or relations). Following this logic, within a given company, the threat for data security can come from any member of staff, and from those employed by external vendors and working within the company (which is of course the case across the IT sector and its multiple partners). This viewpoint can soon lead to paranoia and is difficult to put across, the monitoring of individuals not allowing thorough analysis (for practical reasons and because of the legal framework). Sensitive assets can only be protected as the result of a global policy made up of a series of wide-ranging actions, from the most elementary to the most sophisticated. As a chain is only worth the value of its weakest link, this type of policy must be carefully conceived and relentlessly applied, all the while paying attention to the tiniest detail.

Given the fact that threats are of a multiple nature, a multi-dimensional policy must be conceived and deployed, catering for the physical protection and security of IT equipment and installations, as well as for the protection of data and processes. It is much more than a case of being prepared to face up to complex criminal acts or major accidents (the destruction of installations), since it also involves reacting to daily acts of negligence and to internal risks directly associated with those individuals who have access to critical information. A physical protection policy must be constructed to prevent intrusion within corporate networks and data-processing and storage centers. However, as threats become more diverse and sophisticated, it is increasingly essential to look beyond technical measures alone, and towards raising and maintaining individual awareness of the simultaneously precious and vulnerable nature of information. Through a variety of measures – training programs (particularly for new recruits), the creation of written guidelines for the use of non-material resources, security audits, the personal involvement of managers – behavior can be affected, and improved individual awareness can lead to hardened collective protection.

Chapter 7

New Instructions for CIOs

The quest to change the world of corporations and public institutions so that they can reap the rewards of information technology is a complex activity that now calls on the full commitment of all business lines. That is the reason why there is an ever-bigger question mark hanging over the need to continue running specific "Information System Departments" within company organizations. Indeed, sound collaborative work within a business alone will result in the most being obtained from new information, communications and knowledge technology. The transformation capacity of information tools is such that it must be shared between all operational players within a company. Has the field reached such a degree of maturity that specialists are no longer needed? Is it thus better to continue running a department whose relevance is lost or, on the contrary, to split the remains between business lines and the market? Or might we imagine regenerated information system departments that bring renewed value to corporate IT dynamics?

In the US, it has been suggested that Chief Information Officers" beloved "CIO" abbreviation in fact stands for "Chief of Impossible Operations", or, worse still, "Career Is Over". A true identity crisis is conveyed by the actual situations singularly faced by corporate IT managers, and on a wider scale by their engineers. Recent years have been particularly demanding as we have experienced history gaining pace! Upon completion of the weighty task of preparing the arrival of the year 2000 – in which the forecast disaster was thus transformed into a virtual non-event – CIOs immediately had to adapt to the brutal shock of the New Economy, which caused countless e-business departments to blossom, the latter competing with IT departments rather than complementing them. The ensuing radical disenchantment brought the whole IT industry back down to a harsh economic reality, and saw over-optimistic executive boards reverting to a more lucid analysis of the value for money ratios of "e-business" investment.

With every obstacle to be overcome on this tortuous course, CIOs must analyze and understand the surrounding environment in order to guide their companies in their best interests through the jungle of technology and the excesses of marketing. Indeed, CIOs who deal with quality of service issues and the maintenance of ongoing investment programs cannot build long-term policies simply on the basis of the latest fad.

This controversial theme is subject to fluctuating policies and to whatever managerial methods are in fashion at any given time. Outsourcing has knocked IT engineers off course and has far too quickly become a source of reassurance for executive boards, who are often only too pleased to get rid of some cumbersome subject. Process re-engineering, carried out with the help of a great many consultants, has led to the transversalization of processes and their formalization within ERP systems ... without however changing the practices or the behavior of operational staff. New e-business-focused structures have emerged outside the conventional field of IT. These successive blows to the citadel of in-house IT should not solely be regarded as threats, but also as opportunities. New types of competition, whether from internal or external sources, should provoke IT departments to examine themselves, and aim to merge their undisputed ability to durably manage major corporate information systems with their as yet unproven aptitude for identifying and exploiting new ways of generating value that can be accessed through the use of information tools.

From that point onwards, information system departments will know where they stand and have a notion of their *raison d'être* by providing their businesses with relevant, exclusive services, and doing so better than any other structure could possibly achieve.

7.1. Lessons of the past

Technology is not merely a laboratory issue, but a true aim in itself. It is therefore difficult to forecast technological developments. Even if fundamental trends can be identified, success or failure will depend on the way in which they will combine within the existing social and economic environment.

Pierre Lhermitte has been known to quote a report published by McKinsey in ... 1963! It outlined the factors needed in order to ensure profitable corporate IT management systems:

    — the hierarchical position of the head of IT research;

    — the quality and importance of staff who make up the IT research teams;

– the personal role of the operational managers of each application, and their responsibilities;

– and finally, the impetus coming directly from company managers.

Little has changed since that pioneering period, and McKinsey's words still ring true ... but this should not be a cause for rejoicing! CIOs have to integrate these major trends and manage the contradictions between what is possible and what can be realized within their companies. They are, by their very nature, suspicious of conservatism, since their primary responsibility is that of operating existing systems as cheaply as possible, in order to ensure everyday corporate functions. And yet every time a new product or service is launched, the resulting temporary destabilization can have a harmful effect on service quality. It is always risky to change a single piece of the jigsaw puzzle that software or the technical infrastructure represents. However, if new technology really can improve company performance at a well-managed cost, by providing the desired simplification and robustness and enhancing functional capacity, then it is the CIO's duty to integrate it as quickly as possible. The major problem faced by CIOs is, indeed, that of distinguishing between useful innovations and harmful changes. How does one choose between that which is simply usable and delivered by the market, that which can be used when integrated within a global corporate system, and that which is useful in its own right, in other words which generates value without destabilizing the existing system? How can CIOs be aided in the analyses and choices that they make? By searching through the past and identifying the major questions faced by CIOs, interesting light can be shed on the future. In a world of technology where everything is repeatedly called into question with each step along the road of innovation, it is best to pinpoint constants in order to regulate measurement instruments.

Of the exploitable sources available, two different but complementary documents have been identified. The first was issued by CIGREF and deals with the linguistic analysis of reports published by the association between 1974 and 2001[34]. The IT press sector is the source of the second. Indeed, specialist IT sector publications – and generalist magazines – regularly publish special reviews which assess major technological trends and issues at stake for businesses. It can be fascinating to delve back into the "top ten major issues to be faced by CIOs in the 1990s" as outlined by magazines such as *01 Références* in 1990.

---

[34] Research carried about by CIGREF in collaboration with Anacom, July 2001.

7.1.1. *Key IT issues since 1970, as seen through the eyes of CIGREF reports*

CIGREF, *Le Club Informatique des Grandes Entreprises Françaises*, brings together leading French corporations, each being represented by their IT director. The association was founded in 1970 by a handful of IT directors whose concern it was to stand up to IBM (who at the time had the lion's share of the corporate IT market, without any form of counterweight in the sector). There is no direct equivalent to the organization on a European level in terms of its missions and structure, and it is particularly characterized by the fact it does not incorporate IT suppliers: they can contribute their points of view but are not eligible to join the association. Over 30 years of activities, CIGREF has conducted research into many issues, resulting each year in a number of reports, and a study was recently made into the actual subjects being discussed. This research has been a means of mapping the thinking of IT directors over time, along with their ability to anticipate future trends and circulate the major themes within their corporations. The CIGREF board submits subjects to members of the association who then select which ones to study together. As such, for 30 years subjects tackled have been the mirror image of the issues considered to be the most important in professional and corporate circles by those in charge of IT in major French corporations.

IT Directors are quite naturally concerned by technical developments. Technical focus groups have become an ongoing core element of CIGREF's activities. In the 1970s, the agenda mainly featured technical IT subjects such as teleprocessing, micrography, databases, application portability, workstation development and operation. 1978 saw the appearance of the notion of "information system", in a workgroup entitled "Information System Opportunities and Monitoring". Towards the end of the 1970s, organizational themes were developed, given the economic environment in which several state and private organizations had been set up to take the new dimension of IT into account, and in which telecoms issues were emerging with, in France, the powerful *Direction Générale des Télécommunications* (National Department of Telecommunications). In the 1980s, the information system became the focal point of thinking, around which thematic research developed. Communications emerged around 1981-1982 as a key issue across subjects encompassing network and data communications, messaging systems, PABX, videotex and micro-computing. Cutting-edge subjects then appeared: Ethernet, smartcards and compact optical disks. It was also around that time that autonomous thinking into industrial information systems began: visualization tools for computer-aided design.

In 1984, the key subject of the contribution of IT as a factor of productivity within a company's production cycles was raised by a unit comprising "groups of leaders", and was very much indicative of the way in which the function of this purely technical world had evolved towards lateral thinking about the responsibility of IT across corporations at large. The reorientation was further consolidated by the themes touched upon in the later years of that decade. The "Developments in the IT Function" unit brought together a number of themes centered on the responsibility of in-house IT engineers in the elaboration of consistency across corporate information systems. The notion of cost was also omnipresent, as part of the need to understand and justify escalating IT budgets. The notion of "technology watch" also took on a permanent dimension.

The themes studied throughout the 1990s were evidence of the split in the IT sphere. An ever-increasing number of ever-enhanced subjects (the number of workgroups doubled over a five-year period) continually branched out, as they represented the permanent concerns of a profession that was faced more than any other with the accumulation of technological innovations, within a corporate environment which was still marked by the sluggishness of previous systems. Technical issues are still the cornerstone of CIGREF methods of thinking. Software engineering, methodology and systems quality took root as basic themes in the early 1990s, alongside well-established subjects like the information economy and telecommunications (and the difficult relationship with the state-owned carrier in France), the latter absorbing a large amount of research resources. Links with suppliers became a recurring theme from 1992 onwards, particularly with Syntec, the trade union for IT service providers in France. CIGREF even met Bill Gates officially.

The second half of the 1990s was marked by the appearance of focus groups concentrating on ongoing subjects such as the Y2K issue, electronic data interchange, the single European currency and the 10-digit telephone dialling system. The internet made a dramatic entrance in 1993, with a procession of associated topics such as e-commerce. In 1993, CIGREF launched Cigroup, its own collaborative work tool, and created the CIGREF website. The internet had not, until then, been a major concern for CIOs but CIGREF went on to plough enormous resources into the subject, making new information and communications technology the key subject between 1995 and 2000. It was approached from a number of different angles: communication with decision-makers, user-training, internet systems, broadband links, workflow, etc. CIOs want every means at their disposal to provide users with the best possible solutions by convincing them of the benefits of new technology. Indeed, one of the main issues dealt with by the press and *vis-à-vis* decision-makers was that of France trailing behind other countries. CIGREF was thus much in demand as it was one of the places where the subject was being dealt with in a serious manner. The ERP phenomenon had not hitherto been fully analyzed, but was the subject of a workgroup which collated testimonials of experience gained in that field.

According to the authors of the semantic study of CIGREF publications, "in the CIO/company partnership, reports over the years have shown CIOs to be the engine behind the anticipation of change – but their words are either misunderstood or not believed – while the companies are the brakes, the latter's awareness of the impact of new information and telecommunications technology out of step, and even lagging behind where it should be". CIGREF may have pulled out all the stops in order to facilitate the arrival of the year 2000 and the switch-over to the euro, moving out beyond its natural frontiers, but at no stage did the association cease to "promote the use of information systems as a means of generating value for companies". This study has largely contributed to dispelling the common assumption that CIOs are "conservative", a belief that has been very much promoted by some vendors who believe CIOs thwart the rapid adoption of new technology. As CIGREF has evolved, it has been clear that CIOs are conscious of – and keep a close eye on – technological innovation, but are constantly focused on getting the most for their companies by not yielding to passing fads.

7.1.2. With the benefit of hindsight: the major stakes of the 1990s

The strength of the periodic reviews published by the press is to assess fashionable, thought-provoking topics at any given time. The IT press enjoys this exercise, and going back over old issues can be captivating. Of the many similar examples, the April 1990 issue of *01 Références*, published by *01 Informatique*, provides a particularly full overview of something which was considered at the time to be a vital factor behind corporate IT policies. It was focused on technology watch and the role of the head of information and communication systems, regarded as "one of the only individuals to be capable of sorting through information and of anticipating future trends, thus making the moves necessary to their company's survival".[35] Has anything changed?

First of all, uncertainty regarding the cost of IT systems was put forward as a fragile factor when estimating how profitable investments would turn out to be. The thinking behind how the price of equipment was set by suppliers was shown to be extremely blurred, and as regards software, underestimating the necessary configurations was the norm. To switch from the purchasing cost to the total cost of a system, "The Rule of Pi" could be applied. In other words, the initial forecast cost needed to be multiplied by 3.14159. In fact, it might just as well have been multiplied by Pi squared, that is to say by a factor of 10. In truth, it was clear that nobody really knew, and the author came to conclude that choices were drawn up on the basis of three factors: entry costs and whether these could be broken down into

---

35 *01 Références*, April 1990, "Profession: Technological Watchman", excerpt from Frédéric Barillet's editorial.

modules or reversed, the time it would take to implement the project and, above all, the intentions of those behind it. Such blurred outlines were accepted with some aplomb and showed that the very nature of new technology – and this is a definite constant – was considered to be random. So … we do not know how much it will cost and have even less idea what it will yield, but there's no choice: it's full steam ahead anyway!

The second key issue was standardization. Optimism was commonplace: "on a long-term basis, normalization will allow a full, free competitive environment because equipment will be interchangeable". The OSI (Open System Interconnection) standard was to take root. With the faith of someone who obviously admired IBM, the author demonstrated how the micro-computer operating system OS/2, released in 1987, had "thus become a *de facto* norm within a three-year period" and, similarly, how the IBM-developed program-to-program solution LU 6.2 was about to be granted an ISO norm. As regards operating systems, it was stated that "the winning combination" for the subsequent years would be made up of MS-Dos, OS/2, UNIX and Apple Finder, although not necessarily in that order. Today, OS/2 is the lone survivor, but even this has been convincingly defeated by Microsoft's different systems, of which there have already been five, despite the erstwhile strength of IBM, ISO norms and LU 6.2, whilst Apple has been ousted from the large business market. Without public normalization procedures or even strong agreements within a sector which remains very much hostile to the notion, arbitration is the result of the ups and downs of the market itself. Granted, ten years down the line, the situation is a little clearer in some domains, but application interoperability is still not a simple exercise.

Data location is one of the key IT architecture issues. In 1990, centralized data storage was unanimously condemned. It was claimed that during the decade, the CIOs" crusade to reclaim the data which individual users stored *en masse* on their PCs would be in vain. Referring to one of the many analysts who constantly shape our future, it was said that 50% of top-level data would be stored on personal computers. A top consultant even decisively declared that "centralized processes or data are no longer viable for any application". At the time, it was indeed difficult to stand up to the client-server euphoria or to the wave of anti-mainframe feeling. Where were the internet server resources? Where were the centralized corporate storage facilities such as those of Microsoft, whose worldwide data is managed from Redmond?

Other "major" topics touched upon by the document also reflect the same blind faith in the idols of the era, projecting the influence of short-term trends into the long-term future. Thus, miracles were expected from hypertext, storage on rewriteable optical disks and multimedia with CD-I[36] (Compact Disk Interactive) based computer-assisted training. Automatic translation issues were well-identified. Going beyond technical areas, the special issue had an in-depth look at organizational factors, with reference to the OECD's 1989 report on "New Technology: a Socio-Economic Strategy for the 1990s". The report concluded by saying that the Taylorized model of production organization had to be abandoned in favor of a decentralized structure that favors the exchange of information. Admittedly, the idea is appealing, and the authors considered how to go about bringing new communications tools into play, whether electronic multi-user messaging systems, groupware or computer-assisted tele-conferencing facilities. This approach nevertheless remained very much centered on the IT nature of such tools, coupled with the acknowledgement that failures corresponded to situations in which users did not have the option of going against the uses that the IT department may initially have planned. The "technical system" brought about by IT – still suffused with the aura of major systems – was seen as limiting. The all-comers" award for anticipation goes to one Michel Crozier, who explained that work needed to be done on companies" human systems, because "the stumbling block of this type of communication, which transits through electronic media, is that of solely sending "numbered data"… it is because they relied solely on technical instruments that the Americans have been overtaken by the Japanese". What foresight!

The telecommunications revolution was present, albeit from the somewhat limited prospect of the elimination of paper exchanges between businesses. Electronic Data Interchange (EDI) was to make life simpler for companies, lower the costs of intermediation and improve transaction efficiency. The EEC had forecast that by 1995, 180,000 European companies would have opted to switch to EDI systems. At the time, the future of telecommunications rested on the generalization of RNIS, videotex, teletex and the Atlas 400 universal messaging system, the management of which would be handled by a new breed of specialist – yet to be regarded as a key IT position – the systems administrator. Today, little remains of these promising technical objects, engulfed as they have been by the TCP-IP tidal wave.

Number nine in the list of priorities was information system flexibility, regarded as a major asset for businesses faced with the ups and downs of the market. In decompartmentalised, systemic businesses, key performance factors can include bringing the design period for a new car down to two years, including just-in-time production line provisioning and the synchronization of corporate functions. These fields have gradually become part of an information system's duties, but the outstanding concern of increased complexity could lend credibility to the "small is beautiful" philosophy. On the whole, these ideas are well-observed, because the

---

[36] A system launched by Philips and which met with little success.

problems mentioned are of a permanent nature and have not aged as prematurely as technical visions. It was thus written that "the IT director will go on to become IS manager, will outline the dictionary of data and be the guardian of a vocabulary shared by all departments". This has yet to be achieved, even though the increasing complexity of information systems means that it is ever more important that all company players understand their corporate data.

Nothing in these texts predicted the incredible upheaval that was about to take place on the other side of the Atlantic. Trips to the US were on the wane! What was sadly lacking from the study was nothing other than the internet, the simplicity of which has taken hold of competing technology by creating a vast area for exchange around shared norms! The authors of the study are not to blame, and neither are the CIOs and experts who contributed, because they were working on the basis of the data that was available, and which had been widely manipulated by suppliers. We are still the victims of creative predictions that open up new markets! Therefore, even though it is best to remain humble when carrying out prospective analysis, urging progress in thinking about the prospective and strategic vision of information technology is essential. These considerations should now be founded on more objective bases and more thorough methodologies. Nevertheless, the distinctive feature of this industry is that everyone moves forward blindfold, towards a future that can only be bright. Weaker signals are not granted the curiosity and vigilance they deserve, because the technical world remains a closed shop, overdetermined by suppliers, which does not integrate a user-side approach. This form of instability could be acceptable in a world that is indeed changing, but it goes hand-in-hand with peremptory judgments – if not threats – when one fails to dedicatedly follow fashion. And yet, the technological revolution cannot be triggered by products available on the market, but by the ability of users to make such technical "proposals" part of their everyday practices. History has shown that the adoption of such infamous new technology must be delayed in order to keep tabs on costs and – in a manner more reminiscent of a marathon runner than a sprinter – to reap the benefits expected through the patient and resolute collection of profits, achieved with the active co-operation of users.

7.2. The CIO's missions

In a joint study carried out in 1999 by the Egon Zehnder practice and the London Business School, it was shown that the primary role of the CIO is much more that of being the individual who personifies his/her company's technological policy than being merely a functional leader in charge of managing skills and financial resources. On a parallel level, the CIO must also have the means of improving the integration of the company's complexity, to be able to distribute the benefits of information technology, in a manner which is the most in tune with actual needs, to the heart of key corporate processes. The rise of this "change activator" notion is a recent phenomenon. Dual technical and business expertise has proved to be essential. It is also highly demanding.

7.2.1. *The CIO-teacher*

IS departments are at the heart of their companies, and thus are one of the key vectors of the tough missions at hand. To instill changes, CIOs must learn to synthesize with a view to becoming "bilingual" masters of the language of technology and the language of business and the corporate world, speaking each with ease. However, behind the knowledge communicator and mediator, CIOs must remain action people and bosses, managing the complex nature of systems handed down from the successive waves of technical innovation and managerial modes, who will be judged on their ability to keep the wheels turning whatever the circumstances.

The IT professional is faced with ever more complex tasks, as successive layers of technology pile up on top of each other. In large corporations, systems which have been normalized and are consistent from a technological point of view have now been ruled out. This fact has a tendency to be underestimated – and even denied – by the apparent ease that is propagated by the dominant messages about technology. With the democratization of information, the multiplication of informed opinions of all kinds and the regular coverage given by the general-interest media (even on the showbiz gossip pages!), IT has lost a great deal of its mystery. However, it seems that the pendulum may just have swung too far, because the genuine complexity of the subject is not only being softened, it is being ignored. The debate has shifted. Benefits seem so wonderful that everything has to be obtained before the week is out, and without having to dip into one's pocket! This level of impatience was particularly the norm throughout the dazzling rise of e-business. CIOs must therefore constantly bring marketing-fuelled dreams back to reality, without coming across as grumpy technologists.

Four scenarios for the 21st century CIO

Definition of the scenario	Preference	Probability
The CIO is a senior executive director of a "hybrid" nature, centered on business strategy and the delivery of information technology.	41%	32%
Two functions: a CIO centered on strategy and change and information systems, and a CTO in charge of technology, infrastructures and operations.	29%	35%
The CIO is a functional director, with a career entirely spent working in IT, centered on technical skills, the ability to deliver robust infrastructure and reliable operations.	15%	18%
The CIO is a generalist manager with strong business skills, is open to change and developments, and is backed by outside partnerships and in-house IT skills.	15%	15%

Source: "The New CIO", written by Earl and Vivian (Egon Zehnder, London Business School, 1999).

The consulting and management research worlds have only recently begun showing interest in the role of CIOs. Research – such as quoted above – is now pinpointing the composite role that this atypical corporate actor performs, combining knowledge of what goes on outside the company with full involvement in in-house transformations. As the position has evolved over the past 30 years, the CIO has gradually moved beyond a strictly technical framework, branching out into corporate issues in line with business area transformation and process development. Today's big issue is to consider what managerial profile is best for a CIO. Is it still necessary to choose a CIO from among one's IT peers, a graduate of the technical school but also open to business issues, or is it advisable to recruit a CIO from the ranks of business line managers, choosing someone who is also capable of understanding IT questions and, above all, of directing IT activities? If CIOs are indeed the company technologists, they are also regarded as the entry point for the erring ways and problems of the technological world, and of what many consider to be disproportionately high cost levels associated with such disputed – but indispensable – IT systems. CIOs have sometimes even been regarded as the accomplices of software editors and service providers, since they are in extremely close contact on such a regular basis that autonomous objectivity can disappear. It just goes to show the degree to which it is essential for CIOs to share such necessities and constraints of the like with colleagues from the purchasing departments.

7.2.2. The CIO-leader

It is difficult to strike the right balance between keeping one's distance from the technological world and playing an integral part in it. CIOs should symbolize change at the focal point of a range of business areas which are in constant development. Their mission is not only that of enabling business lines under their responsibility to evolve, but also of steering the development of IT end-user skills, across all corporate strata! But CIOs cannot themselves define their own missions. Within the complex make-up of corporate management, the effective roles of CIOs depend as much on their own abilities as on the room for maneuver granted by their executive boards. That is the reason why management experts – and… executive search consultants – are carrying out an increasing amount of research into CEO-CIO relations.

In a study carried out by Oxford University lecturer David Feeny and London Business School Michael Earl (published by Gartner in 2000[37]), an attempt was made to categorize CEOs regarding their attitudes *vis-à-vis* information systems and their relationship with their CIOs. Seven such categories were identified.

Metaphor	Characteristics
Hypocrite	Espouses strategic importance of IT. Negates through personal actions.
Waverer	Reluctantly accepts strategic importance of IT. Not ready to get involved.
Atheist	Convinced IT is of little value. Publicly "comes out" with this belief.
Zealot	Convinced IT is strategically important. Believes he/she is an authority on IT, too.
Agnostic	Concedes IT may be strategically important. Has to be convinced over and over.
Monarch	Accepts IT is strategically important. Appoints best possible CIO to handle IT.
Believer	Believes IT is an enabler of strategic advantage. Demonstrates belief by his/her own behavior.

Earl & Feeny, 2000

The rise of information system-led process management represents a major opportunity to bring changes across the often vertical nature of corporate culture. It means giving birth to Process Information Officers, capable of constructing transverse systems, and to Knowledge Officers, in charge of making the scattered –

---

[37] *How to be a CEO for the Information Age*, Earl & Feeny, 2000.

and even concealed – knowledge legacy of their companies more explicit and therefore usable throughout all levels of their organizations.

7.2.3. *The CIO-manager*

A CIO's vocation is that of being the corporate player who is the most subject to mutation, and the most apt to seize technological opportunities that will contribute to the profound transformation of processes, organizations and practices. CIOs must remain in the frontlines of innovation, which is the reason why they are natural contributors to the well-mastered construction of the New Economy, knowing how to capitalize on the opportunities offered by the web in the right manner by coupling them with existing technology.

How to be (and remain) a good CIO:

1. Constantly maintain and deepen your qualities as an open, generalist and eclectic manager.
2. Learn to communicate in a precise and convincing manner with all corporate levels.
3. Channel the qualities of IT engineers so that they focus on company efficiency.
4. Keep a constant eye on your company's business needs and its profitability, and remain permanently involved in structural decisions.
5. Do not get so locked in by technical issues that the top management fail to understand you and forget about you.
6. Build an intensive relational network with all key corporate players.
7. Handle your relationship with vendors without being complacent or condescending.

CIOs are faced with the persistent difficulty of having to enhance IT investments. Executive boards feel that IT should be free and service quality is a due! This results in the perverse process of the collectivization of those corporate IT benefits which have directly contributed to improved performance and productivity over the past 20 years, and to the individualization of costs within the IT budget, with fingers pointed at this most spendthrift of sectors! This is the reason why the construction of an information economy on the basis of shared concepts is absolutely vital if we are to get out of the vicious circle in which IT is currently caught, and where it will continue to be denied its status as a vector of progress. CIOs, regardless of their origins, must know how to communicate about the nature and value of what they are creating. The mastery of performance parameters has become an unavoidable dimension of a CIO's skills.

Finally, CIOs pass on knowledge from the technology market to the corporate world. They must see beyond the fads being promoted by vendors' superficial marketing campaigns and hyped by the press, and detect the major trends that will contribute to laying the foundations of change and its timely delivery. CIOs must remain vigilant in their quest for operational excellence and clear-headed in their choice of effective technology, ultimately making them the demanding promoters of quality market products, since they are the guarantors of the end-product *vis-à-vis* the end-users. Their co-operative collaboration with software editors, industry players and service providers must be a reflection of this demand for quality, and be characterized by persistency but not by arrogance.

Chapter 8

New Vision(s)?

8.1. Gurus and a New Economy in a perfect world

In a famous article published in 1966, Fano and Corbato[38] gave a clear-headed description of the future relationship between IT and society. They forecast that computers would play an ever-greater role in human affairs. They believed that communities would conceive systems that would be capable of ensuring various functions – whether intellectual, economic or social – and that these systems would, in turn, have a profound impact on all components of human life. Systems and their associated communities would become so entwined that communities would, themselves, actually become part of the systems, and when combined, IT systems and users would create new services, new institutions, a new environment and new problems. But questions were raised as to what would be the aims of such systems, and what safeguards would have to be set up in order to avoid any kind of deviant activity. They concluded by saying that progress in the field of new technology would raise countless social and technical questions. This vision will sound familiar to those experts who make plans based on the virtues of systems and objects and put them forward, neglecting – through the search for utopia, by forgetting previous waves of innovation, or through sheer blindness – to consider that innovations can also spur on insanity.

---

[38] Fernando Corbato went on to receive the Turing Award in 1991; his son, Steve, is Infrastructure Director on the Internet2 project (see section 8.2.1).

8.1.1. *Shattered dreams?*

Three decades down the line, the questions raised by Fano and Corbato are still relevant. Some philosophers have brandished the threat of the de-realization of the world, a "no-world" in which there are "no time limits, no stocks, no memory, no identity, no institutions, no policies and no reality"[39]. The internet is at the heart of this anxiety, because, in theory, it can achieve what no other type of technology has been able to do: globalization with the disappearance of spatiotemporal frontiers. In 1998, the architect, town planner and philosopher Paul Virilio cut loose in a dark, powerful lampoon against the digital world entitled "The IT Bomb". He claimed it was impossible to clearly distinguish the economic IT war, since it is "part of a single hegemonic ambition to render commercial and military exchanges interactive". Granted, science and technology often have hot flushes and raise their own metaphysical problems: where are we headed? The confusion of scholars is classic. They regularly play at scaring themselves when considering the scale of the collateral damage the tools they have perfected can generate. Philosophers meanwhile are the anxiety-provoking amplifiers of these messages. But nothing can stop the march of science. The unconscious thinking behind technical progress is to aim for a certain type of individual, someone who is consistent, collected, very much a part of a predictable world and comfortably driven by intelligently channeled instincts. However, men still have uncontrollable urges which will escape all the Dr Frankensteins of this world.

Internet gurus, for whom the US magazine Wired has become the *de facto* mouthpiece, have forecast a hundred years of growth and happiness, the web being the philosopher's stone that turns information into gold with no unemployment or inflation and an overriding zen-like state of consciousness. Networks beget distance, sublimating intimacy and rendering it both totally present and totally inaccessible: neat! Cyber-work, cyber-communion, cyber-pleasure... this pure and perfect world is also a pure and perfect market in which only the best survive. Author Pierre Lévy spoke for all enthusiastic internet users when he wrote that "I am very much convinced that the best possible use of digital technology is that of enabling humans to combine their imagination and their intelligence in the name of individual development and emancipation. The collective intelligence project is, by and large, that of the first designers and advocates of cyber-space. In a way, the project is an extension of the Enlightenment philosophy, taking it into new realms" [40]. So the internet is both the Age of Enlightenment and Adam Smith's pure and perfect market. What a mightily heavy dual legacy!

---

[39] Alain Finkielkraut, Paul Soriano *Internet, l'inquiétante extase* (The Worrying Ecstasy of the Internet), Editions de Minuit, 2001.

[40] Pierre Lévy *La Cyberculture*.

And then IT entered the 21st century. The Nasdaq index woke up hung over from the exhilaration of the night before. Job losses (re-)appeared in Silicon Valley. PC sales slowed down, and more and more second-hand Porsches appeared on the market in California. In fall 2001, French newspaper *Le Monde* even ceased publishing its spin-off magazine *Le Monde Interactif*! Were we to believe that the New Economy had come to a premature demise, as announced by smug told-you-so commentators who at the dawn of the year 2000 had been so full of praise for the very same sector? Or were we to acknowledge, with the air of popular wisdom revisited by the digital era, that the limit was somewhat lower than the sky and that the extraordinary growth of the IT industry would inevitably hit a glass ceiling?

Although the jolts on the Nasdaq – which in the 12 months from April 2000 to March 2001 wiped $3,000bn off the slate – were a timely reminder of the fragility of an economy founded on anticipatory calculations of potential profits, it is however also inappropriate to view this brutal realignment as the death knell of the New Economy. This first generation of pioneers may have laid the foundations of a whole new approach which could be consolidated through the subsequent ability of entrepreneurs, the market and, perhaps, politicians to learn from the lessons of the short period of euphoria, and then to apply what they have learnt to long-term prospects. IT entrepreneurs will have to forget the promises of get-rich-quick schemes which were implemented regardless of basic economic laws and which neglected products, clients and the future. Instead they will have to put credible innovations on the market, in accordance with the expectations of users, so that the latter's performance levels can indeed be raised.

8.1.2. *What remains of the dot-com years?*

Of the three engines that powered the New Economy, observers focused their analysis on the area which was most spectacular in the eyes of the general public: B-to-C (business to consumer) electronic commerce. The domain teemed with ideas, attracting enthusiastic press coverage and interest from investors without consumers ever being asked what they thought of it all! And yet, as early as 1999, more dependable analysts – such as Gartner – were already announcing that 95% of dot-com start-ups would fail through market concentration factors or bankruptcy, given their weak business models. Whether or not it is "New", the economy demands that more money should be coming in than going out, even if the use of trickery may delay the inevitable day of reckoning. The story of New Economy trailblazers Yahoo! is a good example. Within a year, the share price had dropped by 94%, its market capitalization dropping from $101bn to $8bn between March 2000 and April 2001, against an estimated turnover of $1.2bn in 2001. One of the major reasons for the market's disillusionment with one of the New Economy's star players was the downturn in advertising revenue which had made it possible to maintain free website access, the drop being indicative of how fragile business models based on free access can be.

E-Business was presented as being an efficient booster for decision-making and action. It was therefore also the most efficient means of rapidly heading in entirely the wrong direction. What is more, behind the tragic story of many a dot-com venture lay the usual demons that haunt companies and those at their helm: weak strategic visions, products and services out of line with consumers" expectations, overestimated profits and underestimated costs outlined in Pharaonic business cases, and, above all, the downright arrogance of company directors who struggled to hide their burning desire for gossip column inches and to immediately cash in on the dividends of their future earnings.

The collapse of those mushrooming companies that had been started up in a quest for inflated stock market values is a lesson in humility and realism. The truth behind the ways the internet is used brings us back to familiar categories of social life: the need to satisfy basic requirements (food, travel, ensuring the safety of one's loved ones and one's possessions) and to participate in community life (exchanging news, photos, getting information and keeping abreast of current affairs), as well as higher level needs (learning, creating and favoring the development of community initiatives, etc.). The internet already provides efficient responses to these needs, and that is the reason why it has already met with success. If the design of tomorrow's tools and systems is focused on providing relevant responses to these needs, value-added goods and services will follow. Market approval and the existence of real, solvent customers continue to be the true engines of innovation. They must never be forgotten.

8.2. The technological outlook

8.2.1. *What a beautiful world!*

The IT rocket's two main engines – power and transmission capacity – have now been well run in. As long as Moore's Law continues to speed up the raw performance of micro-processors, and as long as bandwidth continues to increase – and we may reasonably believe that these two vectors for progress can tap into at least another fifteen years" worth of layers of improved performance – IT will be drawn into a permanent race towards higher performance levels and the relative reduction of costs. At the same time, this dynamic will rapidly render IT a common feature of everyday life and cause its identity to dilute, leaving the path open to industrial concentration and price wars, a classic scenario in markets that are reaching maturity. The phenomenon can already be observed in areas such as components, memories and PCs, as well as for internet access. The PC crisis of 2001 was the first depression in the history of the industry. In 2001, the worldwide computer sales market dropped by 2% in volume, and by more than 10% in value. In these mature markets, the only types of innovation that will enable vendors to progress to more comfortable profit margins are those that customers consider to be genuine.

Although performance/price ratios continue to progress, innovation within technology that is visible to end-customers – whether businesses or private individuals – is a long time coming. What customers really want is a clear shift in exploitable performance. If technology is behind greater speeds of processing and exchange year after year, specifying the measurable gains in micro-processor clock rates is far from being an obvious task. Despite the relative disappointment of users as regards quantitative performance alone, industry responses have mainly been confined to technological feats which continue to fuel the data processing industry. Technology is now progressing in a straight line rather than sequentially. Performance levels can be attributed as much to the heart of the system (the processor) as to peripherals: disk or fixed memory storage, flatscreens, increased power autonomy, greater bandwidth. Ever smaller, lighter, faster and more autonomous, the tools offered by the industry are admittedly attractive in terms of their design and intrinsic capabilities, but the value associated with their use is not increasing at the same rate. It is fundamentally linked to the ability of programs available to contribute to solving the everyday problems faced by those who use them ... without multiplying the sources of irritation and breakdowns.

The product of these various units alone can bring about the necessary shifts that will trigger new performance thresholds in the capacity of the use of tools. One of the major levers behind this acceleration is data transmission speed. In all fields, throughput has hit tremendous levels. Half of the population of Europe can phone the other half using a single fiber-optic cable. Internet2 has followed in the footsteps of VDSL (Very high data rate Digital Subscriber Line) initiatives in France, in laying the foundations of new infrastructures that will lead to the radical transformation of internet use. Internet2, launched in the US in 1996, is a joint effort that has brought universities and private sector players together to develop high data rate technology and define the internet services of the future.

With transmission speeds of a terabyte – a million megabytes – per second, a three-hour film can be downloaded in less than a second. New projected uses have come about with developments in speed and throughput, particularly as regards high-definition video communication. Improved data transport capacity will inevitably bring down prices even if vendors – currently overburdened with debt – are loath to cut profit margins too quickly. Their progress is fuelled by the steps forward made in technical fields. Storage provides one such example. With the advent of extreme miniaturization it is now possible to stock several hours of footage on a digital video camera, or the equivalent of more than 70 CDs of music on an audio player[41]. And simultaneously, storage capacity limits have become less of a constraint through improved compression algorithms. Therefore, the physical curb on portability is constantly dropping away.

Major new and fundamental innovations are currently being worked on to break through the wall of the physical limitations of micro-processor writing. The prospects of this work are now well-identified, and are not far removed from fundamental physics. On the one hand, researchers are working on nanotubes, which are minute carbon rods (50,000 nanotubes placed side by side represent the width of a human hair) that have the same properties as silicon-based components. In their linear state they conduct electricity, and when distorted they act as a transitor. They can be assembled in three dimensions and form far more powerful units than the components that make up today's technology. Researchers are also heading in another direction, that of quantum computing, a product of the digital thinking behind the fastest possible binary processing.

Other promising research has been led into the sense of data. Today, data is nothing more than a series of characters transformed into sequences of 0s and 1s. The search tools at our disposal for the sophisticated tracking down of documents or, better still, a photograph on the internet, have yet to prove satisfactory.

Finally, human/machine interface is the permanent new frontier of IT, as it has been for the past 30 years. Voice and handwriting recognition algorithms are admittedly getting better all the time, but continue nevertheless to disappoint and are not reliable enough to supplant keyboards. Despite major investment in these fields, it is definitely difficult to split something as complex as language into bytes. We can, however, expect further improvements in the next ten years, enabling long-awaited recognition tools to be operational in normal working conditions, with satisfactory levels of reliability and speed.

Data access tool portability and ergonomics should emerge as a key success factor on the market in the years to come. Mobility is one of man's ongoing demands and tomorrow's tools will have to satisfy it. This is the field where wireless communications have a major part to play, in immediate environments, extended local networks and, obviously, in remote networks. The highly personal decision whether or not to take innovations on board is essentially based on the value of their use. The extraordinary success of GSM mobile phones is a perfect illustration of the importance of use-related issues balanced against the cost of possession in the minds of consumers. Technology is not in itself a factor affecting choice when the

---

[41] Apple's iPod uses a 1.8″ hard drive that weighs 50g, contains 5 gigabytes and can store 1,000 songs.

guarantor of the fundamental characteristics of a given product is its large-scale distribution and the presence of several competitors on the market, both factors reducing the risk of ending up in a technological *cul-de-sac* or of being threatened by irreversible malfunctions. From a customer's viewpoint, the state of being a precocious innovator represents a major risk: that of wasting precious time and money getting to grips with a product which is promising but difficult to access … when innovation should make life simpler. Therefore, the domestic and professional IT markets alike will truly be obliged to place greatest emphasis on ease of use. This is the reason why computers – which for 20 years were viewed as a centralized machine and then became more generalized in their current form: the PC with its keyboard and screen – will become just another everyday object, like wristwatches, spectacles, clothes, household appliances and cars. These various objects will all feature miniature flat screens enabling communication with the user and with other machines, and interfaces will be multi-functional. The very nature of the concept of portable computers has changed with the development of wearable computers[42], worn as one might an item of clothing or a wristwatch. This is becoming reality thanks to the success of PDAs – Personal Digital Assistants – of which Palm were the main propagators, and which are now available with built-in mobile phones. But the physical integration of tomorrow's portable, mobile and wireless computers within the everyday objects we use will no doubt go much further than that. Top of the range cars now offer a unique user dialogue system for adjustment of basic vehicle settings and air conditioning levels, as well as telephone, satellite guidance … and even television. In the future, they will enable internet access. The digital processing (capture, analysis, storage, retransmission, reproduction) of all types of data – whether that which can be perceived by humans (texts, 3-D images, sound) or that which cannot be directly perceived (bar-codes, biometric data) – will open up multiple avenues for exchange and communication in all fields of knowledge and of professional and leisure activities.

If technological breakthroughs maintain their current pace, the sole factor which will place boundaries on the otherwise limitless sphere of communicative data is that of human ability. First of all they require being able to give a substantial amount of free time to communication-based activities, which demand a great deal of personal energy: availability, concentration and learning. They also involve the ability to exploit the data gathered in a manner which contributes to one's knowledge or action. However, it has become clear that these machines, however amazing the feats they perform, are more and more time-consuming. Again, the general public will be convinced by the perceived value of the use of technology rather than by technological feats. Their seal of approval will in turn lead to genuine changes in

---

[42] Alex Lightman, CEO of MIT Media Lab spin-off Charmed Technology, has gone so far as to promote wearable computers on the catwalks of the fashion world (http://www.charmed.com).

practices by encouraging arbitration which is simultaneously fun and useful. Users expect progress in the field of use and not in terms of pure power. In order, for instance, to face up to the daily tidal wave of e-mails, what we really need is a tool which would automatically sort incoming messages according to how urgent they are, and that could be configured according to content, sender and also in relation to one's diary. We really need a utility that would select the information available on the internet that is relevant to the context at play. We expect UMTS-equipped mobile phones to come with genuine means of operational assistance that will work when we are stranded in an airport lounge in the middle of a snowstorm! We want tools for online assistance for car repairs, or medical surgery, allowing rapid diagnoses. By submerging information and knowledge processing within actual action contexts in a natural, continuous and reliable manner, the power and intelligence of IT will be of real use.

8.2.2. *Open source software: the alternative?*

The libertarian dimension of the software world has always been at loggerheads with that of the liberals, who support a market which may be free but is sealed by the protection of intellectual property. In the eyes of libertarians, software is indeed the result of intellectual creation but should remain royalty-free. This policy gave birth to the Open Source movement, which has grown substantially since the 1990s and is no longer confined to the world of universities and IT developers. The rise of the web has facilitated both exchange between developers and the large-scale, rapid circulation of programs without the need to resort to costly training and distribution networks. An open source software manifesto was written by MIT researcher Richard Stallman in 1984. The wording was clear: "(…) Software sellers want to divide the users and conquer them, making each user agree not to share with others. I refuse to break solidarity with other users in this way. I cannot in good conscience sign a nondisclosure agreement or a software license agreement (…)."[43]

What is open source software? Open source software meets a set of criteria outlined by the Open Source Software Charter, namely that the source code must remain open and modifiable, the program must always include its source code and respect its integrity, and that an open source license program cannot stipulate that subsequent distribution be subject to royalties or discrimination against individuals, groups of people or an area of application.

It must be possible for independent peers to examine an open source program. It thus undergoes continuous development through successive improvements, eventually achieving levels of power and reliability that are greater than those

---

[43] http://www.fsf.org/gnu/manifesto.html

available on the commercial market. To enable this type of permanent enhancement, it must be impossible to "close down" the software. Such improvements are achieved with the backing of the programming community. Open source software and software which is available free of charge – freeware – are not necessarily the same thing, given the fact that much of the latter is proprietary software distributed free of charge in the interest of commercial positioning. This is the case with browsers such as Microsoft's Internet Explorer and Netscape's Navigator, and with the Sun-distributed office suite, Star Office.

Linux has emerged as an opponent for operating systems from the "Wintel" world, in other words the various versions of Windows and other proprietary systems such as UNIX (IBM's AIX, HP UX, Sun's Solaris) and MacOS. Linux is a free alternative, the use of which is gradually on the rise. The story began in 1984 when MIT's Richard Stallman reacted to the way in which software editors were taking over UNIX by launching the GNU project ("GNU" being a self-referential acronym for "GNU's Not UNIX"!). The GNU project aimed at creating a free, modifiable and improvable operating system, culminating during 1991 in the software designed by Finn Linus Torvalds, a 22-year-old Helsinki University student. Torvalds" program was designed using Minix, a UNIX code run on a 386 processor. He then distributed the source code over the web, requesting that internet users help him make the software more effective. The initial version of the system was released in 1991 and was modestly referred to as version 0.02. Version 0.1 was unveiled in 1994. Torvalds called it "Linus" Unix", and this was soon abbreviated to Linux.

The open source world has undergone active development. Linux is but one example, with an estimated 17 million users worldwide as of the end of 2001. Other tools include PHP (an embedded scripting language for web servers), Apache (web server software) and MySQL (database software). All the aforementioned software is governed by the "General Public License" licensing principles proposed by Richard Stallman in 1991 in order to codify the use of open source software[44]. The principles are those specified in the Open Source Charter and ensure freedom of use and reproduction, and that the authors and contributors to changes are identified. However, the very nature of this type of software means that it cannot be guaranteed.

The cost of open source software is much lower than that of taking out licenses for its commercially-available counterparts. What is more, the manner in which it is conceived means that rapid enhancements do indeed render it robust. Linux can be used both as a server (web, firewall, files) and as a client terminal for office suite needs. Many IT service providers have become specialized in open source-related

---

[44] An example of a license can be found here: http://www.linux.org/info/gnu.html

activities such as the distribution of the software itself, and peripheral products and services (the best-known cases being Caldera Systems, the French company MandrakeSoft, the US leader Red Hat – founded in 1994 – and the German firm Suse, which started up in 1992). Even IBM has made Linux compatibility one of its major areas for development. Linux now runs on all IBM platforms and has become a part of IBM's software offerings such as DB2, Domino and Websphere. However, open source software has yet to make headway in the large company sector, even though deployment has begun across corporate web departments and some state administrations (the French Ministry of Culture and Communications, and state-owned museums). The major issue being considered by the market relates to whether open source software has the means to threaten the dominant position of the proprietary world, thus destabilizing the cozy business model of leading editors like Microsoft and Oracle. Some major players from the dominant industry – such as IBM and Sun – have pledged their support for open source software, without abandoning the economic opportunities offered by the proprietary world. They could tip the balance on the market by giving free solutions credibility.

8.2.3. *Cyborg and the cyberworld: reality and delirium*

The dreams and delirious ideas of many a scientist – who have called on the birth of new generation human beings, electronics-clad bionic creatures who move between the real and virtual worlds – have been made popular by writings on the subject. Cyborg was originally a creation of author Martin Caidin, and was the title of a series of novels first published in the early 1970s. It inspired countless other writers and film directors and led to the propagation of harrowing visions of a world inhabited by ultra-powerful, invulnerable creatures. Isaac Azimov drew up the four laws of robotics and, in his novel "Robot City", went on to describe an ideal metropolis in which humans and robots coexisted on an equal footing. The internet is an embodiment of these fantasies of total control, as portrayed in Hollywood movies like 1995's "The Net". "The Matrix" described a world where virtual reality had taken the place of actual reality, for the immense benefit of an invisible central force.

In less storybook fashion, the imagination of serious writers, like Ray Kurzweil, continues to extend the upward curves of machine power to such a degree that we are bound to see the day when ultra-powerful computers are able to think for themselves. This vision inspired Steven Spielberg in "Artificial Intelligence: AI". Kurzweil believes that we are edging ever closer to a world of thinking robots regardless of the denials of scholars and the anxieties of philosophers. The performance levels of machines will be such that they are bound to escape from the control of their creators.

In visions of the future, bionic creatures do not appear as vectors of humanist thinking but as nightmarish mutants in a violent and decaying world. If science fiction only represents the dramatized projection of our anxieties, it can be said that the tough and chilling picture it paints of IT and of its distant cousin modern biology is unlikely to reassure the detractors of an all-digital world!

8.3. Citizenship and economic development

8.3.1. *Unequal access to internet resources*

According to the high priests of the web, the internet has brought promises of a new, more open world, free from the constraints of history. By diluting time and frontiers, the internet was to call traditional values of sovereignty into question, the sort of values which were elaborated in the 18th century and perceived – thanks to the persistence of nation states, their territories, their laws and police, their currencies and their taxes – as an obstacle to the distribution of ideas and the liberalization of markets. At the same time, virtual micro-communities were to come together freely in accordance with individuals" interests. Thus, in 1996, John Perry Barlow, an internet activist and a Wired companion from the very outset, published "A Declaration of the Independence of Cyberspace", addressing a warning to governments to leave the internet alone, as it is a parallel world which is devoid of the limits faced by the real world. Barlow claims that digital technology detaches information from the physical world, where all sorts of laws relative to property have always originated. His vision was based on the thinking of Pierre Teilhard de Chardin – who evoked "Noosphere" a spiritual membrane encompassing our thoughts in "a single living tissue" – and that of Thomas Jefferson who wrote that "ideas should freely spread from one to another over the globe, for the moral and mutual instruction of man, and improvement of his condition... and like the air in which we breathe, move, and have our physical being, [are] incapable of confinement or exclusive appropriation. Inventions then cannot, in nature, be a subject of property".

Experience, however, has shown the stubbornness of reality and that neither geography nor history has vanished with a wave of the internet's magic wand, to the relief of many an observer. The ideological vision of a utopian world in the hands of a community of enlightened internet users is prone to contradictions. There is a risk that synthesis-like citizenship might end up being smashed into a thousand different facets, with the accompanying hazards of communitarism which are well-handled in the United States but are a far cry from our European culture. And democratic tools must be used in order to monitor the rules which are essential to the durability of complex systems.

Lying somewhere mid-way between the excesses of gurus and the viewpoint of skeptics, we are beginning to gain enough distance to be able to analyze the impact of the internet on development. Nobel prize-winners have taken an enthusiastic but clear-headed look at the realities of the internet world. In a survey, commissioned by Cisco Systems and carried out by Princeton Survey Research Associates[45], 71 Nobel laureates (of the 259 alive in October 2001) replied either by e-mail or over the telephone to a questionnaire on the impact of new technology on education, innovation and global living standards. Although the average age of the laureates surveyed was 72, 89% reported using a computer and the internet. This is noteworthy because it shows that those who look to the internet have a positive image of the tool and its use (those who strongly condemn the internet do not generally use it...). 42% rated the invention of computers and the internet as the greatest innovation in the last 100 years, ahead of air travel and automobiles, telephones, television and motion pictures. Nobel laureates regretted that they were not able to benefit from the internet earlier: 69% believed it would have allowed them to accomplish their research more quickly. 82% thought that the exchange of ideas over the internet would increase the speed of innovation. 91% considered that the internet would offer considerable opportunities for the development of education: 87% thought that networks would have a positive effect on improving learning methods, 93% said that new technology would be valuable in providing students with greater access to libraries, information and teachers around the world and 74% believed that educating students, via a virtual classroom by the year 2020, was likely. Finally, they virtually unanimously believed that the internet would play an important role in improving the quality of life globally over the next 20 years, in the fields of science/medicine (72%), education, global communication (93%) and increased productivity. What were the downsides to this optimistic outlook? 65% expressed concern that advancements in communications technology would make it easier for people to access a person's personal records and information – leading to increased privacy violations – and decreased levels of face-to-face interaction among people (51%). Some worried that the digital divide would persist between rich and poor, urbanites and rural dwellers – regardless of country – and that the internet, despite its educational potential, would be exploited by those who already have the means and resources to access technology, enabling them to expand their dominance in the world.

The first statement of the obvious is that in order to access the internet it is necessary to possess a computer, power supply and a telephone line and be a user capable of exploiting the equipment properly, in other words someone who, at the very least, can read and write. These prerequisites alone cancel out a large proportion of the world's population, one third of which does not even have access to electricity. In OECD countries there is one telephone line for every two

---

[45] http://www.cisco.com/nobel

inhabitants, one for every 15 in developing countries, and one for every 200 in less developed countries. The rapid development of mobile telephony has not – yet – solved the internet access question. The internet exists everywhere where infrastructures already exist: in those cities where prior investments have been made. For instance, 5 of the 27 million people who live in Shanghai and Beijing use the internet, against 4 of the 600 million who live in the 15 poorest Chinese provinces[46]. It is currently impossible to set up high-speed ADSL connections in rural areas worldwide. In France, the number of high-speed internet subscribers is rising very slowly, with estimates even being revised downwards. At the end of 2001, it was estimated that 345,000 would have signed up to ADSL connections and 250,000 to cable access. Come 2005, it is thought that no more than 11% of French households will have signed up to high-speed internet access, compared with more than 20% in the UK and Germany and 40% on average in Scandinavian countries.

The cyberworld reinforces the inequalities of the real world. A 75% concentration of internet users is situated in OECD countries, which make up 14% of the world's population. The US accounts for 5% of the world's population and 40% of the world's internet users, whilst Africa is home to 13% of the world's population and 1% of the world's internet users. Finland is the internet connection world champion, with 108 users for every thousand inhabitants in 1998, compared with one in a thousand in Russia! Furthermore, for operational and technical reasons (security, reliability, power supply) internet servers are concentrated on a limited number of sites, many of these so-called "server farms" being operated by the Californian firm Exodus Communications, who manage half of the major internet sites worldwide[47]. It was rather quickly forgotten that the internet functions well because it is a centralized system.

In 2000, Wired Magazine identified and ranked 46 technological centers worldwide according to four series of criteria:

– The ability of universities and research facilities to train qualified workers and develop new technologies.

– The presence of local or international firms capable of generating sustainable growth.

– The ability of the local population to create new activities.

– The existence of means of funding to enable the implementation of new activities.

---

[46] Source: Human Development Report 2001, United Nations Development Program.
[47] The company was badly hit by the internet crisis and filed for protection under Chapter 11 of the US federal bankruptcy code. Its future is uncertain.

It was established that the US was home to 13 high-potential zones, compared with 16 in Europe, nine in Asia, two each in Australia and Africa, and one apiece in Canada and Israel.

Unsurprisingly, Silicon Valley topped the rankings, followed by Boston, Stockholm, Israel, the Raleigh/Durham region in North Carolina, London, Helsinki, Austin (Texas), San Francisco, Taipei, Bangalore (India) … ahead of New York, Albuquerque, Montreal, Seattle, Cambridge and Dublin. Paris was ranked 28th.

In rankings drawn up in 2001 by Michael Porter and Jeffrey Sachs and published to tie in with the Davos World Economic Forum, Finland was the most competitive country, ahead of the US, Canada, Singapore and Australia. France was number 20. Innovation is not the sole long term competitive factor. Other key factors that make up the global appreciation of a country's outlook include the quality of its higher education system, its tax system, the state of its infrastructures and its openings onto the international scene. The European Commission was late to wake up to the risks of failing to keep up with the US in technological terms, and reacted by launching an action plan aimed at making Europe the most dynamic and competitive knowledge-based economy in the world within ten years. The eEurope initiative was approved by the European Council in Lisbon in March 2000, and covers all performance factors. It supports new infrastructure and services to enable simpler, generalized internet access through telecom liberalization, seeks to equip every citizen with the skills needed to live and work in the new information society by training teachers and providing schools with high-speed connections, aims to set up a legal framework for online transactions, and targets the development of an entrepreneurial culture. The action plan is indeed ambitious, and the program must now be embodied in concrete moves if it is not to get tied down in an exhaustive shopping list of all the underlying myths of the information society.

Information and services distributed over the web are subject to local constraints – primarily in relation to the user's native language – and to the legal terms in force in the user's geographical area. The techniques which are used for the geographical location of internet users now enable servers to comply with local legislation. The ban on Yahoo!'s sale of Nazi paraphernalia in France represents a major precedent in the rising pre-eminence of local laws over the informal – and non-democratic – rules of cyberspace. Granted, this geography-related reality limits the reach of the internet into countries considered to be non-democratic. China thus filters the content made available to its citizens, as do Iran, Singapore and Saudi Arabia.

One of the primary barriers to the development of democracy on the internet is the number of individuals that regularly access the tool, which remains low. Impact measurements have shown that of the 12 million users registered in France throughout 2001, only 6 million were logging on from individual accounts. The democratization of internet access in France is thus increasing at a slow rate. The longstanding core internet user continues to lead the way: predominantly male, urban, educated and belonging to the better-off social classes. The extension of this sociological basis is in line with the number of households who own PCs and the cost of accessing the internet, which remains insufficiently appealing. Meanwhile, public web access is being developed in schools and universities, but remains limited. Much of the French population has no intention whatsoever of linking up to the internet. As of September 2001, four in five French citizens had never been online[48]. This was particularly true of over 65-year-olds and more generally of people earning less than €1,100/month. The digital divide shows no sign of disappearing.

8.3.2. The first hesitant steps towards electronic democracy

This context is hardly favorable to the development of experiments in internet-based direct democracy. Considering the effective exclusion of the majority of the population, pilot schemes have been limited to a handful of small communities. However, some concrete results have shown that the prospect of electronic participation in community life – in its various and diverse forms – should be taken seriously.

8.3.2.1. Electronic voting

Electronic electoral consultation is still a utopian dream. Finland, which is the world leader in internet access and PC-equipped households, has – like most other major democracies – come up against their youth's growing disaffection for going to the polls. And yet two thirds of Finland's young people have stated they would be prepared to vote online. Hence the attempts by the Finnish state to attract this well-equipped, computer-friendly population back to the booths. The country is looking into voting systems that would reconcile the universal character of the ballot – using today's physical polling stations – with remote voting systems via terminals in public venues (post offices, shopping centers and the like) and voting from home or work using the internet. California has also begun moves in the same direction. In Brazil, the municipal elections held in 2000 made use, for the first time, of an entirely electronic voting system, with terminals set up in polling stations. However, the resolution of security and digital authentication issues has yet to reach sufficient levels of reliability for governments to consider generalizing online electronic voting in the near future. Vendors should be drawn to these developments, because a major market is opening up. IBM has already set up an Institute for Electronic Government, Microsoft and Cisco are developing intensive activities aimed at state

---

[48] Research carried out by the French *Conseil Supérieur de l'Audiovisuel* for the Ministry of Finance and Economy.

administrations, and major consulting groups like Cap Gemini Ernst & Young and Andersen have shown great interest in this promising sector.

8.3.2.2. Access to public services

In many industrialized countries – as in developing countries – much has been done as regards access to public services. These programs are part of the wider e-Business group of projects and are aimed at relations between governments and citizens (G-to-C), governments and businesses (G-to-B) and between different state structures (G-to-G). In all cases, the objective has been to facilitate relations between different players by putting all information online in a form that is simple to understand and consult, favoring electronic transactions without any need for paper documents and limiting face-to-face contact with civil servants, thus loosening the tight nature of having physically to travel to offices during often inconvenient opening hours.

In France, a major program was launched in August 1997 to promote internet access to public services. The multi-tiered *Program d'Action Gouvernemental pour la Société de l'Information* (Governmental Action Plan for the Information Society) is aimed at encouraging internet use in schools and businesses, with great emphasis being placed on online state services. The achievements have been remarkable and, according to research carried out by what was then Andersen Consulting, took France to the number one position in Europe and number five worldwide for internet use within state administrations. Public sector sites (1,600 such sites were created over a three-year period, of which 141 were governmental) are of a high quality and attract large numbers of visitors, becoming recognized online tools in the process. More than a thousand different types of forms were online as of 1st October 2001[49] – in other words two thirds of the public forms currently available – while 5,000 of the 17,000 businesses that are concerned with the remote VAT electronic declaration and payment system had already begun proceedings. The French government's objective between now and 2005 is that of transforming all public services into "public tele-services" in order to construct a coherent system for the civil service. It is a case of enabling every citizen and business to prepare, carry out, monitor and archive all administrative procedures online, with the exception of those stages that by their very nature demand physical presence or transmission. On 22nd August 2001, the French Government founded ATICA (*Agence pour les Technologies de l'Information et de la Communication dans l'Administration*: Agency for ICT within the Civil Service), in order to define together the full technical aspects of the development of electronic state administration. Finally, since September 2001, the government has authorized state players to make use of online bidding systems for

---

[49] Source: www.internet.gouv.fr

the purchase of everyday supplies, which represents a major innovation for the conservative world of public purchases.

Similar programs have been developed in internet pioneer nations – the US, Canada, Australia (National Office for Information Economy) and Singapore. However, less advanced countries have also launched ambitious campaigns. Brazil is one of the pioneering nations for online administration, the federal state offering more than 800 online services. In 2000, 93% of the 13 million taxpayers in the country filled out their tax returns on the internet. All of the Mexican state's calls for tender are put online, with the launch in 1996 of a service called Compranet. A similar program exists in Chile, known as Chile Compra. These tools have improved the transparency of public calls for tender and have brought down the cost of processing transactions.

Ever since the Lisbon summit in March 2000, the European Union has made e-Government one of its top areas for action. The ministerial declaration made on 29th November 2001 restated their governments" commitment to the deployment of online services to citizens and businesses, which also implies the transformation of the working methods and conditions of public sector employees. The declaration also underlined the need to go far beyond first generation internet sites and develop totally interactive services: "(…) a dynamic and democratic European society – bestowed with a strong and productive economy – needs its administration to be service-oriented, reliable and innovative at all levels".

As far as local democracy is concerned, French experiments in internet operations have brought nothing but disappointing demonstrations of their potential. Under the leadership of its mayor Michel Hervé, the town of Parthenay launched voluntary internet deployment operations. Rates of internet use have reached 40%, much higher than the national average of 17%. But whilst the development of public access, access to public services and the transparency of communal management are deemed to have been successful, there has been minimal impact on employment prospects in Parthenay, generating just a few dozen new jobs … and the mayor was beaten in the elections held in March 2001! The municipal democracy program set up in the Paris suburb of Issy-les-Moulineaux has been less ambitious, but has given a technological flavor to the town, with an increasing number of IT businesses setting up their headquarters there.

New regulatory authorities are necessary in order to accompany these changes, to protect fundamental liberties and to respect differences.

8.4. Developments in the Third World

The mastery of information and communications technology is still very much a specialty of the developed world. The promises of the internet – and the fast development of mobile telephony – have, however, rapidly enabled some developing countries to shoot ahead and attain commendable levels of technical skill. In Brazil, car dealer networks are less dense, and cars are thus already being sold online. In 2001, mobile phone subscribers in China outnumbered their US counterparts, thus compensating for the limits of the country's embryonic terrestrial network. Cutting-edge skills are being nurtured in India in order to feed the country's IT development, but it has become a challenge to hold on to individuals, many of whom choose to move to the US. It has been suggested that 100,000 IT professionals could leave India each year, generating estimated losses of $2bn. On the other hand, internet-enabled delocalized competency can also sometimes lead to the development of technological centers in struggling areas. Eastern European countries have thus been given the hope of playing a key part in the delocalization of IT services, benefiting simultaneously from the general level of training and from competitive wage bills.

Once again, the key behind growth lies in skills development. Indeed, the internet may be an enormous pool of knowledge, but it can only be exploited by those who can read … and can get onto the network. Unless these two conditions are met, there will be no internet miracle in developing countries or in the underprivileged areas of the world's richest countries.

8.5. Security and freedom: what are the real threats?

The grumpy observers who have denigrated the internet believe it is nothing more than a muddled and chaotic area which houses, at best, licentiousness and crime, and at worst, a boundless exhibition of every base act known to humanity. Examples of pornography, exhibitionism, voyeurism, racism and pedophilia can be found on the internet as they can on any railway station newsstand. In either case, it is a matter of knowing where to look.

The internet is not an area devoid of faith or laws, nor is it a place inhabited by pure and innocent convent girls. The truth is that this network of networks has been created in the image of those who have shaped it and used it: advocates of utopia … and of vice. Consequently, the development of the internet implies that rules of security be clearly defined. All internet users must be able to move around the virtual space in a clear-headed fashion, fully aware of their rights and obligations, with the means of enforcing them at their disposal and the fear of sanctions in the case of untoward behavior. From a legal point of view, this is indeed the case since it is possible to apply the law of every country where the internet is used. This has been put into practice in France, as the aforementioned ban on Yahoo!'s sale of Nazi paraphernalia has shown. The same can be said about cases of pedophilia.

Similarly, citizens must be able to check that state authorities do not take advantage of information technology in order to break public rules. Doubts as to the confidentiality of information exchanged over the web were raised by the publicity surrounding the Echelon network, however enormous the task at hand may have seemed: the network was used by US security agencies to "listen" to goings-on on the internet in the interest of national security. The actual risk faced by ordinary citizens is in fact minute. The risk of a credit card number being misused, even to a limited degree, by a dishonest online trader is greater than that of confidential information being similarly exploited on the network. Many tools exist that reduce the protection of individual privacy and rights to nothing. Technology makes it possible to monitor and identify any individual in a public place, with the use of CCTV cameras linked to facial recognition software. It is technically possible to exploit the electronic traces left by any individual who, when traveling, uses a credit card to pay at a motorway toll or car park, or makes a phone call using a cellular phone. The individual use of the internet leaves traces everywhere, both with the telecom carriers and with the sites visited.

It is currently impossible to develop an IT policy without making use of American products. The security of the US is a subject which has always been of paramount importance to the government ... of the US – now more than ever. Without wanting to sound excessively paranoid, it cannot be conceived that US vendors may have chosen to ignore the national impact of their activities and have refused to contribute to it.

8.6. Press, media and culture

Digitalization primarily concerns the industry producing content: all types of publishing, the press, music and even cinema production are all sectors for which the internet is alternately a threat and a savior. The major financial moves to set up multimedia poles, affecting the new tollbooths to the information society through the simultaneous control of content and distribution networks, have fuelled an action-packed scenario. The supposedly "Gallic" Vivendi Universal has attempted to snatch the leadership from longstanding players such as AOL Time Warner and Bertelsmann. Concentrations and maneuvers of all kinds can be expected in this stormy sector, which has yet to achieve stability. Spectacular technical promises, such as online movies, TV broadcasts on demand and now digital terrestrial TV are struggling to find profitable markets, because of the endlessly-analyzed absence of solvent demand.

The web was also to have killed off the printed press. Instead the sector is still doing well, as it intelligently took the digital revolution on board during the conception of content, before cautiously branching out into the dematerialization of distribution. Within the space of a few years, the working conditions of press journalists have been transformed with the computerization of newsrooms – thanks to computer-assisted publishing – followed by the tele-distribution of newspapers, allowing simultaneous printing in different locations. The general public remains oblivious to most of these transformations in the conception and production processes of information media, but the methods are now widespread and part of everyday life in professional *milieux*, after an initial period of resistance.

The arrival in cyberspace of the leading US newspapers caused quite a stir. On 9th June 1994, The New York Times launched its first-ever electronic edition, following in the footsteps of the Silicon Valley-based San Jose Mercury News, the latter charging for its electronic edition, Mercury Center, its Californian audience being ready for this natural development. Observers[50] were already claiming that major press groups would make a lot of money from the digital revolution, and that before the end of the 20th century we would "no doubt be reading our daily news on our laptop computer screen over breakfast or in the office". The "personal daily" project which was initially proposed by MIT's Media Lab, based on the personalized assembly of data automatically gathered by an intelligent agent on the web – which Rupert Murdoch found to be an attractive concept – may not have become generalized in the form of a newspaper, but has inspired countless customizable internet portals. Net-based electronic publishing projects have not had the fantastic levels of success that had been expected, but they have, however, had far more convincing results than their predecessors who had to work with technology which failed to reach the necessary standards, such as videotex[51]. The versatility and multimedia character of the internet provide the press with a technologically credible platform. The distribution of written news on the internet has become a practical reality. In differing registers CNN, *The Economist*, *The New York Times* and *Le Monde* have all developed their own convincing styles. The question that remains is whether the presence of press publications on the internet – a medium which is expensive to develop and maintain – can be an economically viable option. Free site access is certainly not sustainable, and the use of advertising to provide funds has rapidly shown its limits. The subscription method appears credible although it lacks flexibility. "Pay-per-page" may be an even more promising system as long as payment is both secure and transparent. In the field of information – and for the overall development of e-commerce – online payment

---

[50] *Courrier International*, Issue no. 189, 16th June 1994.
[51] Viewtron, launched in Miami by Knight-Ridder in 1981 and integrated within AOL in 1992, and by IBM and Sears with Prodigy in 1987.

must be through the use of tools which are both straightforward and reassuring for customers. At this point in time, the smartcard is the tool which is best suited to such an essential function.

The big question for the future concerns the durability of the physical media used for digital data. Newspapers and books can be stored for centuries, provided the conditions are adequate. Will this also be the case for CDs, CD-ROMs and DVDs? How about the other formats which have come and gone? What about digital photo and video formats? It is our duty to remember, and to do so it is essential that stable conditions for archiving data be defined. This question has been raised by archivists and historians, and is all the more relevant as, by favoring the present, recording formats are being rendered obsolete. In this field, once again, major collective action is needed in calling for normalized standards.

8.7. Health and education

The hopeful prospect of a fairer society continues to drive genuine scholars. Their social conscience has led them to pay greater attention to the global impact of innovation on society than to the immediate effects of fluctuating share indices ... and although they are often the first to reap the rewards of the stock market, their ambitions remain intact. Modern IT can, indeed, bring profound change to health and education, the key components of society. These two areas had hitherto regularly been considered to be the carriers of transformation in current practices, but had failed to cause a major wide-scale shift in practices. At best, partial experimentation had cleared the way in some areas, thanks to a handful of pioneers who were often isolated in their professional field, and working with little or no support from their peers.

There have been in-depth transformations in the field of medicine with the increased power of digital examination tools such as ultrasound, optical and MRI scanners. However, the progress that might have been expected in medical diagnoses through the digitalization of medical data has been thwarted by the fragmentation of data across multiple partial databases, the reluctance of practitioners in the field and social security organizations to share the data they have generated and collected, and the taboo subject that is the confidentiality of personal medical data.

As regards education, the endemic lack of equipment in primary and even secondary schools in most developed countries – not to mention the total impoverishment of developing countries – has resulted in isolated, sporadic and experimental practices that have been launched without any kind of structured long-term vision of how learning tools can become an integral part of educational curricula. This groundwork has been carried out by isolated pioneers with little backing from their establishments, and has often been met with criticism from colleagues. Happily, a number of magnificent examples of internet use have nevertheless emerged, despite the difficult context. Many primary schools in France produce modern-day versions of the class newspapers and letter-writing schemes which one Célestin Freinet introduced early in the 20th century. Technology provides an extra element of quality which enhances the work of pupils, and perfectly fits in with a respectable educational approach. In the world of secondary education, many websites have been set up by enthusiastic teachers, putting their personal knowledge online for the sheer pleasure of sharing it with others. Initiatives of the like remain isolated and receive little publicity.[52]

However, a lack of equipment must not alone shoulder the blame. In the educational world, as in the corporate world, tools must provide an appropriate response to actual requirements. Other than problems relating to equipment, networks, power supply and maintenance – a constant source of struggle for teachers – the fact that a school has internet access has little significance if teachers fail to exploit the tool properly by making it a part of their pedagogical processes. Otherwise, the internet in schools will be nothing more than a buzzword that will remain in fashion until the next trend comes along. Many towns, counties and ministers have yielded, but learning problems prevail! In a study, carried out by French magazine Newbiz and published in September 2001, 62% of teachers and 70% of the parents surveyed acknowledged that the internet is not used within schools, even though a majority stated that it was as much a priority as learning other traditional subjects. Just as many believed that the internet would not change current pedagogical methods, at least in the short term. However, in the school year 2000-2001, France did introduce a "Certificate in IT and the Internet" for primary school pupils, aimed at specifying a number of significant skills in the field of information and communications technology and validating children's ability to master these skills. A pilot group of 50,000 pupils sat the examination, which will become compulsory in all schools nation-wide in 2002-2003. The merit of this – extremely general – tool is that it draws up a baseline of skills considered essential in order to draw benefit from the use of the internet and personal IT. It is the primary school equivalent of the ECDL (European Computer Driving License), which is aimed at adults and provides a tool for self-assessment of computer literacy, was introduced in Finland in the 1980s and is now present throughout Europe.

---

52 The work carried out by a society of teachers in France deserves particular recognition: CIIP (*Association Coopérative pour l'Information et l'Innovation Pédagogique* : Co-operative Association for Pedagogical Information and Innovation) and their website '*Le Café Pédagogique*' (http://www.cafepedagogique.net).

We are only just beginning to tap into the enormous potential of internet tools for elementary and adult education alike. Work must now commence at an institutional level – beyond that of lowly internet militants and enthusiasts – leading to the implementation of permanent practices that might, in turn, become part of everyday procedures in educational establishments

.

Conclusion

... And ending with a perfect cadence! IT will long continue to fuel debates in boardrooms and endless chatter in staff canteens. IT products are no longer confined to laboratories and air-conditioned rooms, but have simultaneously become a fantastic tool for social transformation and a brown product available off the shelf in household appliance superstores. Everyone has their own experience of IT and their own tale to tell about some endless, ruinously expensive project ... or the printer that kept breaking down. IT is a subject which is in constant growth, with an ever-increasing amount of experience being gained. It is thus tremendously difficult to have a clear idea of this ongoing procession of impressions and judgments, which are as wide and divergent as the differing levels of growth of IT in individual households, which may not have led to rising levels of competency but have at the very least brought about higher levels of information and demands. This reflection now complete, it is clear that the time has come to emerge from prehistory, and for IT to become a natural tool in the corporate world, deserving neither the excessive praise heaped on it by sellers nor the indignant condemnations leveled by many users. Today's computers are immeasurably smaller, faster and cheaper than in the 1950s. The question has not changed: how can computers be used to improve the way we do things that we previously did without them?

IT is a powerful tool that must be harnessed without any kind of apprehension or prejudice, for the service of the essential resources that are information, communication and knowledge.

For this to be achieved, the thinking behind the choice of corporate IT and information system use must be carried out in a context which is down-to-earth, mature, serene and well-informed. By intelligently breaking away from market-led approaches, it is a case of pinpointing the essential issue at stake: how to build and run the effective tools and systems that are needed in order to make and implement conscious decisions ensuring the company's sustainability and development. Indeed, the sole judge of the quality of an IT and IS policy is the conscious, controlled performance levels consequently gained by the company and measured according to the criteria deemed appropriate. The quality of these criteria will be a means of assessing the commitment and informational culture of the company directors. However, this area is by no means any different from the other components of a corporate policy.

There is also an urgent need for a rise in the awareness levels of political decision-makers. In terms of supporting education, collective awareness, more transparent choices and thus increased maturity in society at large, or the defense of citizens against the excesses and threats of unsupervised technology, society needs political leaders who have an in-depth understanding of the stakes and threats posed by the information society, and who do not resort to blind, irresponsible promotion.

The technological saga will continue. Men and women will still consider technology to be an additive that boosts their personal achievements, although there will be much frustration, rejection and lack of consistency along the road. However, despite its ongoing imperfections, IT will leave a profound mark on 21st century society by providing the basis for an unprecedented expansion in human knowledge. Will IT further the development of human conscience? The answer lies with us.

"Science without conscience is but the ruin of the soul."
(François Rabelais, c. 1494-1553)

References and Bibliography

Literature dealing with IT and the information society could in itself provide an interesting subject for research. On the whole, bookshops stock IT books for IT people ... anything other than that is difficult to find.

Books with titles like *Mastering Office XP* and *The IP Routing Guidebook* do not prompt considerations about the information society, but tend to be the work of specialists who seek to propose operating methods that only too often simply paraphrase the original user manuals published by the manufacturers. Very few study books are aimed at non-IT specialists. It seems that bookshops do not consider accessible IT books to be a winning formula! Of the books which are available, many are North American publications – the IT publishing sector there being very active, and the books having substantial print runs. In most cases, universities are the source, while the most fashionable publications are often by authors who have day-jobs as consultants, and whose writing is backed by their employers.

Naturally, the web has become the primary source for IT-related information. Many original documents can be found online, and many enthusiasts use the internet to share their culture and experience. There are many online IT museums. Sites provided by vendors include an increasing wealth of resources, and it must be emphasized that some, like IBM, have made particular efforts to make their archives accessible. Finally, state administrations, public organizations and educational institutions have made a high number of documents available to the general public. All of the above makes researching a book like this an easier and faster process ... all in the name of productivity!

North American sources

Janet ABBATE, *Inventing the Internet,* The MIT Press, 1999

Bernard H. BOAR, *Strategic Thinking for Information Technology: How to Build the IT Organization for the Information Age*, John Wiley & Sons, 1996

David CAMINER, John ARIS, Peter HERMON and Frank LAND, *LEO: The Incredible Story of the World's First Business Computer*

Martin CAMPBELL-KELLY and William ASPRAY, *Computer, a History of the Information Machine*, BasicBooks, HarperCollins, 1996

Manuel CASTELLS, *The Rise of the Network Society*, Blackwell Publishers, 1996

Manuel CASTELLS, *The Power of Identity*, Blackwell Publishers, 1997

Manuel CASTELLS, *End of Millennium*, Blackwell Publishers, 1998

Paul E. CERUZZI, *A History of Modern Computing,* The MIT Press, 1998

Michael DERTOUZOS, *What Will Be*, HarperCollins, 1997

Michael DERTOUZOS, *The Unfinished Revolution*, HarperCollins, 2001

Simson L. GARFINKEL, *Architects of the Information Society, Thirty-five Years of the Laboratory for Computer Science at MIT,* The MIT Press, 1999

George GILDER, *Telecosm,* The Free Press, 2000

Detlev J. HOCH, Cyriac R. ROEDING, Gert PURKERT, Sandro K. LINDER, *Secrets of Software Success,* Harvard Business School Press, 1999

Ray KURZWEIL, *The Age of Spiritual Machines*, Penguin, 1999 (www.books.mcgraw-hill.com)

Michael LEWIS, *The New New Thing, a Silicon Valley Story*, W.W. Norton & Company, 2000

Bernard LIAUTAUD, *e-Business Intelligence*, McGraw-Hill, 2000

Rosabeth MOSS KANTER, *e-Volve!,* Harvard Business School Press, 2001

Hasso PLATTNER, *Anticipating Change, Secrets Behind the SAP Empire*, Prima Tech, 2000

Arthur B. SCULLEY, W. WILLIAMS, A. WOODS, *B2B Exchanges,* ISI Publications, 1999

Daniel E. SICHEL, *The Computer Revolution, an Economic Perspective*, Brookings Institution Press, 1997

Paul STRASSMANN, *The Politics of Information Management, Policy Guidelines,* The Information Economics Press, 1995

Don TAPSCOTT, Art CASTON, *Paradigm Shift, The New Promise of Information Technology,* McGraw-Hill, 1993

Don TAPSCOTT, *The Digital Economy, Promise and Peril in the Age of Networked Intelligence*, McGraw-Hill, 1996

Don TAPSCOTT, *Blueprint to the Digital Economy, Creating Wealth in the Era of E-Business*, McGraw-Hill, 1998

Don TAPSCOTT, *Growing Up Digital, The Rise of the Net Generation*, McGraw-Hill, 1998

John THORP, *The Information Paradox*, McGraw-Hill Ryerson, 1998

Recommended for CIOs only:

Thomas H. DAVENPORT, *Information Ecology*, Oxford University Press, 1997

Jerrold M. GROCHOW, *Information Overload!*, Yourdon Press Computing Series, 1996

Peter WEILL and Marianne BROADBENT, *Leveraging the New Infrastructure*, Harvard Business School Press, 1998

French sources

Simon NORA, Alain MINC, *L'Informatisation de la Société*, La Documentation Française, 1978

Jean-Pierre CORNIOU, Nathan HATTAB, *Qui a Encore Peur de l'Informatique?*, Eyrolles, 1989

Marc GUILLAUME, *Où Vont les Autoroutes de l'Information?*, Commissariat Général du Plan, Descartes & Cie, 1997

Yves LASFARGUE, *Techno Mordus, Techno Exclus?*, Les Echos Editions, Éditions d'Organization, 2000

Pierre LEVY, *La Cyberculture*, Editions Odile Jacob, 1997

Pierre LHERMITTE, *Le Pari Informatique*, Editions France-Empire, 1968

Pierre LHERMITTE, *Conséquences Prévisibles du Développement de l'Automatisation de la Gestion des Entreprises*, report submitted to the *Conseil Economique et Social*, Journal Officiel, 14th March 1968

Armand MATTELART, *Histoire de la Société de l'Information*, Repères, La Découverte, 2001Joël de ROSNAY, *L'homme Symbiotique*, Seuil, 1995

Claude SALZMAN, Xavier DALLOZ, *Les défis de la Net-Economie*, Dunod, 2000

Jacques VERNAY, *Chroniques de la Compagnie IBM France 1914-1987*, IBM France, 1988

Weronika ZARACHOWICZ, Pierre-Xavier GREZAUD, *Global Village, A Qui Profite la Révolution Technologique*, Editions des Arènes, 2001

Technical books for IT engineers:

Corinne CAUVET, Camille ROSENTHAL-SABROUX, *Ingénierie des Systèmes d'Information*, Hermès, 2001

Jean-Louis TOMAS, *ERP et Progiciels Intégrés*, InterEditions, 1999

General documents

Angus MADDISON, The World Economy: A Millennial Perspective, OECD, 2001

Making New Technologies Work for Human Development, Human Development Report 2001, United Nations Development Program (UNDP)

"Machines à écrire", Autrement, no. 146, June 1994

Le Travail au XXIe siècle, Mutations de l'Economie et de la Société à l'Ere des Autoroutes de l'Information, edited by Gérard BLANC, Dunod, 1995

Paul VIRILIO, *La Bombe Informatique,* Galilée, 1998

Reviews, periodicals and internet sites

All the major IT magazines have websites which complement their paper publications:

- L'informatique Professionnelle

- CIO

- Computerworld

- 01 Informatique

- Le Monde Informatique

"Annals of the History of Computing" Institute of Electrical & Electronics Engineers (IEEE): http://www.computer.org/annals/

Governmental sites

http://www.europa.eu.int/information_society

http://www.minefi.gouv.fr

Acknowledgements

Above all, I would like to thank Martine, Marine and Alice for their patience throughout nine months of work, pressure, suitcases filled with books during our holidays – before the piles built up everywhere else – and the endless hours spent in silence on the internet.

Thank you to my IT colleagues at ANPE, Sollac, Usinor and Renault, in recognition of their acceptance to be managed by a demanding amateur who would occasionally be critical of the profession.

Thank you to my CIO colleagues at CIGREF and the Research Group, to my friends the permanent staff at CIGREF and the association's two General Managers Pierre-Yves Le Bihan and Jean-François Pépin, and to my friends and accomplices at *Informatique Professionnelle* Magazine for the years spent thinking, working, questioning and doubting ... without which there would be nothing but slogans.

My immense gratitude goes out to two of my loyal proof-readers, Sébastien Bachollet and Jean-Michel Atzel, for bravely accepting to carry out such an essential and methodical task, and to all those whose advice and criticism enabled me to refine my analyzes, most notably webmaster *emeritus* Claude Rochet, the tireless explorer of ideas.

My thanks go also to the vendors, without whom IT would not exist. I wish them continued progress towards the creation of true added value ... *qui bene amat bene castigat*!

***

The translator would particularly like to thank David Pike for the endless stream of e-mail attachments and phone calls full of words of wisdom, advice and constructive criticism. I think the expression is "beyond the call of duty"!